More Praise for *Chasing Chaos*

"A fresh, very readable, highly personal account of the trials and tribulations of a young aid worker as she confronts the daily realities—the good, the bad, and the very uncomfortable—of life dealing with some of the most important humanitarian challenges of the last decade."

—Ross Mountain, Former United Nations Deputy
Special Representative of the Secretary General and
Humanitarian Coordinator

"Not only is Jessica Alexander a wonderful writer—her clear, evocative prose transported me into refugee camps in Darfur, war trials in Sierra Leone, and post-earthquake Haiti—but she is honest about the complexity of 'doing good,' without being defeatist. Funny, touching, and impossible to put down, this book should be required reading for anyone contemplating a career in aid, and for all of us who wonder how we can make a useful contribution to a better world, wherever we are."

—Marianne Elliott, author of *Zen Under Fire:
How I Found Peace in the Midst of War*

"You'll start *Chasing Chaos* because you are interested in humanitarian aid. You'll finish because of Jessica Alexander's irresistible storytelling: her honesty, her humanity, her wackadoodle colleagues, her dad. I loved it."

—Ke ___ Sex *(and Other
De* WITHDRAWN *from a War Zone*
ty

"A no-holds-barred description of what it is like to travel to world disaster sites and engage in the complex, challenging, nitty-gritty work of making a difference across lines of culture, class, age, gender, and perspective. In telling the story of her decade as a young and passionate humanitarian aid worker, Jessica Alexander also manages to tell us the best and the worst of what this work is like and to speculate on the aid establishment—how it has changed, where it works, and what its limits are. A must read for anyone with global interests—and that should be all of us."

—Ruth Messinger, president, American Jewish World Service

"*Chasing Chaos* examines the lives that aid workers lead and the work [that] aid workers do with honesty, clarity, and warmth. While the book is peppered with hilarious anecdotes—it is also salted with tears. Honest, genuine, heartfelt tears. This life and this work that aid and development workers embark upon so often oscillates wildly between stomach-bursting laughter and shoulder-seizing weeping—*Chasing Chaos* captures these oscillations, and the doldrums in between the ends of the spectrum, perfectly."

—Casey Kuhlman, *New York Times* bestselling author of *Shooter*

"The compelling quality of *Chasing Chaos* is Alexander's honesty, sharp observations, and conversational prose. With humor and insight, she shares the intimate details of her everyday life. Even if you're a seasoned traveler, this entry into the world of humanitarian aid organizations—the good, the bad, and the frustrating—is fascinating."

—Rita Golden Gelman, author of *Tales of a Female Nomad*

"A hardened idealist's challenging look at the contradictions, complications, and enduring importance of humanitarian aid."
—Robert Calderisi, author of *The Trouble with Africa: Why Foreign Aid Isn't Working*

"In *Chasing Chaos*, Alexander takes us to a place where few outsiders can go, cracking open the rarefied world of humanitarianism to bare its contradictions—and her own—with boldness and humor. The result is an immensely valuable field guide to the mind of that uniquely powerful and vulnerable of beasts: the international aid worker."
—Jonathan M. Katz, author of *The Big Truck That Went By: How the World Came to Save Haiti and Left Behind a Disaster*

CHASING CHAOS

JESSICA ALEXANDER

❖

CHASING CHAOS

my decade in and out

of humanitarian aid

B\D\W\Y

BROADWAY BOOKS

NEW YORK

Published in the United States by Broadway Books, an imprint of the Crown Publishing Group, a division of Random House LLC., New York, a Penguin Random House Company.
www.crownpublishing.com

BROADWAY BOOKS and its logo, B \ D \ W \ Y are trademarks of Random House LLC.

Library of Congress Cataloging-in-Publication Data

Alexander, Jessica.
Chasing chaos : my decade in and out of humanitarian aid / Jessica Alexander. — First edition.
pages cm
1. Humanitarian assistance—Sudan—Darfur. 2. Sudan—History—Darfur Conflict, 2003- I. Title.
HV555.S73A44 2013
361.2'5092—dc23
[B] 2013008182 5243248
ISBN 978-0-7704-3691-9
eISBN 978-0-7704-3692-6

PRINTED IN THE UNITED STATES OF AMERICA

Maps by David Lindroth, Inc.
Cover design by Maayan Pearl
Cover photographs by Kurt Drubbel (desert); © Ben Walsh/ Corbis (car)

10 9 8 7 6 5 4 3 2 1

First Edition

TO DAD

and

TO MOM, *who is with me wherever I go*

CONTENTS

All Skin and Grief

I awoke as I did every morning. The call to prayer erupted at 5:30 a.m. and was so loud I could have sworn the muezzin set his amplifier right next to my pillow. But the scratchy voice that shrilled through the old speaker came from the roof of the adjacent mosque.

Someone make him stop. Please, just make it stop.

When the muezzin paused to take a breath, a chorus of chickens, goats, and a baby crying in a house nearby filled the momentary hush. I peeled the mildewed towel from my face—the one I had drenched with water and placed on my forehead before bed. It was the only way I could fall asleep in the smothering Darfur heat. Every evening I'd dunk my pajamas in water and lie on the foam mattress, eyes shut tightly, reveling in the cool wetness clinging to my skin, hoping I would fall asleep before it evaporated into the dry night. But that almost never happened.

As the muezzin continued, I got out of bed listlessly; I had to get to the camp early that day. Close to one hundred and twenty thousand displaced people lived in camps around the city of El Fasher, the capital of North Darfur; twenty-four thousand of them lived in the camp where I worked, Al Salam. Families would be sitting outside the registration tent this morning, already lined up and waiting for the camp processing to resume. Since the other two camps—Abu Shouk and Zam Zam—were at full capacity, we had to make room for the new arrivals. We registered, screened, and distributed food to the weary families as quickly as possible, but each day an endless flow of colored specks in the sandy distance moved closer to the camp: men and women carrying babies in their arms and bundles on their heads, donkeys trudging slowly by their side. It was a war. People kept coming.

I went to the small bathroom in our compound, thinking that maybe, miraculously, the water would work. I turned the small faucet, hoping for a trickle, but it coughed and sputtered. My calves and armpits hadn't seen a razor for weeks. My hair hung in oily clumps around my face and smelled like dirty dishwater. I pressed the lever to flush the toilet, but it went limp beneath my fingers. The day before we'd accidentally left the lid open and bugs had swarmed around the seat. Today the lid was down but it still smelled like rotting shit.

I brushed my teeth with the bottled water we had on reserve. Lila, my Kenyan colleague who lived with me, walked into the bathroom and saw me, water bottle in hand. "Still?" she asked. She was wrapped in a bright pink sarong, holding soap and shampoo, hoping to take a shower.

"Still," I said through a mouthful of toothpaste.

The water problem was supposed to be fixed days ago, but as with everything in Darfur, we waited.

"Adam, *mafi moya*," I had said some days before. (*"there is no water."*) Adam, our Sudanese colleague, was responsible for maintaining the guesthouses where we lived. "When is the pump going to be fixed?"

"Hello, Testicle." Adam couldn't pronounce my name—Jessica—so it always sounded as if he were calling me a testicle. "Water will be there today!"

"Adam, you said that yesterday and the day before and we still have no water." I was so tired and defeated that the words came out flat and quiet.

"I know. Tonight, *inshallah*!"

Inshallah—God willing—qualified most Sudanese commitments. "*Inshallah,* I'll be there." "It will be finished by the end of the week, *inshallah*." "Your visa will come tomorrow, *inshallah*." If God willed these things to happen, they would. In my experience, God tended to be unwilling.

Dressing in my baggy, worn-out khakis and long-sleeved shirt, I didn't need a mirror to see how awful I looked. With a layer of sweat and dirt already covering my face, my skin couldn't absorb the SPF 55 sunblock smeared on it, so I walked into the unrelenting sunshine with a filmy white clown mask.

As it did every morning, breakfast consisted of a hard-boiled egg and a cup of Nescafé. Lila was already sitting inside the small kitchen. It had been ransacked. Canned goods were scattered everywhere and the floor was sprinkled with flour and rice; their ripped burlap bags slunk low. "Are you kidding me? *Again?*" I said. "Those *goddamned* cats."

Street cats roamed our compound, keeping away the hedgehogs who scurried through North Darfur like squirrels in Central Park. Before Darfur I had never seen a hedgehog; they looked like miniature porcupines. Some people thought they were cute; to me they were prickly nuisances, leaving stinky turds under our beds and in the back of our closets. But the cats were worse. We locked the door to the kitchen every night, but they managed to slink under the small crack at the bottom.

Lila crouched down to sweep the mess. I grabbed a match and went to light the stove to boil water for our eggs and coffee. It wouldn't take. I tried again but only a rapid *tick-tick-ticking* came from the stovetop. Lila sighed, "I told Adam last week that we were running low on fuel."

"Can you remind me what he gets paid to do around here?" I asked, still flicking the stove, the anger rising in my throat.

Lila looked up and shrugged with the same resignation we all embraced to survive the lack of control over our most basic needs.

Having lived in Darfur for close to seven months, I felt at turns dizzy, tired, and depressed. A low-level rage had been slowly building for weeks. I had seen people's burnouts turn them nasty and cynical. But really I just wanted some water. To get the rank smell of my own body out of my nose. My sanity relied on so few things here—water and fuel being the primary ones. It felt as if even these were too much to ask for.

But it wasn't only the loneliness or the living conditions; it was the unrelenting feeling of futility within the enormity of this war. The work my colleagues and I were doing for international humanitarian agencies wasn't ending the country's real problems: the merciless horror of fire, rape, and murder that rode in on horseback. All we could do was provide a few flimsy plastic sheets, rice, and oil to fleeing farmers and their families, some who had walked two weeks to get here. Some came from Chad, some from the Nuba Mountains to our east, others from one of the many small, nameless villages scattered across the dusty Darfur canvas. There was an endlessness to the crisis, and I was exhausted.

It was 2005 and the Darfur crisis had already displaced nearly two million people and claimed the lives of another seventy thousand. People were terrorized off their land by the Janjaweed, the government-backed militias who set fire to farming communities, landing their residents in displaced persons camps throughout Darfur.

"Salam Alaikum," I said to Yusuf, the guard who lay outside the door to our compound. He slept there each night, supposedly protecting us. It was like plopping Grandpa on a rocker in front of our door. If there weren't teenagers with AK-47s kidnapping and murdering people, it would have been a funny joke.

"*Alaikum Salam. Keif Elhaal?*" he asked cheerfully, standing up—how are you?

If I had known the Arabic to say, *I haven't bathed in a week, haven't eaten in a day, my fatigue has reached hallucinatory levels, and it's 6:30 a.m. and I'm headed to the camp where I'm pretty sure I'll have to face thousands more people and tell them that we don't have enough supplies for them. So, actually, Yusuf, I'm pretty shitty. How about you?* I would have.

But the only response I knew to this question in Arabic was *Kulu Tamam*—all is good.

Nothing around me was good. Like the horse who was slowly starving next door. Every morning when I passed it tied to the tree outside our neighbor's compound, I wondered whether the animal, all skin and grief, would be alive when I returned. The family still used it to carry bundles of firewood, sacks of grain, barrels of water—whatever could fit on the rickety cart they strapped to the horse's back. Its neck drooped low and its spine and rib cage jutted out in sharp relief, loose hide sagging toward the ground.

It was a short walk from the compound where Lila and I lived to the office. Woolly scrub bushes lined the roads; I trudged through the rust-colored earth, kicking up cinnamon sand with each step. Children often teased us expats on our walk to work. Sometimes they'd run up behind us and laugh and giggle screeching "*Khawaja! Khawaja!*"—white person. Other times they'd sneak up close, touch our hair, and run away. The soldiers who worked for AMIS (African Union Mission in the Sudan) had corrupted some of the boys and it wasn't uncommon for them to yell "suck my cock" or "big tits" when white women passed. The rowdier ones sometimes even tossed rocks at our backs. But they were gentle tosses, meant to get a rise out of us, testing us to see how we'd react.

This morning, I saw a bunch of them in the distance.

Not today kids.

I walked past them.

They waited until my back was to them and two pebbles hit me—one on my shoulder and the other on my heel.

You little shits. That did not just happen.

I snapped, all the indignities and frustrations of weeks past converging into a bullet rage. My back teeth clamped down so tightly it felt as if they had welded together. Whipping around, I seized a dusty fistful of rocks from the road and cocked my arm. We froze, staring at each other that way; like a Wild West showdown, for what seemed like minutes but was only seconds. I can't imagine what I must have looked like to them: a crazy white lady—frayed, displaced, and alone on their streets. They turned and scurried down the dirt road, laughing at me, skipping and pushing into each other, turning back to get another look, and running farther and faster away. I tossed the rocks aside, my hands stained brown from the scooped earth.

I need to get the hell out of here.

Hot Pockets and Sunny D

By now I've heard it all. "You're like a young Mother Teresa," a family friend—a corporate lawyer, a doctor—will say, cooing over me and telling me what amazing work I do. "You're just like Angelina Jolie," they tell me. "The world needs more people like you," a friend will remark while looking through my pictures.

I am a humanitarian aid worker. I've organized food and shelter distributions for tens of thousands of people displaced by conflict. I've bargained with stubborn customs officers looking for bribes to get shipments of lifesaving supplies across borders. I've managed programs to provide children education opportunities in the aftermath of war. I've slept in tents with rats and gone many a hot West African day without bathing. But most of the time I work behind a desk staring at budget lines and spreadsheets cataloguing the number of jerry cans delivered or latrines built. I write a lot of reports and send plenty of dull e-mails. But I'm not a famous actress, I'm no hero and I'm certainly not a saint.

Yet, I can't blame people who make grand assumptions about the lives of aid workers. When I first started in this career, I was equally unsure about what this life would look like. As an undergrad at the University of Pennsylvania, the only exposure I had to humanitarian aid was a chance encounter with a Peace Corps flyer in the student center. I entered college in 1995, during the Clinton years, when graduates were receiving job offers from multiple banks and international humanitarian crises like Rwanda and Bosnia happened somewhere far, far away.

In college everyone was studying hard to break into more straightforward fields—business, media, law, medicine—and initially I was happy to follow a more typical professional track, knowing that would please my parents, who were both doctors—my father an MD and my mother a PhD—and had similar expectations of me and my two younger brothers. After graduation, I had no idea what I wanted to do. I did some temp work; I babysat on the side; I browsed the LSAT study guides at Barnes and Noble. I even auditioned for the Rockettes. I showed up for the first audition with seven years of childhood tap dancing lessons under my belt, plus a freshly printed resume featuring my college GPA and spring semester internship at NBC Studios. All the other girls were professional dancers. Somehow, I made it to the second round, where I stood shoulder to shoulder with fifty other girls exactly my height and weight doing high kicks and double pirouettes. The stage manager informed me they'd call if I made it to the next audition. They never called.

Soon after, I got a job as an assistant marketing executive at a New York City–based advertising agency. On my first day of work, I revolved through the doors of the midtown office building and found myself in a soaring atrium. I felt as if I were on a movie set, playing the part of a young girl just starting out in the city. My heels echoed as I crossed the sunny space, clutching the briefcase my mother had bought me—a real gift, for my first real job. I was giddy by the time I pressed the elevator button.

But the fantasy vanished quickly. I was assigned to the Totino's Pizza Rolls account—not to be confused with their Party Pizzas or their Pizza Stuffers. Those were covered by other departments. But our department? Our department *owned* the Pizza Roll.

I spent my days researching the frozen pizza market, analyzing the cuisine preferences of our consumer base in the Midwest: White Castle and Wendy's. Once, I had to go to the supermarket and buy out the entire frozen pizza aisle. I carried stacks of freezing cardboard boxes back to the office, microwaved them all, and sat in the small kitchen taste-testing them myself. When I wasn't stuffing my face with our own soggy, salty brand or comparing the fat content of Totino's to that of our competitors, I was watching their ads. The singsong jingle—"What you gonna have? Hot Pockets!"—was the soundtrack to my life.

I switched jobs a few months later. My new employer was a marketing consultancy firm, and my client list included Fidelity Bank and Sunny Delight. Instead of tasting mini-pizzas, I was leading focus groups with pre-retirees to discuss their financial plans, and ten-year-olds hyped up on Hi-C and Sunny D. Technically, this was a promotion, and although I didn't feel like I really belonged there, it was more money than I could have ever imagined making fresh out of school. I didn't really know what else to do, anyway.

❖

Then, in May of 2000, my mother died, a week after her fiftieth birthday. I was twenty-two. All the clichés turned out to be true: what once had seemed important no longer mattered at all.

My mother had first been diagnosed with lymphoma five years earlier, when she was forty-five. It had felt then like the thing she was most upset about was having her life fantasy—the dream she had built with Dad over the past twenty-five years—crushed by disease. The whole cancer thing just wasn't part of their plan. Or her personality: Mom had always defied exhaustion and illness. She would burst through the front door after work and yell in a singsong eruption through the house, "Hello! *Kids!* It's *Mom*! I'm *home*!" In the car, she played the cool radio stations—Z100 and Power 95—and tapped the steering wheel to Marky

Mark or Madonna. When I was a kid, she always had enough pieces of gum in her pocketbook for me and all my friends, and at our birthday parties she stuffed everyone's little plastic goodie bags until they looked like trick-or-treat take-ins. Mom could make even the most mundane tasks fun—whether it was taking out the trash or learning the state capitals before a social studies test—there was always an accompanying song or dance move. As we grew older, my girlfriends all wanted to be her friend, and my guy friends thought she was hot.

At the height of her illness, Mom threw on a wig, put on makeup, and forced herself to get up and go, if only to show everyone else that things were all right. If she did have moments of mental frailty, it was behind her bedroom door. With us, she put on a happy face and bubbly voice; she was still the blonde beauty Supermom. I knew she was sick, but I never actually believed my mom could die. I just assumed she'd beat this just like she took on every other obstacle—with determination and fervor until she won. At that time, Mom was more than a mom. She was my friend. I went to her for boy advice; I called her from the high school lobby pay phone during teenage meltdowns. She was the person who advised me on everything from what topic to pick for my English paper to what I should wear to prom.

But eventually the illness caught up with her. Parties were cancelled. Vacations were called off. My youngest brother decorated her hospital room with his newly won tennis trophies from matches she wouldn't have dreamed of missing a year ago. She wore a pin on her jacket that explained exactly how she felt: "Cancer Sucks."

During my senior year of high school, I would come home and gently turn the knob to her bedroom door. She'd be in bed, lying on her back, the comforter tucked under her chin, her wig on the bedside table. The sunlight from the window grazed the tips of her blonde buzz cut. It looked as if it had been sprinkled with gold glitter.

No one says *cure* when they talk about cancer—at least they never did to my mom—and even during her healthy stretches, there was always a pestering voice in the back of everyone's head. *This may not be the end of it.*

Mom fought hard. One morning while I was getting ready for school, I heard her arguing with Dad in their bedroom. The door was closed—they didn't want to worry us—but I opened it anyway.

"Jessica, tell your father that I am not going back to the hospital!" She was on the floor, still in her nightgown, sitting next to a large red stain on the carpet. She reached into a bucket full of sudsy water, holding a rag that was also stained red. She pulled the rag at both ends furiously, dripping pink suds onto the floor. Mom started sobbing again. I went over to console her. Dad stood at his closet, already dressed for work. As a doctor, he was used to seeing patients in the hospital, trained to deal with them in a removed, clinical way.

He now had to adjust to sharing a home with a chronic patient. Bedside manner is taught in medical school, but no one tells you what to do when the person you're treating is your wife.

"Honey, you just threw up a lot of blood. We have no idea what is going on," Dad said.

"I feel fine!" She knew Dad was right; she was arguing with the cancer. Eventually, Mom gave in. Not only that time, but time and time again. There were weekly stints in the hospital for radiation, then chemo; then more radiation. Daily, it seemed, doctors drew her blood to check low red blood cell counts and high white blood cell counts until the thin blue veins in her arms collapsed and they had to start poking her legs. She went to an herbal specialist who gave her immunity-boosting teas. Her hair fell out and then grew back again, only to fall out twice more. She gained weight because of the steroids they put her on, her face puffing and swelling. They cut open her chest to install a shunt, then cut her open again to remove it when it got infected. She had a bone marrow transplant that landed her in the hospital for three months. It failed. The lighthouse in my life switched off.

Even though we had had five years to come to terms with her illness—and the chance that she might not survive it—after my mother's death I was in more pain than I could have ever imagined. I spent a lot of time in bed. To me, ours was a fortunate, normal family, with weekend soccer practices and dance recitals, neighborhood barbecues, and plenty of sleepover parties.

Thursday nights, my brothers and I took breaks from our homework and jumped into bed with Mom and Dad, where we'd share a fresh bowl of popcorn and watch *Seinfeld* together. Weren't happy endings just part of this story? This wasn't supposed to happen to the Alexanders or to my indestructible mom.

I thought about the news of Mom's death spreading through town—the lady who did her nails, the checkout person at the grocery store, the receptionist at her doctor's office—all the people who had known her well. I imagined how shocked they must have been to learn that Mom, the woman whose laugh you could hear in the next room, was dead. The two images just didn't belong together. For a girl raised in a sheltered New England town, protected from tragedy, with a mother who could do anything, it was the first time I contemplated that bad things could happen to us, too.

❖

If I could die at age fifty, I wanted a more meaningful profession than the one provided by Hot Pockets and Sunny Delight. I had inherited Mom's vivacity, her can-do spirit, and the memory of her strength emboldened me with newfound nerve. I wanted to live life to the fullest, and that meant breaking the conventional course that I was charting. Impulsively, and against the advice of my father and all the career counselors I had met with at Penn, I quit the marketing firm without another job in the wings. I didn't know what I was going to do next, but I also didn't care.

That summer I decided to go to Central America— alone. It was my first time traveling by myself, and my first encounter with such foreign conditions: I jammed inside busses filled with people and chickens. I got welts on my arms and legs from insects living inside my mattress. I bartered for fruit at the market in a language I barely spoke. It wasn't all that exotic, as there were plenty of backpackers and tourists in the towns I visited. But during that trip, something clicked. I was for the first time encountering inequality close up— visiting towns where there was no running water and where treatable diseases went untreated. I met expats who worked in these countries, embracing a different and intriguing way of life. I saw something out there far bigger than my own New York existence, and I wanted to be a part of it. I returned home determined to pursue aid work.

At the time, I'm not sure I understood what I was getting into. Even now, it's hard for me to distill my feelings into a single, succinct motive. Part of me was enticed by the idea of traveling to foreign places and being part of a global community. I imagined my life abroad would be filled with adventure and rewarding, intellectually intriguing work. Another side of me *was* looking for a way to dodge the painful repercussions of my mom's death. A career that would bring me to the most extreme places on earth could do just that. I would be distracted, from the grief that still lingered at home, and inside me. There was other suffering out in the world, and I wanted to touch it. Whatever my intentions, subconscious or not, they led me to the conclusion that the traditional grind could wait: I was young and free and animated by a newfound sense of possibility—the urge to move out into the world, and to be moved by it.

I started my search confident that I would easily find work. How hard could it be? But every opening posted online, even entry-level ones, required field experience. Some asked for a master's degree. I sent résumés and letters every day; all went unanswered.

I was shocked and humbled. Back then, I assumed that "helping people" who were poorer than me and in need of whatever the well-off and educated could offer would be something anyone could do. I had no idea what the jobs entailed or what it meant to be qualified for one. People advised me to go into the Peace Corps, claiming that was the best way to get the field cred I needed to break into this industry. I balked at this: a month traveling around Latin America I could handle, but I wasn't exactly prepared to commit to living in a remote village in Burkina Faso or Guatemala for a whole two years. Not at this point, anyway.

❖

After months of rejection letters, I found a public relations job at a small but growing international development organization in New York. I had just spent a year doing marketing. I figured that I could handle PR. It was an entry-level position, and it would get me in the door.

The first few weeks on the job were unlike anything I'd ever experienced. The office culture was nothing like the corporate environment I had just left: small, windowless cubbyholes were packed with up to three senior staff members. Junior staffers sat in the hallways, surrounded by stacks of books and papers. Cabinets with half-shut drawers exposed a haphazard filing system. The photocopy machine broke all the time and we always had to wait several days before someone would come to fix it. But everyone who worked there was young, smart, and dedicated. They casually referenced their recent trips to Guinea or Gabon, and I'd scurry back to my computer to look up whether those countries were in Asia or Africa. They spoke authoritatively about HIV in Uganda and microcredit in India, female genital cutting in Senegal and child rights in Afghanistan. Just overhearing their conversations made me feel smarter.

The new job helped me move past the loss of my mom; so did a new relationship. I started dating Michael, a kind and soft-spoken man a few years older than me. I had met Michael within weeks of returning from my trip to Central America. He was the most patient, comforting person I could have been with during those months. In 2002, after a year and a half of dating, he proposed. It was the night of my twenty-fifth birthday, and I said yes. With my job at the development agency going well and my new fiancé, I felt as if everything were finally coming together.

But one day on the job, I realized there was a lot more to it and maybe it wasn't *all* so together. I presented a press release about a program we ran in response to Hurricane Mitch. Our work was based in Tegucigalpa, the capital of Honduras. I spent hours researching the place, the local agency we were partnering with, and determining how we had helped the people affected by the storm. "So," I began, "the article will focus on the work happening out of Tegu-whatever-it-is, not as much in the rural areas."

The Latin America Program Manager—a young woman from Honduras—looked up. "You mean Tegucigalpa?"

"Yes, Tegoo . . ."

"Te-goosy-galpa," she said slowly, as if pronouncing it for a three-year-old.

I repeated the capital slowly back to her, left the press release on her desk, and walked out of the office. If I was planning to stay in this field, maybe a master's degree wasn't a bad idea after all.

People Died This Way

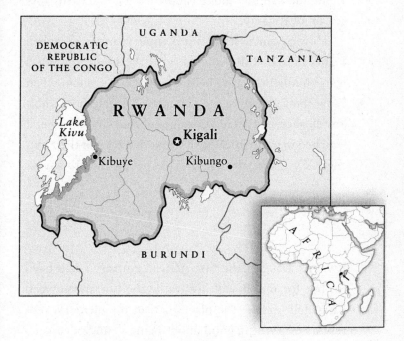

I was sixteen when I pulled *TIME* magazine out of the mailbox. The cover read: "There are no devils left in Hell. They are all in Rwanda." Rivers overflowed with dead bodies. Neighbors hacked each other to death with machetes. Children were separated by tribe, and those from the wrong ethnic group, butchered. A pregnant

Tutsi, the article reported, was cut open and the infant inside her ripped from her womb.

I gazed with disgust at the images from this country that, at the time, I could neither pronounce nor find on a map. But it was May; I had my PSAT scores to worry about and summer jobs to apply for. I could easily forget about Rwanda.

I didn't understand until nine years later, when I saw church walls stained with the blood of Tutsis who huddled together before grenades hit them, when I saw their belongings—a comb, a coloring book, hollow clothes—scattered throughout that church, when I watched men rip thick bush with one swing of their machete. Only then did I know that people died this way.

Rwanda was not the first African country I had been to, but for me, it will always be the one whose spell I first fell under—the place that, in my memory, represents everything good about being young, idealistic, and free.

I arrived at night, tired after an eighteen-hour journey from New York for the start of a summer graduate school internship. I had enrolled in a masters program the previous fall and in between my first and second years went to put my studies into practice. The fat Belgian man sitting next to me was snoring in his seat, bored by an experience he clearly had too many times. I was on the edge of mine, straining to make out the blurry capital city below—Kigali.

Although Rwanda is small—slightly smaller than the state of Maryland—its ten million residents make it Africa's most densely populated country. Rwanda is called *les pays des mille collines*—the land of a thousand hills. The sequined lakes of Rwanda had been described to me as some of the most magnificent places on earth. As excited as I was to see this beautiful place, I was nervous, too. Yet I could easily imitate my more experienced graduate school classmates talking about Rwanda and what I'd be doing there in that casual, cocky air they affected so convincingly. I had to get all of the necessary shots for the first time—the names of which were terrifying enough (yellow fever, typhoid, hepatitis) and spent an absurd amount of money on anti-malarial drugs. I even bought an East Africa guidebook and a new backpack for the occasion.

The primary languages spoken in Rwanda, a former Belgian colony, are French and the local language, Kinyarwanda. Although English was made the third official language in 1996, most people didn't speak it. My French vocabulary consisted of "merci," "merci beaucoup," and "voulez-vous coucher avec moi." The French phrase book I brought was of no help either. I ruffled through it on the flight, but "I'll have the fondue" was meant for someone going on a glamorous Swiss holiday. There was no translation for "The goat stew is full of gristle. I am unable to eat it." The index unhelpfully had no entry for "explosive diarrhea" or "convulsive vomiting."

The stewardess sent me off the plane with an "au revoir!" as perky as her tailored starchy blue uniform. I walked slowly down the stairs and onto the tarmac, taking in my first breath of the honeyed African air. Above the terminal, the neon lights spelling out Kayibanda International Airport flickered like a No VACANCY sign on a roadside motel in the middle of nowhere.

I walked to the terminal casually, trying to act as if I were as cool landing in Kigali as I would be landing in Denver. I shifted my new backpack from one shoulder to the other in what I hoped was a laid-back sort of way, as if the biggest thing on my mind was the fact that my bag was too heavy. I put my hair in a low, messy ponytail, trying to invoke my mental image of a seasoned field girl.

I had imagined chickens walking through the terminal. Instead, there were fluorescent lights, tiled floors, customs booths that efficiently ushered people through them, a swift conveyor belt that whipped our luggage around. I was impressed. But once I pulled my suitcase through customs, everything changed. Throngs of people waited outside, pushed up against the metal gate. Shabby dogs wandered through the crowd and locusts flung themselves around the lights overhead, forming green halos. A few children played beneath the lights, and every so often a boy reached up, plucked a locust from the air, and popped it in his mouth. The rest of the kids laughed and shrieked.

And then I saw my name. On a sign held by the smiling driver sent to pick me up. He wore a blue UN T-shirt and matching oversized baseball hat. I waved, he pointed to his sign, I nodded, he smiled and folded it under his arm.

"I Alfred," he said.

"Hi. I'm Jessica," I said, reaching out to shake his hand. "Thank you so much for coming to get me!" He didn't understand a word of what I was saying, but through nods and smiles we seemed to be communicating brilliantly. I had a friend and I felt safe. Alfred grabbed my bag and led me through the crowd to the car.

The inside of the Land Cruiser smelled of diesel fuel and hot plastic. Alfred revved the loud engine and pulled out onto the brightly lit airport road. We passed large billboards advertising everything from milk to tires to condoms. As Alfred made the first turn into Kigali, it got dark like a country road at night. A labyrinth of dusty wooden stalls sold water bottles, lampshades, bed frames, bags of rice, and electrical plugs. Open fires dotted the sides of the road, and white hazy smoke steamed up from the piles of smoldering trash. The air smelled like melting plastic and burning rubber. Neighbors milled along the sides of the roads, talking, resting, braiding hair, sucking sugarcane. Black faces and white eyes were illuminated by candlelight.

Alfred and I didn't talk much.

"Are you from Kigali?" I asked.

"Yes, yes." He nodded.

"Do you live here with your family?"

"Yes, yes."

"Where in Kigali do you live?"

"Yes, yes."

After about fifteen minutes, we pulled up at a squat building. It didn't really look like a hotel at all: there was nothing distinguishing it from any of the other ones we had passed. The hotel sat so close to the road there was no place to park. I looked at Alfred with some confusion when he killed the engine right there in the middle of the road. But traffic swerved around us indifferently. Alfred quickly got out of the car to get my suitcase. I was embarrassed by its size and weight as we clumsily lugged it up to my room on the second story.

He opened the door to my room and held it as I entered. It was small; the concrete floors and walls were painted a dull red color. A single bed covered by a mosquito net sat in the center, a mirror hung crookedly on the wall next to it. A short stack of wooden drawers hugged the corner of the room. To the left was the entrance to the bathroom, which held a toilet, a sink, and a barrel of water that came up to my chest.

Alfred showed me how to tuck the mosquito net under my mattress so that no bugs got in, checked that the bucket of water in the bathroom was full, flicked the light switch on and off, and finally pointed to his watch—his promise that he would be back for me in the morning to take me to the office. *Wait!* I almost said out loud, almost reaching out to tug on his T-shirt. *You're leaving? Don't go . . . please?* He shut the door quietly behind him and left me there, alone and tired.

My suitcase took up most of the floor space next to my bed. I needed a shower and found my shampoo and soap, neatly packed into Ziploc bags, and walked into the dark bathroom. A small pail floated on top of the bucket of water in the bathroom. I dunked it into the water. It was chilly, certainly colder than body temperature, and colder than anything I had ever deliberately dumped over my head before. A cold shower I could handle; I had taken many of those at summer camp. I used to tiptoe in and out of the cool stream, lathering up and rinsing off. But now I stood still, holding the full pail over my head, cringing with goose bumps in anticipation of the cold spank on my skin. I shivered as the first splash of water trickled down my hair onto my back.

The next morning Alfred arrived exactly at the time he promised and seemed as excited to see me as I was to see him. I jumped in the car and he quickly pulled out onto the city traffic.

When I was a kid, my dad invented the "Ten Things Different Game." We'd arrive at a new place, usually Florida to visit my grandmother, and Dad would ask me and my brothers to find ten things that looked different than at home. "The trees—they're palm!" "The weather—it's hot!" "The houses—they're condos!" "The people—they're all old!" As Alfred navigated my new city, I could tell it wasn't going to be difficult finding ten things different in Kigali.

By half past seven the streets were already crowded with people, either on bikes, on foot, or behind the wheels of cars that looked more like demolition derby rejects. Some had smashed windshields; others had doors held on with duct tape. Some were missing doors altogether. But no one cared—the attitude seemed to be, if it drives, I'm driving it. Without regular electricity, there could be no traffic lights, no signals—just random merging, staccatoed honking, and suffocating fumes.

On the connecting side streets were crowds and crowds of people: women walked slowly, balancing heavy bags brimming with rice or flour on their heads. Some had tied babies tightly to their backs with colorful swaths of cloth, the children's little heads bobbing side to side, like metronomes. Others held large buckets of sloshing water, their shoulders taut, their arms pulled straight down. Young children skipped to school in bright blue and pink uniforms, wearing small backpacks that hopped away from their backs with every step. Older students walked slowly and carried their books close to their chests. Some men dressed formally in baggy suits and polished shoes, holding shiny briefcases with silver buckles. There were no sidewalks that I could see, so foot traffic converged with cars, and they seemed to move together according to a single frenetic rhythm that everyone could feel but me.

Before I came, people told me that I'd be able to tell the difference between Hutus and Tutsis. Hutus were stereotypically squat and short while Tutsis were long and lean. Others said that you'd never know the difference. For centuries, distinctions between Hutus and Tutsis wouldn't have been apparent to outsiders: they shared the same cultural practices, lived next to one another, attended the same schools and churches, worked in the same offices, and drank in the same bars. A considerable number of Rwandans were offspring of Hutu-Tutsi marriages. Alfred was of medium build and normal height—I didn't know which ethnic group he belonged to. But as I noticed the giraffe-like features of some of the women and men throughout town, I thought, *those must be Tutsis.*

NINE YEARS HAD PASSED SINCE the 1994 genocide during which the Hutu ethnic group systematically exterminated their Tutsi neighbors. Around eight hundred thousand Tutsis were murdered in the space of one hundred days—five times as fast as the Nazis had exterminated people during the Holocaust. Without killing machines like gas chambers, without trains that could carry carts of people to their deaths, without sophisticated telecommunication equipment to transmit orders, the Rwandan population managed to turn on itself in some of the most savage and barbaric ways possible at a record speed.

The pulse of violence had been beating for decades. In the 1930s, Belgian colonial officers issued identity cards, which classified Rwandans according to their ethnicity. Under Belgian colonial rule, the administration favored the Tutsi minority for educational opportunities and high-powered positions within government and civil society. When the Belgians finally granted Rwanda independence in 1962, the Hutu majority took control, and a group of Tutsi exiles in Uganda formed the Rwandan Patriotic Front (RPF). Throughout the early 1990s, they staged attacks to overthrow the Hutu leadership. But the genocidal killing spree was ignited after the plane carrying President Juvenal Habyarimana, a Hutu, was shot down on April 6, 1994. He was returning from Tanzania, where several African leaders had gathered to discuss peace accords. It is still unclear who actually fired at the plane, but the president's death threw fuel on a conflagration that was already slowly burning. Lists of Tutsi families had been prepared, machetes and guns were stockpiled, and within twenty minutes of the downed plane, Hutu extremists started their hunt.

The Interahamwe (meaning "those who attack together") became the name for the thirty thousand or so Hutu extremist Nationalists who participated in the killings. The propaganda radio commanded Hutu brothers to kill the "Tutsi cockroaches" and spread messages of fear throughout the country: "You must fight these enemies, really ravage them, in short, defend yourselves." The international community largely looked the other way while the massacres were happening. On April 21, 1994, the United Nations reduced its forces from 2,500 to 250 after ten Belgian soldiers who had been guarding the Rwandan prime minister, Agathe Uwilingiyimana, were killed with her. The United States refused to acknowledge the acts in Rwanda as genocide, because if they did, international law would have required them to intervene. President Clinton had just lost eighteen soldiers in a fight over a downed Black Hawk helicopter in Mogadishu; he wasn't about to put more American lives at risk for another group of warring Africans.

By July 17 when the RPF defeated the Rwandan army and Interahamwe, eight hundred thousand people had been killed. Paul Kagame, the leader of the RPF, took military control of the country, and two million Hutus fled to neighboring countries for fear of retribution. I arrived in 2003, an important year in Rwanda's history for two reasons: the country adopted a new constitution in May and held its first post-genocide presidential elections that summer. Kagame won with 95 percent of the votes cast.

When I arrived in Rwanda that June I was still a student, a year shy of receiving my first master's degree.

I had come to Africa for the coveted summer graduate school internship. I didn't sign up to go in a fit of passion, or out of a desire to escape to the most far-flung exotic place I could get a job. I wanted a good job, where I'd learn, make some contacts, and try out life "in the field."

In classes, the "field" was the reference point for everything. "Yeah, but in the field, it's totally different," someone would huff, referring to a microcredit loan project they worked on in Angola. "It's fine to discuss women's empowerment in this ivory tower, but *in the field* there's just so much more to it," others would bemoan, citing stories from a maternal health clinic in Bangladesh. If you weren't there to see it, to live it, you really had no authority to talk about it. Even though I did my reading, diligently highlighting the important passages, I would bite my tongue and stay silent in class, knowing I lacked the requisite field experience.

Many of my classmates had already worked or traveled overseas, and they talked about their summer job prospects in Ethiopia and Iran as if they were deciding between a job in New York or DC. Danger, discomfort, remoteness—these things were less important than a chance to work in the latest disaster. As for me, I was coming to Rwanda to work for a UN organization that dealt with refugees, an internship that a professor had encouraged me to apply for after I wrote a paper about the region.

Surrounding East African countries had bloody

histories well before the Rwandan genocide erupted. Over the years, thousands flocked to Rwanda seeking refuge, and by the time I arrived in 2003, Rwanda was providing material assistance to close to thirty-five thousand camp-based refugees, the majority of whom were Congolese and the rest Burundians. This agency was mandated to protect the people who crossed the border into Rwanda seeking refuge. I soon learned these were the people I would be working with during my internship—and not Rwandan refugees, as I had assumed from the beginning, and *still* assumed, as Albert and I pulled into the office driveway.

WE WAITED AT THE ENTRANCE of the three-story compound for uniformed guards to lift the heavy gate and wave us along. Inside, I took a seat in the lobby while someone summoned Kassim, the man who had hired me. We had communicated a few times over e-mail after my professor had put us in contact. Moments later, he appeared. A short, balding Lebanese man, he wore a pressed shirt and khaki pants and his glasses slipped down his nose as he put his hand out to greet me. "Jessica!" he said enthusiastically. He hadn't asked my name, but it was a pretty safe bet: I was the only white person sitting in the lobby.

I followed Kassim to the third floor, where he led me past half a dozen rooms along a corridor. The building was cleaner than I expected, the walls and tan tiled floors smooth and shiny. Kassim's office was a huge room with a large window overlooking one of the forested ridges surrounding the city. Lush green light spilled in from outside.

"Wow," I gasped.

"Yes, it's not bad. Here, have a seat." He pulled a chair out across from his desk. "Do you want some coffee? Tea?"

"No, thank you."

"I'm going to have some. Henry!" Kassim yelled. A short Rwandan man wearing an old collared shirt and faded khaki pants appeared in the doorway.

"Tea, please," he said. Henry scurried away.

A huge map of Rwanda and the surrounding countries hung behind Kassim's desk. Red pushpins dotted the map. He stood up and pointed to it. "Let me get you oriented. We're here," he said, pointing to Kigali. "This is where we process all of the resettlement cases, handle all of the urban cases, and coordinate the camps in the country. In this camp, Kiziba, there are fourteen thousand refugees from Congo who have been here for over five years. We do a lot of GBV [Gender-Based Violence] programming there. In this one—" he pointed to the red dot near the Burundi border—"Burundi refugees live. We manage both of those camps. You'll visit them and see."

I listened intently, took out my notebook, and started jotting down words: *urban cases, two camps, Kiz-something.*

"We have field offices here and here," he said, indicating one town near the border with Congo and another near the border with Burundi. "We also have a temporary field office here in Kibungo but will be closing it by year end." This red dot was in the southeastern part of Rwanda, close to the Tanzanian border.

Tanzania usually had an open-door policy for refugees, but the massive influx after the 1994 genocide had them reconsidering their usual protocol. As Kassim explained, now that Rwanda was a stable country, Rwandans in Tanzania could no longer claim refugee status and the Tanzanian government went so far as to call them illegal immigrants. Beginning in 2002 the Tanzanian government removed these people from Tanzania, all twenty-three thousand of them, in a period of three months. Although organized by the United Nations, the repatriation to me seemed nothing more than a glazed-over forced removal of the Rwandan refugees for the benefit of the Tanzanian government.

After so many years in another country, most people didn't have roots or family to return to. Their land and homes in Rwanda had been reallocated to others, and basic social services—health care, schools, water—were lacking. "We've been dealing with the returnees there, registering them at the border, providing them with initial supplies, and making sure they are safe to return. There are only a few left who need to be processed and given NFIs [non-food items], so in a few more weeks we'll be shutting down that office," Kassim explained.

He sat down and sipped the tea that Henry brought on a big round brassy tray.

"So I hear you are good writer," he said.

"Sure, I guess . . ."

"Well, we need a good English writer here to write up the refugee status determination interviews."

I spent much of those early days pretending to understand the lingo before hustling back to my desk to figure everything out before anyone caught on to the fact that I had no idea what they were talking about. But now, sitting across from Kassim, I listened intently, nodding without fully comprehending, and eventually, I caught on: in Kigali, close to twenty-three hundred urban refugees and about three thousand asylum-seekers of various nationalities were receiving limited assistance. Those were the cases I'd be working on.

"A lot of the interviews were conducted by non-native English speakers, so we need someone to correct them in solid English so that they're in good shape to send to Nairobi."

Again I nodded. *Nairobi, English, interviews.*

"OK, I have to go to a meeting at UNICEF now, but Katrin will show you around and get you started."

Kassim yelled for Henry, who appeared within seconds, as if he'd been standing behind the door waiting for his next order that whole time.

To Henry: "Get Katrin!" Then, to me: "Have you found a place to live yet?"

"No, I'm staying at a hotel."

"Oh, OK." He paused. "I'm sure you will find something soon."

"Do you know *where* I could find something?" I asked.

"It's hard to get a temporary rental here. I don't know. Ask around. I'm sure it will work out." I wasn't as sure. Who was I supposed to be asking?

Katrin appeared at the door and Kassim introduced us. She was a tall, stocky woman from Ukraine who looked only a few years older than me. She had cropped blonde hair, a plump face, and a wide smile.

Kassim seemed relieved to get me out of his hair and ushered us out of his office. "Show her around and give her that extra desk in your office."

I followed Katrin as she led me from office to office introducing me to the staff, people representing a mixture of cultures, races, and backgrounds—some from Canada, Europe, other African countries, and many Rwandans. The staff at the time totaled sixty-one, the majority of them being locals. The Rwandans at the office were happy to meet me and stopped whatever they were doing to chat. "Welcome to Kigali," they said.

Programs for refugees happened in the camps, out in the countryside. The Kigali office was where the basic administration, such as financial procedures, donor reporting, IT, and HR, took place. My office with Katrin was spacious enough to fit two desks, and we both faced a balcony overlooking the busy street. The tall bookshelves lining the walls were filled with

unmarked blue binders. Katrin had a tackboard next
to her desk where she had hung a typed paper titled
1951 Refugee Convention, a scribbled note marked
"Nanny" with a phone number, a typed list of office
extensions, and a small photo of a snowy city which I
guessed was somewhere in her home country, Ukraine.

Katrin handed me at least fifteen forms to fill out:
waivers to ride in agency vehicles, registration for my
computer, forms for taking pens and staples from the
limited supply closet. I signed confidentiality agree-
ments about the refugee cases I would interview and
report, and was given a five-minute security briefing by
the Rwandan security advisor: don't talk to strangers,
don't eat anything weird, and don't walk around alone
at night. Any questions?

Noticing the way my African colleagues were
dressed, I regretted having packed so many "field
outfits." I had figured I would need comfortable and
disposable clothing, but now looked down abashedly
at my sensible brown linen dress, as wrinkled as an
elephant's hide after days of travel. The Rwandan
women were amazingly put together and stylish. They
dressed traditionally, in long skirts and fitted shirts
decorated with loud greens and oranges, shocking
purples and yellows—colors that white women could
never pull off. Our skin was just too pale. I learned
later that the secret ingredient to their outfits was
wax—it was put in the cloth in order to repel dirt and
prevent wrinkles.

❖

My first week in the office, I'd walk around introducing myself to people at the canteen, in the bathroom, along the hallways. Perhaps it was because I was painfully naive, annoyingly exuberant, green to the point of repulsion that everyone but Kassim pretty much ignored me.

"Hi! I'm Jessica," I practically screamed at a woman standing at the printer one day. She looked a few years older than me, her hair overgrown and tied in a loose ponytail. She wore faded khaki pants that hit her mid-calf and a loose, colorful shirt that looked like she had bought it in India or Nepal.

"Hi," she replied, "I'm Susan. Ugh," she said, looking at the pages coming out of the printer. "There's no toner left. I told Henry to get some a week ago."

I shrugged. "What are you working on here?"

"Women's health."

"How long have you been here?"

"Too long. Two years."

"So how do you like it? How has it been?"

She seemed annoyed that I was even speaking, let alone expecting her to respond. "I don't know. I mean, lately bad days have turned into bad weeks, which have turned into bad months. The time just kind of goes, you know? I'm just so ready to get out of here," she sighed, ripping up the pages coming from the printer and throwing them in the trash.

I had thought all these people would be so happy

to be here. I certainly was. I wanted to hear how they ended up in Rwanda, what they knew about the place, and how they got into this career. Where were they before? Where were they going after? "I'm here for the next couple of months. I'm sitting down the hall with Katrin. If you want to have lunch or anything some time, just let me know."

"OK," she said, smiling weakly.

When the sun went down I sprayed myself with DEET because I heard that this was the time when mosquitoes were the worst. "Have you ever gotten malaria?" I asked Katrin one evening as she was getting ready to go home.

"Yeah, twice." She said it as if she were talking about getting a cold.

"Was it bad?"

"Yeah, it feels like death. Well, the first time did. The second time wasn't so bad."

"Are you taking anything? I'm on Malarone."

"No. I don't take anything. After you're here for so long, you just stop. That stuff will destroy your liver." She turned around to watch me rubbing the repellent onto my skin. "Sorry, can you spray that stuff outside? It's getting really stuffy in here."

❖

That week, I plunged into the blue binders lining our office wall. Refugees arriving at the camps were given refugee status on a prima facie basis, meaning due to the urgency of the situation, it wasn't possible to determine refugee status for each individual and therefore they were accepted as a group. But for those who came to the capital, where they either had friends or relatives or thought that they could find work, their status as a refugee had to be proven through a Refugee Status Determination interview. Each applicant's file came in a red folder with a passport-sized photo stapled to the front. Inside were photocopies of whatever documentation he or she had and a draft of their interview transcript. Kassim was right—many of the English translations were indecipherable—but I sat with the files until I could make whole sentences out of the notes.

Determining refugee status was not a fast process at all. Staff in the Kigali office interviewed the applicants, wrote up their cases, and put them into the red folders. When they were edited and approved in Kigali, the folders were sent to Nairobi where they then had to be approved for a second time. The Nairobi office was the regional hub, processing thousands of asylum seekers from all over East Africa. Rwanda wasn't its only concern, and things moved slowly. For resettlement cases, once that hurdle was cleared, there were more. The red folder was sent to Geneva, where someone at the global headquarters would have the final say. The whole process could take more than a year.

It was hard to believe that humans could endure the trials written in these pages: if they themselves hadn't been mutilated, or subjected to rape or torture, they had witnessed it done to their relatives. I couldn't imagine which would be worse. As I read, I kept flipping back to the small photos stapled to the front of the red folders, trying to match the events to their stoic faces. I didn't know then, but I would be meeting these people in the coming weeks, and I would be hearing their stories—their voices—myself.

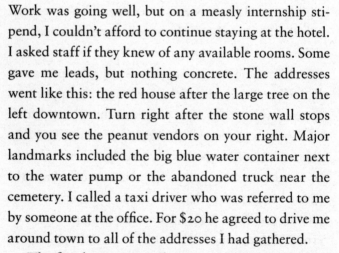

Work was going well, but on a measly internship stipend, I couldn't afford to continue staying at the hotel. I asked staff if they knew of any available rooms. Some gave me leads, but nothing concrete. The addresses went like this: the red house after the large tree on the left downtown. Turn right after the stone wall stops and you see the peanut vendors on your right. Major landmarks included the big blue water container next to the water pump or the abandoned truck near the cemetery. I called a taxi driver who was referred to me by someone at the office. For $20 he agreed to drive me around town to all of the addresses I had gathered.

The first house I visited was a good mile and a half off the main road. There was no running water, but the woman who owned it told me I could use her bucket and walk five minutes to the river each morning. I thought I could probably do a bit better. I got back into the car to go to the next address: after the petrol station near the soccer stadium. But that place didn't have a finished floor and the door didn't shut all the way, so there would be no way to lock it at night.

After a few more failed attempts, the taxi driver could tell I was upset and took a detour to show me his sister's house. We pulled in and he pointed me to a half-constructed room. As I walked over a pile of chipped concrete, I noticed that the roof wasn't finished. It was a nice room, just no roof over it. I pointed up. "No, no, don't worry," he said. "Nothing gets in!"

That night, I returned to my hotel room and from inside my mosquito net I listened to the shouts, laughter, and life on the street. It felt cozy under there, like the sheet-fortress my brothers and I built over our bunk beds as kids. But my brothers weren't with me now and I wondered if this was the plight of all aid workers on their first missions. Was this some rite of passage, the refugee agency's version of an initiation? Because I felt like a displaced person. And sleeping alone did not help my loneliness.

Ever since Michael proposed earlier that year, we had been living together in his studio apartment in the East Village. For a time, we were happy and in love. But once I started graduate school, I found myself surrounded by peers from Senegal and Ethiopia, Kazakhstan and the Czech Republic. Even the Americans, having spent years in Mauritania and China, Ukraine and Somalia, were worldlier than anyone I had ever met. I tried to talk up my recent work trips outside the United States, but in reality I had spent more time in Cancun and Jamaica over spring break than anywhere else. The more engaged I was with this new cohort, the less I wanted to settle down. I didn't so much change my mind as recognize it: I hadn't known how much I wanted to do, how much I wanted to see.

But the snowball had already started picking up speed and I was too scared to stop it. We went shopping for linens, registered for plates and silverware, designed our invitations. All the while, my panic intensified. I couldn't even get excited about my new Carolyn Kennedy–esque dress.

A FRIEND FROM COLLEGE HAD gotten engaged a few weeks before me. One night we met at a bar to talk about wedding planning. I practiced facial exercises beforehand—the open-mouthed smile, the brow raised in delight—to help me look as though I had risen to her level of excitement. I tried to mimic it in the mirror, but really I just looked like a jackass.

When I arrived, my friend was already at the bar drinking. "I got you something!" she exclaimed, as I approached our table.

I hadn't gotten her anything. "You're so thoughtful. You really didn't have to!"

"Oh, no, it's really nothing—just some fun stuff for us to go through." She reached into her bag. "Here!"

She pulled out a copy of *Modern Bride,* heavier than my tenth-grade world history textbook. She opened to a dog-eared page.

"Michelle's dress was just like this! Except the lace was lower down, you know? Like around her hips . . ." she said, swiveling her hands around her waist.

"Uh-huh," I said nodding. We turned the thick, glossy page.

"We just saw these dishes at Bloomingdale's. What do you think? Are they nice enough for dinnerware? Or more like porch summer barbecue?"

"I'm probably the wrong person to ask about this," I said. "But yeah, I think they're probably nice enough for dinnerware." I was trying, really I was, to get up for this. But she could tell.

"You know what you should do, Jess?" she said, closing the magazine and earnestly taking a sip of her white wine.

Get a handgun?

"You should go on theknot.com."

"What is that?"

"It's this really fun website. They give you all of these cool ideas—off-the-cuff stuff, things you wouldn't think of. Like sprinkling glitter on the tables instead of candles."

"OK, what is it, the N-O-T dot com as in, 'I do . . . *not!*'" My sarcasm went unnoticed.

"No—it's knot. As in, tying the knot."

The next day, I sat down at my computer and went right onto theknot.com. What harm could it do? At least I was doing *something*. I typed my name in the first box, my fiancé's in the next, our wedding date, my budget, and—*poof*—it was done. I was registered!

What I didn't realize was that theknot.com sends daily e-mails checking up on you. The next morning when I opened my inbox, screaming from the monitor was my first e-mail from theknot.com. Subject line: *Jessica! Just 207 days until your wedding!*

I felt like I was choking. I could see a rope coming out from the screen making a tight noose.com around my throat. I couldn't breathe. I felt dizzy and light-headed, but not in the way that I had when Michael proposed six months ago. This was in the bad way. This was in the way that I thought I was going to puke.

I had to call this off. No matter how many hours I spent awake listening to Michael sleeping next to me, trying to convince myself otherwise, every day that brought us closer to the wedding, the more nauseous I felt. A voice inside me compelled me to continue living on my own, to immerse myself in this career, and in the lifestyle it required. My twenty-five-year-old self felt sure it wasn't possible to do that *and* be married at the same time. It was the first time, but certainly not the last, that my personal life would take a backseat to this career.

I never regretted breaking off the engagement. But

as I lay under that mosquito net in Kigali, where I didn't speak the language and where I couldn't find my way back to the airport if my life depended on it, I wondered whether it was, in fact, the right decision. Being alone at times like these really sucked.

❖

But finally, through friends of friends who had worked in Kigali before, I found Gloria, a Rwandan woman who lived downtown. She ran a local women's organization for widows of the genocide, and told me to meet her at its offices one evening after work. When I arrived, she walked proudly up to me and shook my hand. "So you are Jessica?"

"Yes," I said. "It's so nice to meet you."

"Well, let's go." She was not a chitchat kind of person, and getting to know Gloria over the coming months would take time and patience. She wore a perfectly tailored bright yellow dress, the color popping off her dark skin, and carried a small black patent leather purse. She was a round woman and her steps were slow, as if she were waddling. Gloria had a driver, a boy in his teens who was already sitting in the driver's seat of her beat-up white car. She opened the passenger door and pushed the front seat forward so I could get in the back. "Skinny ladies in the back," she said. I slithered inside. The car made an audible sigh when she sat down in front. My seat back did not stay upright, so I sat supporting myself by holding onto the back of hers.

"This is Juma," she said, pointing to the driver. He looked at me in the rearview mirror and smiled. "He doesn't speak English." Juma pulled onto the main road, crowded with people walking home from work.

"Have you been to Remera yet?" I didn't know what Remera was. A restaurant? A store?

"I don't think so, no."

"That is where we live, Remera." It was a neighborhood. We drove down the bumpy road, the back of my seat jumping with each pothole. Dust from outside seeped into the sides of the car and puffed up around us. After a fifteen-minute drive through rush-hour traffic, Juma pulled onto a side street that was a short distance from the office. He slowed down at a gate and beeped. A young man, Gloria's guard, opened it, and Juma pulled into the driveway. "Come on," she said, holding the front seat forward for me to get out of the car.

I entered her small, simply decorated house. The living room held a long black pleather couch which faced a large entertainment console that looked as if it came from a 1987 Sears catalogue. Its cabinets held an old radio and a small television. At the far end of the room was a dining room table with plastic coverings still on the chairs. On the small table next to the couch, a bouquet of fake flowers sat on top of a doily. Things were tidy, and everything seemed to have been placed deliberately. One bulb hung from the ceiling and moths swarmed around it.

We walked to the back of the house, passing a small, dark kitchen area and two other bedrooms. Gloria opened the door to what would be my room. The furniture was simple: a dresser, a plastic table, and a small bed draped with a bright pink cover.

"One of the women at the widow center made this. It's part of our livelihood's work," she said proudly, tucking in one of the corners. She reached up to open the small window close to the low ceiling. "There is a screen so you won't have problems with the bugs."

Gloria offered me tea. I accepted and as she walked back from the tiny kitchen, holding a mug, she said, "You will eat with us, you will be part of the family." I moved in that night.

Gloria was not married, but she had two daughters who lived in Nairobi, where they went to private school. She shared this house with her sister Betty and Betty's family—a son my age and two little grandchildren. Gloria was a prominent woman in the community and, by all local standards, was rich, with a car, a driver, a maid, and a guard.

Later that night Betty returned home and Gloria introduced us. Betty smiled kindly as she put out her hand to shake mine. She did not speak a word of English but it didn't matter. I was immediately at ease. Sitting in Gloria and Betty's living room, sipping bland tea, and listening to them speak Kinyarwanda—this was the first time since coming to Rwanda a week ago that I felt at home.

THAT FIRST NIGHT BETTY AND I sat in silence in the living room with our mugs of tea. Every so often we looked up at each other and smiled. On the wall were two photographs, one of a man and another of a woman, both of whom appeared to be in their early thirties. I pointed to them and gestured with a shrug of the shoulder. "Who are they?"

She looked up slowly and first motioned to herself and then pointed to the ground. Gloria walked in and translated matter-of-factly. "Those are Betty's children. They were killed in the genocide."

I looked back at Betty. Her face was down, her eyes gazing into her mug.

Betty's house was now filled with walking, talking reminders of her children's deaths—her two grandchildren, whom she was raising. From the living room we could hear them bouncing around the bedroom, giggling and screeching. I took out photos of my family from my backpack to show Betty. I pointed to my brothers as she took the small album from me and brought it closer to her face so she could see.

Betty pointed to me in the picture with a somewhat confused but animated smile. *This is you?* She looked down and then again at me, and shouted something to Gloria in French.

"She says you are very pretty," Gloria yelled back to me from the other room.

"Oh, *merci*." I blushed. Sure, I look pretty in that photo, at my brother's graduation, with makeup and blown-out hair. I looked down at my dusty garb and ran my hand across my sweaty face. *Of course she doesn't recognize me.*

She pointed to my mother and father, looked at me, and smiled again. At first, I wanted to shout back to Gloria—"How do you say '*My mother died*' in French?"—but I didn't. I just pointed to my mother's photo and then pointed to the ground, exactly as Betty had done. And she just knew—that strange expediency of not speaking the same language.

I came into work the next morning relieved. "I found a place to live!"

"That's great!" Katrin said, I think more grateful that I wouldn't be pestering her for leads anymore.

"Yeah, it's close by here, with a lovely family."

"Family? Oh, who do they work for?"

"Well, she runs a local NGO for widows of the genocide, and she lives with her sister, grandchildren and nephew."

"Wait," she said, turning away from her computer screen to look at me. "You're living with a Rwandan family? Are you serious?"

"Yes. What?"

"You have a lock, right? I mean, you haven't left anything valuable there, have you?"

"I don't know. No. But, I mean they're really kind. I'm not worried."

"Well, I've heard some bad stories. Do you want me to hold some of your valuables at my house?" I was supposed to trust a woman who had practically ignored me for an entire week over a family who had graciously welcomed me into their home?

"No, but thanks. I think it will be OK."

I could expect this reaction from Katrin because I noticed she kept a cool distance from nationals. She wore rubber gloves when she went to the refugee camps to greet community leaders and children. "Who knows what they are carrying," she would say. "I have an infant son and can't bring home any viruses or anything."

AT HOME, BETTY'S GRANDCHILDREN—a boy and girl, ages five and ten—followed me everywhere, anticipating my every move. I swear they would have sat on the floor and watched me pee if Gloria hadn't been there to scold them when they followed me into the bathroom. Betty's grandson knew five English words. They were by 50 Cent: "Go, shorty. It's your birthday." When the electricity worked, they sat watching one channel, which aired the local news and *Big Brother Africa*. I tried to communicate with them in their language, Kinyarwanda. When I'd open my mouth to say "*Murakoze chane*" (thank you very much), they'd smile, puckering their lips and averting their eyes. But within seconds, unable to contain their giggles, they would burst into hysterics. Was it my pronunciation? My voice? My accent?

Before bed, they came out of the room they shared with Gloria and Betty carrying combs and gestured for me to sit down so that they could brush my hair. They each took a side and every so often stopped to quietly stroke my head to feel the wispy texture. They touched my white arms with intrigue, losing themselves in their curiosity. When they looked up to see me smiling at them, they would turn away, clutching their embarrassed smiles with both hands. I was the first white person they had ever gotten this close to.

Betty was a nurse and more soft-spoken than Gloria. She was older and her eyes revealed years of grief. She walked slowly but authoritatively. Her hair was tied tightly in cornrows on her head, and she had a large space between her teeth, which only made her occasional smile even more endearing. She paced the house humming, which sometimes turned to singing, like she was lost in her own head, not noticing or caring that others could hear her. Gloria's nephew Lawrence also lived in this house. He was close to my age, spoke English, and worked at a bank downtown. Every morning he'd sit at the breakfast table before any of us were dressed wearing the same white button-down shirt, green pants, and a checkered blue tie that stopped mid-belly. He called it "dressing smart." Lawrence asked me a lot about America. He wanted to know what music we listened to and which movies we watched, what my friends did and what we ate. He looked at the pictures of my family and asked what they did, what our house looked like on the inside. He wanted to know whether I had ever seen snow and what it felt like, how many channels my TV had, whether I had met Michael Jordan or Madonna. I thought back to the questions my college friends at home asked before I left—Was I scared I would encounter lions? Did I have to pack my own water there? How was I going to charge my laptop without any outlets?—and Lawrence's curiosity didn't seem so absurd.

But I quickly got a sense of why my colleagues shrank with horror from the rigors of living with locals. The interior of Gloria's house seemed to be made of unfinished surfaces, crumbling walls, and floors that never got clean no matter how diligently they were scrubbed. The bathroom always had a soggy feel and a tangy odor. There was a toilet, but flushing it meant pouring in a large bucket of water at a rapid enough speed that it all gurgled down in one swallow. I'd usually find someone else's turds floating at the top. My bed smelled like earth and if I sat down on it when the light was shining through the window, a mushroom-puff of dust arose from inside.

I walked home from work every day. It was about fifteen minutes from the office to Gloria's by foot, and the road I took to get there was lined with half-constructed houses. That's how people built their homes: when they had enough money to start, they'd put down a foundation. Then they waited until they had enough money to build the first wall. And then the second, and so on. Although there were banks in town, people didn't usually make enough to save money the way I'd known people to save in America. All over, homes were in various stages of construction, grass and weeds growing inside the open rooms. I wondered how long it took some of these people to finish, and how old they would be when they finally moved in.

Children followed me during my walk home. All that was needed was for one to spot me and scream "*Muzungu!*" and kids of all ages would come streaming out of their homes to walk with me. "How are you?" I asked. Some only knew one answer to this question: "I am fine!" You could tell whether children attended the morning or afternoon session of school because regardless of what time it was some would always shout "Good morning!," while others inevitably greeted me with "Good afternoon!"

Initially, I was flattered. They wanted to be near me and get to know me. I had scores of new friends! I also noticed that in addition to their salutation they repeated the same phrase, "*Mpa amafranga.*" I imagined it meant something like, "Isn't this a beautiful Rwandan day?" But when I discovered that it meant "Give me money," I was deflated and a little heartbroken. These children saw me as a walking ATM, not a friend. Newly cynical, I learned how to say *"Nt ama-franga nfite yokuguha"*—I have no money to give you. Within a few days, I was walking home alone.

Loneliness followed me into the nights. Gloria was often out to dinner, networking and fundraising for her organization, and Lawrence usually worked late, so I was left with Betty who, although lovely, could only communicate silently, through smiles and nods. It was dark by 6 p.m. and without a car, without friends, I had nowhere to go but bed, where I would read and listen to the same twelve CDs again and again. The monotony of those nights was unbearable. The hours passed slowly, like honey dripping off the back of a spoon.

At the office I would overhear Katrin on the phone making plans for the night—"Yeah, I'll see you there. Tell Mark to come! I haven't seen him for ages!" She'd walk out with Susan, reminding me to lock up before I left. I felt right back in seventh grade, when Elise Levine sat me at the unpopular table at her Bat Mitzvah.

I'd usually eat lunch by myself at a local restaurant down the street from the office. After a few days the Rwandan waitress, a gorgeous, slender, tall young woman who dressed in clothes much more stylish than mine, took pity on my palpable loneliness. She already knew what I was going to order—a Diet Coke and a plate of rice and stew—and would have it prepared for me when I arrived.

I was so desperate to speak with people that one

afternoon, in a fit of bravery—as if loneliness had suddenly been converted into courage—I approached an expat woman who looked about my age sitting at the table across from me.

"Hi, I'm Jessica."

"I'm Nisha," she said, looking up from the papers she was reading.

"Sorry to disturb you, I just moved here and . . ."

"It's hard at first," she said, smiling.

I laughed. "Yeah."

It turned out Nisha was as friendly as she looked. She smelled of sweet perfume that I got a whiff of every time there was a slight gust of wind. Her dark hair was pulled back in a tight ponytail. She had been here six months working for an NGO, she told me, and lived in a house downtown with her husband.

"Hey, I'm having a dinner party tomorrow night. Why don't you come over and I'll introduce you to a bunch of people?"

I almost got out of my chair and hugged her.

"Sure! But, I don't have a car. I don't even have a phone!"

"Well, don't worry, I can pick you up here after work—I pass right by here on my way home—if you don't mind coming before the other guests get there. We can cook together!"

I would have scrubbed her floors if she asked me.

"Thank you so much! What time should I be here?"

"How about six?"

"Perfect. See you then!"

I almost skipped back to the office, thinking about what I'd wear to my first dinner party, what I should bring, whom I would meet.

The next evening, Nisha pulled up to the restaurant right on time and I piled into her beat-up Jeep. We arrived at her house, which sat at the bottom of a steep drive, and I tried not to gasp as she showed me around. The place was palatial, her sunken living room with its high ceilings felt larger than Gloria's entire house. Every room was a museum to the places she'd traveled: African masks of different shapes hung on the wall, waist-high wooden giraffes stood in the corner, colorful tapestries were used as tablecloths, African designs dotted the salad tongs. It was an impressive display, and you got the sense she wanted to impress. I've been to *all these places,* the artifacts said.

We entered the large kitchen and she opened the refrigerator. "Oh good, she managed the pasta!" Nisha said. "Last time you should have seen the mess she made of it!" Nisha was referring to her cook. And when she said that we'd be cooking, she meant making a salad, and this was because she didn't trust her cook to wash the vegetables in bottled water. All of the other items for the dinner party—the large pasta dish, grilled chicken, vegetable stew—were already prepared. The table was set and all we had to do was light the candles with the matches placed neatly next to them.

Nisha offered me a beer and we went out to her porch. "Tim will be home any time now," she said. Her husband Tim was still looking for work in Rwanda. Nisha had gotten a good job here and he had followed her out, hoping to find work when he arrived. "Next posting is his turn," she explained. "Once my contract is up here, I'll follow him wherever he gets work. But I like it here. I hope we can stay for a while. At least another year."

Eventually the guests arrived—ten people in total, all of them aid workers from various agencies. At some point I went to the bathroom and as I was coming out heard someone calling my name. "Jessica?"

It was Katrin. "I didn't know you were coming here! I just came straight from the office! I would have given you a lift if I knew you were coming!"

By now, I had shared an office with this woman for three weeks. Nisha had been warm and inviting, a quality that I would certainly find in others, but most people, once they learned I'd only be there a few months, were distant. Looking back, I couldn't really blame Katrin; keeping some degree of distance from the short-termers was how we dealt with the transience of this existence. Eventually I, too, would begin to regard people the same way—anything to protect myself from the constant emotional jolts of this life. Maintaining personal stability became important in ways I'd never imagined, and in ways I wasn't at all prepared for.

AS THE WEEKS WENT ON and I got to know more expats, I realized how odd my living situation actually was. Most expats lived like Nisha, in spacious houses situated behind high walls, some with barbed wire at the top, others with broken glass bottles crammed into the cement. They had guards who opened the gates when they returned home, and generators that ensured they always had electricity. The houses that I visited had porches and backyards, air conditioners and DVD players, stereo equipment that rivaled my dad's surround sound system at home. At dinner parties like these we drank alcohol from Italy and ate cheese from France. The expats sat around, complaining that their guard was caught sleeping *again,* that their driver was on the verge of getting fired after being late *again,* that so and so came into work drunk *again.*

"I just can't wait to get to Jinga this weekend," one would say, inhaling a cigarette deeply.

"Where's Jinga?" I asked.

"You've never been to Jinga? Oh, it's *fabulous.* You have to get there before you leave. It's the start of the Nile not far from Kampala. We go rafting there." She turned to her friend, "Edward, you cannot fall out of the boat this time!" Her tone was so detached, as if we were living in some parallel universe, no part of which resembled the Africa that I had imagined from home.

❖

Eventually, with my personal life under control, I was able to settle into work. Rwanda seemed to have closed the chapter on the genocide. The identification cards introduced by the Belgian colonialists that differentiated between Hutus and Tutsis—like the yellow stars that classified Jews during the Holocaust—were abolished. People no longer referred to themselves as Hutu or Tutsi, but as Rwandans.

Still, it was impossible to meet someone who hadn't been touched by the genocide in some way. Taxi drivers spoke candidly about family members who were slaughtered. Opening their desk drawers, my colleagues removed pictures of siblings who had been murdered. Waiters told stories about living in the crowded Tanzanian embassy, or hidden beneath a canopy of banana leaves, during the hundred days of hell.

Somehow people went on with their lives. They got dressed in the morning and went to work. They sent their children to school, if they could afford the fees. Some worked Rwanda's soil to feed their families. Their resilience and ability to put the past behind them with such stoic resolve almost seemed unnatural. I didn't think anyone I knew at home could be so brave, so dignified after seeing what humans are capable of.

For the aid community, though, the Rwandan genocide had been eclipsed by new conflicts. Afghanistan was the disaster of the day and donors redirected funds there. For aid workers, the allure of Rwanda was long gone—there were newer, more exciting places to work.

Although thousands of cases still needed to be processed, both within and outside of Rwanda, the office was operating with the amount of funding and staff that would suggest that the refugee crisis had nearly been solved. And so while people continued to flock to the office seeking help, while camps were still overpopulated, and while resettlement cases remained unresolved, the agency was being forced to scale back—closing field offices, letting employees go, stopping certain programs altogether—because donor attention and money had shifted elsewhere.

From my window, I watched dozens of people, many of them from Congo, Uganda, or Burundi, waiting outside the office, in order to find out if they were eligible for benefits as a refugee, or follow up on a resettlement request, or make an appointment for a refugee status determination interview. Women sat on the ground breast-feeding. Men, their shoes freshly shined in preparation for their interviews, milled around, reading in silence or chatting with friends. People were patient and calm. Occasionally they stood up to stretch, but mostly they just sat for hours on rocks around the office compound, in the hot sunlight in hopes of getting some kind of help. Whatever that help might be, they believed, it sure was better than where they came from. Looking at the stacks of file folders on my desk and then over at the ones spilling out of the cabinets all along the hallway, I knew that these were only a few of the many who waited. And I knew that they'd be waiting for a long time.

After I had spent a few weeks rewriting refugee status determination interviews, Kassim decided that I was ready to conduct interviews on my own. Uganda had been colonized by the British, so English was the spoken language, and it was to their cases that Kassim assigned me. These were just initial interviews to get basic information—where they came from, what happened to them, when they left and how they got to Kigali. Later in the process someone else would ask more pressing questions to determine if their stories were true, if it really was too dangerous for them to stay in Uganda, and if they could, in fact, seek legal refuge in Rwanda.

My first few interviews, I shadowed Katrin. "You have to ask them for details. You have to ask them to describe who they campaigned for and when," she instructed me. "What they did and where. What happened to them to make them flee. It may sound harsh, but do you know how many people come in here trying to claim refugee status who don't actually qualify?"

One day, we interviewed a man in his early forties who came with his five-year-old daughter. He wore a wrinkled suit, she a blue frilly dress, and white ribbons in her hair. We walked into the interview room, and his chair screeched loudly as he pushed it back to stand up and greet us. We both shook his hand, and then Katrin motioned to him. "Please, sit."

I colored with the man's daughter at one end of the

long wooden table while Katrin interviewed him at the other. This man's wife had been jailed for campaigning for the opposition party in Kampala, the capital of Uganda. After she was released, she and her family fled to Rwanda, where she was granted resettlement to the United States. She went. Her husband and daughter were still waiting to get their resettlement statuses confirmed. If they returned to Uganda, her husband feared that he, too, would be thrown in jail.

"How exactly did you come here?" Katrin asked.

He looked up at the ceiling and raised his eyebrows, recalling the route.

"Did you go through any other countries on your way?"

"For how long was your wife in prison?" Katrin inquired, while nodding and scribbling his answers.

And then in a higher pitch, "Where was her prison exactly?"

"Do you remember the names of her prison guards?"

This gentleman, a former teacher, answered slowly and deliberately, sometimes pulling on his tie as he spoke. When Katrin finished the interrogation, he quietly asked a question of his own. He looked at his daughter, who was sitting in my lap, and then back to Katrin: "When can I tell her she can see her mother again?"

"We will do what we can as fast as we can," Katrin said.

He nodded and waited, in a moment of deep thought. Then the man stood up, walked toward where I was sitting with his daughter, scooped her up, and held out the picture she had drawn.

"How pretty!" he said cheerfully. He turned to me and cupped my hands in his. "Thank you. Thank you." I hadn't done anything, and felt funny receiving a thank you. Maybe he thanked me because I looked more sympathetic than Katrin, who was still at the other end of the table scribbling notes. The man looked defeated. I wondered how long he had waited for this interview, how he must have anticipated it with such hope, thinking that by the end there would be an answer, some kind of resolution to his messy life. He walked out still holding his daughter in his arms. Giggling, she waved back at me over his shoulder. I felt ashamed by my powerlessness. *I'm just an intern,* I wanted to say to him. But he wouldn't understand. Katrin handed me the file and said, "I used to cry after every interview. But it gets easier. You just see so many like them."

But it didn't get any easier. I walked out of most interviews speechless and nauseous. I met with teenagers who fled after their family members had been killed, struck with machetes until they choked on their own blood. I met with a boy who saw his cousin's "manhood" cut off, and another who fled after returning home to find his house burned down and his father's decapitated body behind it. I met dozens of people like this during my short stay in Rwanda. Similar cases came through this office for more than fifteen years.

❖

The work in Kigali was going well, but I was still itching to go to the camps. Kassim and I had agreed that for my internship I would work in two other areas, including Kibuye, the town where Kiziba—the camp that held fourteen thousand Congolese refugees, and one of the red dots I'd seen on Kassim's map that very first day—was located.

Eventually, my pleas were heard, and everything was arranged: I would be going to Kibuye at last. Kassim would be accompanying me on the two-and-a-half-hour journey from Kigali. Even though he had been in a senior position here for over a year already, this was his first visit to the camp, too. He sat in the front seat of our air-conditioned Land Cruiser, equipped with radios, bottles of water and peanuts, and a medical kit.

Over the weeks, I had gotten to know Kassim. He was in his late forties and recently divorced from his wife of eight years, the details of which he never explained. He hated working in Rwanda and this was his first, and probably last, mission in Africa. "Africans are lazy," he said on my first day there. "You'll see." I wondered why he had come here in the first place; why he decided to move to this country, this continent. To him, Rwanda was just another posting, a chance to make a break from his ex-wife, a promotion he couldn't refuse. Here he could save a lot of money and climb another level in the bureaucratic UN system, all the while living in his gated house, with maids and cooks, keeping his head down until his posting was over in a year.

We made our way along a paved road, passing women with babies on their backs and bundles of firewood or food on their heads. Young children carried bright yellow jerry cans full of water under their little arms. Some balanced them on their heads. Until now, I had only seen the city, and the people there, for the most part, looked healthy and well-fed. Outside Kigali, the signs of poverty were more apparent. Homes made of mud dotted the hills, distended bellies weighed children down, rags and bare feet were the uniform. Most children were out of school—it was summer—and makeshift football fields sprouted up everywhere. Boys played barefoot, or in flip-flops, with balls made of plastic bags or banana leaves rolled together. Women stopped pounding maize in preparation for dinner to look up at our car as we passed through their villages. Others continued working their land as we drove by, their backs extended in perfect angles, knees bent and arms outstretched in positions that would make a yoga instructor envious.

Out of the car window I saw men sitting on the side of the road, taking rest under the shade of a tree. Others strolled topless; their stomachs were lined with muscle like the rows of a xylophones.

Each inch of the Rwandan terrain was terraced and cultivated, making a patchwork of undulating shades of green. In the mornings, the mist rose and hung between peaks, like steam that lingers after a hot shower.

At late day, the sun hit the hills in such a way that it seemed as if lightbulbs were glowing inside them.

It was the dry season. Whenever a vehicle drove on the dirt roads to and from villages, it sent clouds of ruddy earth swirling into the air and left everything in its path blanketed with dust. A few months earlier, a mandate was issued by one of the humanitarian agencies ordering drivers not to exceed 30 kilometers per hour on dirt roads, so as to limit the spray produced by moving vehicles. It sent the wrong message to go into a community, run a workshop about health and safety, and then on the way out leave everyone coughing and choking on dust.

TO REACH THE CAMP, we pulled off the main road and drove up a dirt one for forty-five minutes, switchbacking our way up the steep mountainside. With each turn we got another view of the twinkling lake and the taffeta grasses below. Just over the perch, I could make out the lush hillside sprinkled with plastic sheeting where the community of refugees resided. We passed through the security check—a piece of string held up by two twigs. A refugee, hired as a guard, slowly got up from his chair and lowered the barricade to the ground. We drove over it with our truck.

The driver parked in the center of the camp where a clinic, three schools, a water hole, and some administrative offices stood. Immediately, screaming children surrounded us on all sides. *"Muzungu! Muzungu!"*

Within seconds, I had one child holding each finger, all of them wanting to take me somewhere, to show me something. The little ones at the back were desperate to get in on the action, too, as were the adults slowly making their way over to the vehicle. It was rare that a foreigner came to the camp—usually, Kinyarwanda-speaking local staff led food distributions, held community meetings, and managed day-to-day affairs. Some stared like Gloria's grandchildren did, as if I were a celebrity walking down a crowded street. Except they didn't have cameras or cell phones that took pictures. They had their eyes, which followed my every move.

Kassim got out of the car, looking alarmed, as if he had been handed someone else's child and that child had just pooped in its diaper. With a nervous chuckle he muttered, "I wonder how the mothers keep their kids apart? Don't they all look the same to you?"

I smiled weakly at his attempt at irony, the all-black-people-look-the-same joke. But he was panicking, and I realized he was serious.

❖

I had imagined refugee camps to be like this. Homes made of mud were crowded together in tight clusters. They looked as though they just sprouted from the earth, like human-sized sand castles. Cracks on the walls created a zigzag pattern, like a large road map. I couldn't imagine how these homes didn't melt in the rainy season, but somehow a combination of cement and mud held them together. The alleys between them were lined with sewage, and children ran up and down the pathways, dodging the soggy strips on either side. Windowpanes were made of the tins from cooking oil containers that read "Gift of USA," which was how the United States labeled its food donations so that recipients were certain to know where their meal came from. Some camp residents played makeshift board games or cards, squatting among goats and chickens in the alleys. Already a layer of brown dust caked my pale skin and linen clothes, but the residents looked clean and fresh, their faces smooth, their skin radiant.

For clothing, most people at the camp made do with Salvation Army donations—mementos of experiences they had never had, expressions they had probably never heard. Adults wore "Don't mess with Texas" T-shirts and shirts that said "Shit Happens." Kids dressed in novelty jerseys ("Co-ed Naked Field Hockey: We Know How to Handle Sticks") and keepsake boxer shorts ("I boogied my pants off at Jenny's Sweet 16"). And once I saw a grandmother wearing a T-shirt emblazoned with the words "Tug my Jugs."

DURING THE WEEKS I SPENT in Kibuye, I worked out of the agency's three-room field office. It was run by Meredith, a French-speaking Canadian woman in her late thirties who had already been there close to a year. She worked with two Rwandan program staff and one administrative staffer. I was the only other person in the office with whom she could communicate in English and I think she appreciated it.

"You know, I don't even know if that camp population figure is right anymore. We've been using it for over a year now, and I don't know when the last census was even taken." She revealed this on my first day in Kibuye, as we sat in her small office by Lake Kivu. Refugees moved fluidly in and out of the camp, so we never knew at any one time how many people were housed there. But Meredith was concerned about an emergent underground market, where people traded and forged their ration cards, adding additional children or relatives to get more supplies.

That became my task—to reregister families and check the agency's records. With a team of three Rwandan staff, we went door-to-door numbering houses with white chalk and writing down how many people lived inside. It was a simple job that didn't require a lot of skill, but it allowed me to explore the camp, enter people's homes, see how they lived. Most families crammed inside these small cracked homes, pushing all the mattresses to one side, where they'd sleep close together. When I visited, it was usually the women and girls who were at home, cooking or braiding hair, sweeping the floors, nursing infants, pounding cassava.

After visiting for a few weeks, I started to be recognized by camp members. They invited me into their homes for tea, let me hold their babies, asked me to take their pictures. Many people in the camp confused me with Melanie, a Canadian girl who worked for another organization. She had cropped blonde hair (mine was long and dark) and she was a good six inches shorter, never mind thirty pounds heavier than I was. No one would have ever confused us back at home, but I tried not to be insulted when people shouted "Mel!" as I walked through camp. I remembered Kassim's observation that all their children looked the same. They thought that of us, too.

Sometimes driving through the country, I saw groups of men dressed in flamingo pink uniforms jogging or walking in unison. The first time I saw them, I asked my colleague whether there was a circus act in town.

"They're the Hutu prisoners. That's the prison uniform. Those bastards."

By 2004 (after I had left) fewer than 5 percent of the 120,000 Hutus imprisoned for allegedly participating in the genocide had been tried. Those detained included men, women, and children. A handful of people thought to have wielded especial power during the genocide were brought to the International Criminal Tribunal for Rwanda (ICTR) in Arusha, Tanzania. The rest were crammed into Rwanda's prisons. Harsh conditions contributed to the deaths of more than 1,000 inmates during 2000. At the pace local courts were proceeding, human rights organizations estimated that prosecuting all these people would take more than a century.

Gacaca was the traditional communal law enforcement process that handled village or familial disputes—everything from theft to marital issues, land rights, and property damage. The word *gacaca* means "cut grass" in Kinyarwanda, to symbolize the outdoor gathering place where the community would come to deliberate. The government realized that in order for economic recovery to begin, the thousands of men biding their time in jail had to come back to their communities and work. They hoped the *gacaca* courts could speed up the process.

The day I came to listen to a *gacaca* trial, I recognized the pink uniforms on the men standing on the back of a pickup truck, holding onto the sides for balance as it pulled into the community center. When the truck arrived, wives, children, and friends ran to greet the prisoners. The men embraced their spouses and swooped their children up in the air to cuddle them. They shook hands with neighbors and laughed with their siblings. These were not the monsters I had imagined. Some were quiet and shy. Others seemed charming and friendly. These looked like normal men—men who had lost themselves for three frenzied months, and did the unspeakable.

But *gacaca* forced these men to speak. In order to get a reduced sentence, the accused had to admit his crimes in front of his peers, neighbors, and family. It was the surviving community members who acted as the witnesses, lawyers, and jurors. Nineteen judges, mostly women—appropriately, and inevitably, given that when the country started to rebuild in 1995 an estimated 70 percent of the population was female—determined the credibility of the accused and decided their punishment. I sat with a translator on the edge of the hill, looking down on the fifty or so community members who had gathered on the grass to listen to the prisoners disclose their crimes and implicate those who had participated with them. Those who confessed and whose confessions were deemed truthful were either immediately released or had years shaved off their prison terms.

That day we heard from a man who was accused of murder.

"He killed six people. Two of them children," my translator whispered in my ear.

Without flinching, the man described how he and his group staked out a strategic place in the bush. They confronted everyone who passed and asked for the identity cards. If the person was a Tutsi or did not have a card, his group killed him on the spot.

He told the judges about a woman who hid Tutsis in her house. The woman eventually betrayed the Tutsis she was sheltering and told his group where to find them. Although he denied having participated in the murders himself, the man on trial admitted that the men he was with had gone into the woman's home and killed them all.

"The leader of their group told them to kill quickly," my translator whispered, "because in the neighboring town they had finished the job of eliminating Tutsis long ago. It was a competition. His group was ordered to pick up the pace so that no Tutsi was left."

While children roamed through the crowd, radios played softly in the background, and cows passed through the judge's circle. The accused spoke freely and mildly about the murders he had committed, as if he were merely commenting on the weather.

The community didn't get up and scream. They didn't run up to the people who killed their family members and rip their eyes out. They sat quietly and listened, poised and calm, and then stood up one by one to cross-examine the prisoner. "I saw you kill my cousin." "You took my goats." "You went in a truck with my brother and then I never saw him again."

The next man on trial named the people he killed. None, he said, were children. A woman from the crowd remembered his involvement differently, though.

"You came and knocked on my door. You came into my house and tapped the side of my arm with a machete, telling me to shut up while your friends searched the ceiling and under the bed for my son. And when you found him, you killed him." Surrounded and supported by her remaining friends and family, this woman pleaded with him to admit to this act.

Finally, he responded. "I didn't actually kill the child," he told her, "but I was in the group that did. Bring the Bible here so I can swear on it."

Although it was a small town, I met more aid workers in Kibuye than I had in Kigali, and on our days off it turned out there was a lot to do: take boat rides on Lake Kivu, drive to the tea plantations, visit the mountain gorillas. I crossed the border into Congo for $30, which seemed like a lot of money, until an American friend reminded me that it was essentially a cab ride from the Upper West Side to Brooklyn and to get over it. I got over it. In Kibuye I awoke to the sounds of birds and chickens, walked to the office on a path beside the lake, read on the porch at sunset while frogs and crickets softly announced the end of the day.

My posting after Kibuye would be Kibungo, a small border town near Tanzania, where the majority of the more than twenty-three thousand Rwandan refugees were returning from Tanzania were lodged. It was there that I fell in love.

I MET CHARLES AT THE field office, a small building on the side of the road whose staff oversaw the returning refugees. Charles's parents had fled Rwanda to Uganda in the late 1950s, when the wave of violence between the Hutu and the Tutsi struck the country. He was raised in the capital, Kampala, where he went to the English school. He was tall and smart and funny and didn't care that I was American. He wasn't like the other Rwandan men who had either asked me to get them a visa or to marry them within hours of our meeting.

Charles supervised aid distributions to returning refugees in Kibungo, and I was sent there to help him. The refugees were loaded onto the backs of trucks at the Tanzanian camps, driven over the border and dropped off in Kibungo, where they were registered and supplied with food (rice, oil, and salt) and NFIs (the non-food items that Kassim had explained)—bars of soap, cooking materials, tarps with which to make temporary shelters. In most cases, the refugees' property in Rwanda had been taken over by other families and their belongings lost. Everything they owned, they carried.

One evening, a scheduled food delivery was delayed and the repatriating refugees waited overnight without anything to eat. When we arrived the next morning, they flocked to the car, surrounding it before we had even parked. They were frantic and flailing, shoving papers in Charles's face, speaking wildly, each one needing help and attention. With the calm of an airline ground attendant after a flight has been cancelled, he walked through the crowd, writing down the requests, assuring each person one at a time.

There were limited resources, and he had to distribute

them to a group of people whose needs far exceeded our ability to fulfill them. He spoke calmly to women and touched the noses of their babies strapped to their backs. He organized people into distribution lines more efficient than the checkout lanes at Whole Foods. I was assigned to the soap detail, and handed three long bars, stacked like Jenga pieces, to each tired but grateful recipient.

A huge truck rolled in minutes later and dumped bags of corn, rice, maize, seeds, and oil. Charles split the returnees into groups of twenty. Each group was given a three-month ration of food, which they were left to distribute among themselves. Women took off their cloth head wraps to use as makeshift bags for carrying rice. Others untied their overskirts to do the same.

Charles instinctively knew when people were cheating and would pull them out of line only to see they had indeed forged their ration cards or were taking more than their allocated share. He was in control—and there was nothing more attractive.

BECAUSE HE WAS RWANDAN, CHARLES earned only a few hundred dollars per month. Although this was considered a good salary, my school stipend to support my internship was double that, despite the fact he was seven years older, ran a field office, and had been working in this industry for close to a decade. But his generosity was endless, and he never mentioned money or the disparity between our incomes. His friends greeted me warmly, and at their homes brought me trays full of drink and food. When I'd look to him for help finishing a plate loaded high with rice, goat meat, and beans, he would laugh. "Eat up," he'd say. "You need to get fat like a real African lady."

When Charles walked into town, everyone seemed to know him. People stopped to greet him, slowed down on their bikes and rolled down their windows to shout his name and wave. Whether it was because he had helped out the daughter of a friend who needed money for school, or lent another some cash so he could repair his house, or taught someone's child English, they all adored him. Street children followed him around like eager puppies.

Our friendship quickly budded into a romance and we snuck around the office, kissing behind closed doors and leaving notes for each other on our desks. I was as awed by Charles's skin as Betty's grandchildren had been with mine. His limbs were long and narrow, and I stroked them slowly and intently.

When he undressed for the first time in front of me, I couldn't help laughing out loud at his choice of underwear: classic tighty-whities. He looked ridiculous. "What is so funny?" he asked.

"You! That underwear! My brothers used to wear underwear like that in middle school!"

"What do they wear now, those shorts things where

your balls hang down? My dear, goats let their balls hang down. Do I look like a goat to you?"

If I stepped out of line, he would threaten to sell me to his neighbors. "I could get a pretty good price for you, you know. About fifty goats. So you better behave yourself," he'd joke, tapping on my chest. He called me a silly white lady when I did something stupid. I called him my Tutsi prince.

A few weeks into our relationship, he invited me to Uganda to meet his family, especially his sister, who had just had a baby. I accepted immediately.

We sat next to each other on the ten-hour bus journey, listening to music—he taking one earpiece, me the other—and talking about our families and friends, about how we grew up and who we had known and loved. Outside, the rolling hills of Rwanda gave way to the flat lands of Uganda. When we stopped at a roadside stall outside of Kampala, he got off, saying he needed water. He came back with cookies.

If someone had told me a year earlier that I would be on a rickety bus crossing the border into Uganda, sitting next to the Rwandan I was falling in love with and whose family I was on my way to meet, I never would have believed it. It was ridiculous how fast I transitioned into this world, how much these kinds of moments would sit with me and continue to lure me back to these foreign places again and again and again. Rwanda was so far from New York and the life I had been leading there, so vastly distant from the life

I might have continued to live. But instead I was here, and it didn't matter that my entire body was cramped up on the metal seats of a hot, crowded, smelly bus: there was nowhere else I would rather have been.

But we both knew that this romance would be short-lived. Charles couldn't move to America, and I had to go back to school. I desperately wanted to return his kindness by showing him around New York City. But he was reluctant—he had too much pride to stand on line at the US embassy and to be talked down to by "those assholes at the visa counter."

"Why would I want to go to America?" he'd say. "I have a good job here, I have my family, my friends. What do I want there? To be treated like a second-class citizen? No, thank you." I tried to tell him that a visit with me would be fun. He laughed as he pictured it. "I can just see the look on your father's face when you bring home an African man! He'd turn whiter than he already is!"

When it was time to leave, I went to the airport with a few expats I had met who were also leaving that day. The destinations written on the boarding passes in my hand—Brussels, then New York—seemed like other planets.

But I was now certain of one thing: after graduate school, I was coming back to Africa. Of all the discoveries I had made over the past few months, perhaps the most important was just how much I still had to learn.

Charles surprised me and showed up at the airport

to say good-bye. I ran to him when I saw him entering the terminal with his confident bouncy walk. We sat together holding hands until it was finally time for me to board. I started to tear up.

"Stop that," he said, getting up to hug me. He held my face in his hands. "I will see you again. I promise you that."

Does Everyone You Work With Have Dreadlocks?

NEW YORK CITY, 2003

I landed at JFK International Airport on August 14, 2003, in the midst of one of the largest blackouts in American history. Mine was the last plane to touch down before they shut the airport.

My dad had left work early so he could pick me up when my flight got in at 8 p.m. But I didn't walk through the sliding doors of the Terminal until 2 a.m. Beleaguered but happy to see me, Dad greeted me with an enormous embrace. His hair was pushed up on the side he had been sleeping on while he waited. The flowers he brought had already begun to wilt.

We drove over the Whitestone Bridge in the purple moonlight and looked out at the charcoal silhouette of Manhattan across the river. The city seemed abandoned. The Empire State Building was dark; the Chrysler Building unidentifiable. Manhattan had lost its sparkle.

The next morning, from the comfort of my father's

Connecticut home, I watched endless images of a blacked-out New York City flicker across the television screen. People went without air-conditioning, computers, flushing toilets, refrigerators. They slept on the sidewalks because they couldn't make it up the stairs to their apartments at the tops of skyscrapers. But New Yorkers could rest assured that these things would be functioning soon enough. They knew that the lights would return, that the city would once again run as usual. People stuck on sticky, crowded trains that stalled under the East River may have had to wait for hours to be retrieved, but eventually the subway cars were towed back into Penn Station by a diesel train. In the places I had just come from, the best you could hope for was that a group of teenage boys strong enough—and willing—would come along and push the train back into the station.

The New York Times even tried to make this comparison: "By 9:30 p.m., the New York Marriott Marquis in Times Square resembled a refugee camp. The hotel was evacuated earlier after its backup generator failed. More than a thousand people clustered outside the entrance . . . Hotel employees passed out pillows, cups of water, fruit, and stools. Tailgate parties started spontaneously on the curb. There were six-packs of beer and bottles of water, sandwiches and pizzas, coolers of drinks floating in tepid water."

Six-packs? Pizza? Pillows? This was unlike any refugee camp I had seen.

My summer in Rwanda was nothing: a blip on the screen of a lifetime. But when I came home, I found myself overwhelmed by American excess. I didn't start wearing Birkenstocks and Che T-shirts, or reeking of patchouli oil. I didn't reference Nicholas Kristof in every conversation. I didn't flick light switches just to revel in the miracle of electricity or sit there turning the water tap on and off amazed by how easy we had it. But there were certainly things I noticed.

Back in New York, I knew how to approach a bank teller, or a checkout person, I knew how to navigate the supermarket and could find soap in CVS in less than a minute. When I went to get my license renewed, even the DMV seemed well organized. I responded to ten e-mails in the time it took me to open one in Kigali. Even the subway was a joy, since I could count on it coming and not breaking down. Table service was speedy and efficient. I noticed the streets with new appreciation. Not only were they paved so smoothly, they were all painted with yellow lines! No one cared about me, no one looked or stared, no one approached me for anything. I was back, anonymous in New York City, and I loved it.

It wasn't until I began interacting with my college friends that I noticed a change in my attitude. In college, Africa was essentially one big continent to me, a blur of indistinguishable countries. If you had asked me then where Kigali was, I would probably have said somewhere in the Caribbean. So I wasn't too surprised by the way some of my friends reacted.

"Do you think this is your calling?" one asked at a bar. He was a corporate lawyer at a prestigious firm in New York.

"Like as in being a nun?" I asked.

"Well, you know what I mean," he said, looking over my shoulder at a girl in a tight shirt. "I just don't understand why you feel the need to go so far. I mean, do you ever want to just work on domestic issues? Why don't you work on problems in America?"

It was a fair question, and one that I would consider later in my career, long after I started to burn out. But at the time, I hadn't really questioned my motives, whether I was doing this out of altruism or doing it because I enjoyed the adventure of it all or some combination of both. My answer years later would be more complicated, but then his question offended me.

"Don't *you* feel like you should be helping your country then, too?" I asked.

"Well, yeah. But you're in this field."

I guessed he meant the "doing good" field.

"So," he continued. "Does everyone that you work with have dreadlocks?"

I thought about Charles a lot, but struggled to explain him to my friends. "You mean he was African? Like born there?" When I said yes, a college friend leaned in, concerned. "You used protection, right? Aren't they all HIV positive over there?" Another one asked if he was a tribal leader, as if he were a character in *The Gods Must Be Crazy*.

One night, sitting in an Upper East Side apartment with some girlfriends, I recounted my affair with Charles and told them that I had invited him to visit me here.

"I have to write this letter of invitation for him to give to the embassy to get a visa," I explained. Although Charles had been reluctant to deal with the embassy nuisance, when I got home I convinced him to at least try.

"Well, what does this letter hold you to?" my friend Melissa asked, sitting on her plush bed, surrounded by more pillows than I could count on one hand.

"What do you mean?" I asked, confused.

"Well, I don't know. What if he messes up? Are you responsible?"

"I guess so. But how would he mess up?"

"I don't know . . ."

"No, what? Like how could he mess up that badly?" I asked, thinking she knew something I didn't.

"Well, what if he robs a bank or something?"

"What if he robs a bank?" I repeated. "You mean because he's African?"

"No, I mean, you know, what if he jaywalks? I don't know. I just don't want you to get in trouble."

"Meliss, you said *rob a bank*." I wanted to believe

that this was just hyperbole, a simple turn of phrase—
that my friend couldn't possibly have meant what she
said.

Charles never did get to come to visit. But after that
night, I finally understood something. That maybe
these people—these people I had been close to, these
friends—and I were starting to part ways.

Zulu X-Ray India 9

WEST DARFUR, 2005

I signed my contract to work in Darfur shortly after an American woman stationed there was shot in the face. She was traveling along a stretch of desert that a steady march of aid workers bearing relief supplies had transformed into a makeshift road. On the way from Khartoum to a remote village in Darfur, she was ambushed by members of the Janjaweed, the government-backed militia that was systematically terrorizing the Darfurian population and driving them out of their homes. It was a group of these soldiers, perched in the mountains above the casually improvised road, who had sprayed bullets into the side of the American woman's Land Cruiser. One of them went through her cheek. I was scheduled to travel that very same route, on my way to the very same village, only a few weeks later. It was 2005, and I had just finished graduate school. This would be my first *real* job in the field.

If I wanted to keep doing aid work, I had to go to a place like Darfur. Touring the countryside of Rwanda nearly a decade after the genocide was like doing a desk job in the Green Zone, never facing actual combat. Hardship duty stations like Darfur, the Democratic Republic of the Congo, or Northern Uganda were where you moved up in the ranks and built your résumé.

I had no idea what to expect. I knew that I would be working in Zalingei, the capital of Central Darfur. Zalingei's small population—about thirty thousand people—was outstripped by the number of refugees in the IDP (Internally Displaced People) camps that had been set up nearby. The NGO that employed me was running three programs in the camps: one for children, one for women affected by violence, and one that delivered water and maintained sanitation facilities. I was hired to oversee a study about the lives of children in the camps, the results of which would be used to help our organization plan a youth program. I had conducted research with children a year earlier, during a summer internship in Mozambique—not too shabby, but not exactly world-class credentials. But while I didn't have much experience, the agency didn't have a lot of money to spend, and I came cheap.

Most Sudanese are practicing Muslims and the country's penal code is based in large part on conservative sharia law. I rummaged through the sale racks at GAP, Old Navy, and H&M, seeking not only scarves to cover my head but skirts that reached past my knees, loose, long-sleeved shirts that didn't reveal my cleavage, and baggy pants suited for a missionary.

Meanwhile, I asked myself the questions people always ask themselves when they start new jobs. Will I be able to do the work? Have I just convinced them that I'm qualified, and will they find out that I'm really not? At that point I couldn't know, but in this case, however, there was the added anxiety of knowing these questions would be answered in a war zone.

❖

The night before I left for Sudan was one of those perfect New York evenings. It was May, and everyone in the East Village seemed to be out on the streets. Beneath canopies of blooming trees, bikers weaved through traffic and hipsters leisurely walked their dogs alongside mothers pushing infants in expensive strollers. Conversation—life—seemed to ricochet off every building. I breathed deeply, trying to absorb these final moments of metropolitan comfort.

Before going to the airport, I stopped to say good-bye to Joanna, my best friend. She spun out of her office's revolving door quickly, leaving a tough day behind her, and appeared beside me on the sidewalk.

"You're smoking now?" she asked.

"Yeah, I guess," I said, looking at my Marlboro Ultra Light. "It just seemed appropriate." I was nervous.

"Can I have one?" She lit it. "These are gross. It's like puffing air." She usually smoked Parliaments.

We walked down the street; I lugged my suitcase, which now felt like a permanent appendage, behind us.

"So, Jo—" I began.

"Yeah?"

"Since I'm probably not going to get married anyway, and well, even if I do, I'm not having bridesmaids, this is I guess the equivalent of me asking you to be a bridesmaid . . ."

"What is?"

"Well, you know, if something should go horribly wrong, will you speak at my funeral?"

"Dude. Shut up." She rolled her eyes. "You're not going to die. It's going to be fine."

"I know. I know. I'm just like—" I started to well up.

"Jess, come on. Look, if it's awful, you leave. Simple as that. You can leave whenever you want. There's nothing to prove here."

"I know I can." This was a lie—I just didn't know

it yet. How could she or I have known then that leaving Darfur was almost as difficult as breaking out of a maximum-security prison? That once you got into the country, the government had to issue an exit visa, which they did at their whim, and their pace, before you could leave. Furthermore, flights from Darfur to Khartoum were often cancelled because of bad weather, malfunctioning engines, delayed itineraries. You never really believed you'd gotten out of there until the rickety wheels hit the tarmac in Khartoum and the shaky ten-seater came to a final halt.

"I'll write you every day," she said.

"I don't know how bad the connection will be."

"I'll still write you—oh, don't cry."

As I hugged my friend, I wondered why I was doing this. Why was I voluntarily going to a remote part of the Sahara Desert where there was a war, where an American was recently caught in a spray of random gunfire, where I knew no one, where I didn't speak the language, where I had to get a new passport because I couldn't enter the country with the Israel stamps in mine? Was I going for humanitarian values? Right then, I didn't feel compelled by them. I didn't necessarily feel connected to the plight of Darfurians, either. This was what I needed to be doing for my career; it just happened that Darfur was the place I would be doing it.

I wished Joanna could come with me to the airport, but she was going off to meet a guy for dinner. I would be long gone after her date and wouldn't be there to get the debrief call—to hear whether he was balding or had bad breath, if he was a good dresser or a bad kisser. She was headed to the Lower East Side and I was going to JFK.

My father had insisted on coming to the airport with me, and after buying sufficient magazines, candy, gum, and water, we sat down for a cup of coffee. Dad's white hair had thinned since Mom died. He wore it full and puffy in the front to mask the growing bald spot in back. Still, his skin had few lines; it was plump and soft like my grandmother's—an Alexander gene that I hoped I had inherited. Even though loss still hovered over him, Dad was relentlessly energetic, embracing each day with legitimate joy, and retained a curiosity about the world that for most other men would have been buried with his wife. I so admired his optimism and patience that one year on New Year's Eve I called to tell him my resolution was to be more like him.

Dad reached into his jacket pocket and handed me an envelope.

"What's this?" I asked.

"It's some money."

"I have money, Dad."

"I know, but you never can have enough cash on you."

"Dad, I don't want your money."

"Jessica, it's in case of an emergency. I don't want you to be without US dollars. US dollars talk," he said, shifting his hands around the coffee cup.

He could tell I was about to start arguing and cut me off. "Look, what was Saddam Hussein carrying when he was found in Iraq? A suitcase full of American dollars. You can give it back to me if you don't use it. But I want this on you in case you have to get out of a jam."

I thanked him and put the thick envelope into my bag. I didn't want to think about the kind of jam I'd have to use it in.

We walked to the security line casually, neither of us wanting to acknowledge that this was it. But when we finally got there and saw the NO UNTICKETED PASSENGERS ALLOWED sign, it was time to say good-bye. I hugged him for a long time.

"Bye, Jay. I love you," he whispered.

"I love you too, Dad."

I walked through the metal detector, and looked back at Dad, still standing where we had parted. He touched his upper lip and rubbed it. I could tell he was crying. We waved good-bye again, and I blew him a kiss. I walked around the corner toward my gate before he could see that I was tearing up, too.

❖

My flight arrived in Khartoum at 3 a.m. As soon as I stepped off the plane I was enveloped by the dry, searing heat of a brick oven. My bag had to be scanned before I could bring it into the country. I was warned not to bring a camera or alcohol because they would be confiscated: alcohol because Sudan is a dry country, a camera because the government didn't allow anyone except journalists with permits to record what was happening inside the country. Pornography and pork weren't allowed either. People who worked for the UN could flash their light blue *Laissez-Passers* and walk in without a hassle, their suitcases usually stuffed with boxes of wine or bottles of spirits.

I was picked up by a driver from the agency and taken straight to its compound—a two-story building: the office downstairs, and the expat guest residence upstairs. The residential floor held a few bedrooms, one bathroom, and a small kitchen. A terrace overlooked the narrow street below, and a pack of cigarettes, a couple of coffee mugs, and a few scattered papers littered the small deck table. It was 4:30 in the morning by the time I was shown my room. I turned on the air conditioner, climbed under the mosquito net and onto the foam mattress, and passed out immediately.

Three hours later I awoke to a knock on my door. "Hello?" A female face appeared in the doorway. "Oh, you arrived. Good. I'm Sheila," she said. All I could see was a short woman in jeans and a bright green shirt charging toward me.

"Hi," I said, still groggy.

"Sorry to wake you. Mustafa needs your passport to get your travel authorization approved before we go to Darfur. Do you have it?"

"Yeah, hold on," I said, getting up and going through my bag. "Here you go."

She took it from me. "We're all working downstairs," she told me, moving toward the door. "Come down when you're ready."

In the office below, doors swung open, then shut again—loudly. I could hear the whir of a copy machine, and a phone that wouldn't stop ringing. Sluggishly, I detached myself from the foam mattress and resigned myself to the day.

I MET THE OFFICE RECEPTIONIST at the bottom of the stairs. A pudgy Sudanese woman, she wore a blue-gray scarf around her head, then draped low across her body, like a dress. She smiled warmly, as if she had been expecting me, and showed me to the small office that I would be sharing with a Sudanese man named Mohammed. He looked up from the document he was reading. "*Salam Aleikum,*" he said. He wore glasses that were too big for his face, with thick plastic rims that magnified his eyes.

"*Aleikum Salam,*" I said back, and sat down to plug in my laptop. I had to start preparing for the assessment I would be doing in Darfur and send some e-mails to my colleagues there. Mohammed helped me get organized, showed me the passcode for the Internet and where to get tea. At eleven, he looked up from his computer and said, "Would you like to join us in *feitur*?"

"What is that?" I asked.

"It's our breakfast. Just come," he said, waving me along. Sudanese drink tea in the morning and wait until eleven to have their first meal. I hadn't even thought about food all morning, but as soon as I heard the word "breakfast" I realized I was hungry. I followed Mohammed outside to the lawn in front of the compound. A group of Sudanese colleagues gathered around a large bowl filled with grayish bean soup. As I approached them I realized I was the only foreigner there. At once, they dipped pieces of bread into the murky puddle and stuffed it in their mouths, chewing and slurping loudly. Mohammed tore off a piece of his bread and handed it to me. I followed their lead, dunked it into the soup, and let the dull lentil mixture fill my mouth. The bland mush needed salt. I grinned and swallowed. My colleagues were pleased.

AFTERWARD, SHEILA BURST INTO our office, her sweaty hair sticking out of the ponytail and poking up around her neck. "Abdul left for the day without telling me. Now there's no one to go to the bank." I could understand her annoyance but it seemed a little extreme, especially since Abdul left after hearing his uncle had been hospitalized. "I'm going over there now," Sheila grumbled. "God knows when I'll be back with this traffic." She stormed out.

Mohammed looked at me through his glasses and giggled. I did, too. *What the hell is she so pissed off about?* In the coming days, I'd hear Sheila yell at the administrative staff, demanding explanations, which they struggled to provide in English. Nothing was ever fast enough. She walked out of offices huffing, leaving the people inside rolling their eyes.

Sheila was in her midforties, and the lines on her face revealed years of smoking too many cigarettes in scorched settings. I wouldn't realize until much later that Sheila was a character I would see on many future missions: a burned-out, middle-aged woman, who had either divorced or never married, who didn't have children because she had spent her reproductive years in rain forests or deserts. Aid workers had a name for women like her: humanitarian widows.

One morning, Sheila and I sat on the terrace having a breakfast of yogurt and granola. After finishing hers, she got up and brought the dishes to the sink. "You know," she sighed, "this is the third day in a row that Fatima has not been here. I come to these places so I don't have to do things like this." The dishes clanked as she rinsed them hastily.

In places like Sudan, Sheila and other expats could afford luxuries that would have been beyond their means at home—cooks, maids, drivers. They didn't struggle with mortgages or car payments, food and labor was cheaper, and many UN employees received school allowances for their children to attend private schools. Houses came with swimming pools and gardens, guest bedrooms and terraces. It was a trade-off for sure: families often had to bounce around the world, chasing contracts and emergencies, to places they might be reluctant to bring children. But if they were able to settle down, any attendant annoyances—your car breaking down, a leak in the roof—could be taken care of by someone else. You could always hire people to maintain the infrastructure of your daily life. Tasks like doing the dishes just disappeared.

The next morning, Fatima's sister came in to tell Sheila that Fatima was still very sick and wouldn't be able to work that day.

"Well, when will she be back?" Sheila insisted.

Fatima's sister looked at her feet and shrugged.

"OK, well, tell Fatima that we're going to have to start looking for a new lady."

Two days later, Fatima's sister returned to the office. This time it was to tell Sheila that Fatima had died of typhoid. Later that afternoon, an e-mail was sent around to all staff to make sure that our vaccinations were up-to-date.

It would take a few days before the government approved our travel authorization for Darfur—standard procedure for anyone who wanted to move around the country—so I had some time to explore Khartoum. The call to prayer reverberated through the city five times a day, as muezzins filled the sky with their chants, echoing high above the crowded streets. At noon, the sun bleached the city white. It felt too hot to move, and most people stayed indoors. Later, when the sun's glare lifted, the city glowed gold and copper.

At that time, in 2005, there were multiple wars going on in Sudan, the largest country in Africa. Eleven years after the international community vowed "never again" to the Rwandan genocide, a similar catastrophe was happening in Darfur. Land disputes between seminomadic livestock herders and crop farmers who practiced sedentary agriculture had been going on for decades. In February of 2003, two opposition groups— the Sudan Liberation Army (SLA) and the Justice and Equality Movement (JEM)—assaulted a military airport in El Fasher where they captured a general and destroyed multiple aircraft. The raid came after months of conflict, during which opposition groups attacked army vehicles and encampments to protest the consistent economic marginalization of the region and the ongoing attacks on local villages by the Janjaweed, the government-backed militias formed by nomadic Arab tribesmen.

By the time I arrived the conflict had claimed fifty thousand lives and driven more than 1.96 million into Internally Displaced People (IDP) camps in Darfur and another 200,000 to refugee camps in neighboring

Chad. According to the United Nations, Sudan, with its already huge IDP populations from its earlier and ongoing North–South civil war, had the largest internally displaced population in the world.

Although terror gripped the countryside, Khartoum itself was free of street crime. It was massive and sprawling, a web of wide roads—some paved, others simply strips of dusty orange earth. It seemed unsuitable for living, yet somehow on this vast, scorched expanse a city, fed by rivers of oil wealth and billions of dollars of Chinese loans, was functioning. Multistory buildings were going up on every corner. There were plenty of restaurants: Thai, Indian, even Italian with a separate gelato shop. Although alcohol was forbidden, the sole Chinese restaurant secretly served beer out of teapots.

It felt as if the entire aid world had descended on Khartoum. In graduate school, I applied for unpaid internships, consultancies, and part-time jobs doing work no one else wanted to do. The agencies had seemed so inaccessible and elite then. But in Khartoum, they were everywhere, more than two hundred of them, their names and logos stuck to the sides of white Land Cruisers, flapping on flags jutting from their antennae, and on the tall gates that surrounded their large compounds.

After a while, the names of agencies working all

over the world began to sound like bids for distinction. CARE got its name from its beginnings, when in 1945 the organization rushed care packages to survivors of World War II. Others, obviously inspired by CARE, opted for other one-word descriptors: Concern, Plan, Goal, and PATH.

If agencies worked for children, they let you know it. There was War Child, Peace Child, Invisible Children, and HANCI (Help a Needy Child International). You'd walk out of the airport and see people holding signs for incoming staffers: Save the Children here, Feed the Children there. Religious agencies found their way too, and most made their denominational affiliations explicit (World Vision, a prominent Christian agency, was a rare exception): there was Church World Service and American Jewish World Service; Samaritan's Purse, Catholic Relief Services, and Catholic Agency for Overseas Development, Islamic Relief.

People complained of getting lost looking for the DRC (Danish Refugee Council) and showing up at the nearby NRC (Norwegian Refugee Council) office. Sometimes a heavy accent made it hard to tell if someone was looking for ARC (American Refugee Committee) or IRC (International Rescue Committee), two streets away.

Meanwhile, Doctors Without Borders (which we Americans called Doctors Without Borders, Nurses Without Panties and the Brits called Nurses Without Knickers) became the model for dozens of other organizations. Around the world there were Engineers

Without Borders, Reporters Without Borders, Teachers Without Borders, MBAs Without Borders, Veterinarians Without Borders, Mothers Without Borders. I had even heard of an agency called Clowns Without Borders. Aid workers started referring to each other this way—our gay friends were Queers Without Borders, the assholes Douche Bags Without Borders.

And those were just the NGOs. The United Nations had its own army of acronyms too: UNICEF (United Nations Children's Fund), UNFPA (United Nations Population Fund), UNHCR (United Nations High Commissioner for Refugees), WFP (World Food Programme), WHO (World Health Organization), UNDP (United Nations Development Programme), OCHA (Office for the Coordination of Humanitarian Affairs).

A typical UN meeting would be a two-hour "After Action Review" or "Impact Indicator Breakout Session." We'd play UN Bullshit Bingo, betting packs of cigarettes on how many times these phrases would be said.

"I call 'strategic objectives' and 'reach a consensus,'" someone would say on the way to a meeting. "Fine, but I get 'humanitarian architecture' and 'accountability mechanism,'" someone else would say. Another voice would chime in from the back of the Land Cruiser: "I won on 'performance framework' last time—I'm gonna ride that horse again."

The same overflowing fishbowl of agencies traveled from one disaster to another. It felt oddly similar to the Greek system in college—there were the "good" agencies, the "exclusive" agencies, the agencies that kept to themselves, and the ones that threw big parties; the rich agencies with their fancy compounds, air-conditioned bedrooms, regular Internet access, and dozens of white Land Cruisers parked in their lots. Each agency had a reputation and a place somewhere in the industry hierarchy. But the pecking order varied from country to country. Just as SigEp could be cool at WashU but lame at Michigan, so, too, could Save the Children be great in Darfur, but terrible in Aceh. It really just depended on who was there.

One afternoon, I sat on the terrace with Caner, our young Turkish security advisor who traveled between field offices to monitor the security situation. In addition to the daily updates he received from the humanitarian community, Caner often prepared his dinner and ate it outside with the drivers and guards. "It's the only way to stay informed about the threats," he'd say. "Those are the guys who really know what's going on."

While sucking down three cigarettes on the balcony, he outlined the dos and don'ts of life in Darfur. First, there was curfew. "You have to be out of the camp by 5 p.m., and curfew to get back to the compound is 10 p.m.," he said, stubbing out his first cigarette in a Coke can. This wasn't the Mom-won't-let-me-hang-out-with-the-cool-kids-in-the-parking-lot-outside-Dunkin-Donuts-after-ten kind of curfew. This curfew was in place because 10 p.m. was when the militia, usually drunk and wielding heavy artillery, came out to patrol the streets.

"We advise staff not to wear flip-flops to the camp," he continued.

"To protect my feet from the stuff on the ground?"

"Well, yeah, there's that. But really it's because you won't be able to run as fast if something happens."

Cell phones didn't always work in Zalingei so we would have to communicate on walkie-talkie. Caner handed me a sheet with the military alphabet and told me my new identity—Zulu X-ray India 9. "We're on Channel 5. You have to alert base every time you enter and leave the camp, anytime you go anywhere in a vehicle."

As he explained the lingo—*Oscar,* for instance, meant "office." I stopped him. "I don't think I can say 'over and out' with a straight face."

"You need to respect the rules of the radio," he said blankly.

"It's not like we're in the military or anything." He didn't budge. I tried again. "Base, this is Zulu X-ray India 9. Arrived safely at Oscar. Do you copy?"

Playing base, Caner replied, "Copy that, Zulu X-ray India 9. I hear you Lima Charlie."

"Lima Charlie?" I asked.

"Loud and clear."

From New York City or Geneva, the field is anywhere outside of the bureaucratic headquarters. Once you land in Africa or Asia or Latin America though, the field is anywhere beyond the capital city. So being in Khartoum wasn't really being in the field. Heading out to Darfur, though, especially the remote town of Zalingei, definitely qualified. And once you took trips from there, out to even more isolated communities, you were no longer considered in the field. You were then one step further. You were in the bush.

Since the American woman had been ambushed, the drive from Khartoum to Darfur—a long trip across open desert—was deemed too dangerous. I was to fly instead, which meant getting from Khartoum to Zalingei would be a two-step, three-day process. First, I would take a plane to Nyala, the capital of South Darfur, and from there a helicopter to Zalingei.

My flight was supposed to leave at 6 a.m., which meant we had to check in at 4 a.m. After a 3:30 wake-up call, the last thing I wanted to deal with besides airport turmoil was a cranky Sheila. "I'm too old for this shit," she muttered as she got into the car, hurling her bag onto the backseat. Although the sky above us was still dark, the temperature was already 80°F and climbing. At the airport, an airplane cemetery—remnants of plane parts that hadn't made it, their noses pressed in, wings knotted and twisted—had been left at the end of the runway for all to see. I struggled to believe that this was really the less dangerous option.

THE DAY WAS HALF GONE by the time Sheila and I landed in Nyala, where I was to spend the night before my helicopter ride to Zalingei the next morning. Just outside Nyala, the second largest city in Sudan after Khartoum, is Kalma camp, which at the time housed more than 130,000 IDPs, making it the largest stand-alone camp in Darfur.

It was a short drive from the airstrip to the compound, and groups of IDP tents lined the sandy road. Other buildings the color of earth blended into the brown landscape. There was hardly any vegetation whatsoever; I couldn't imagine anything but a cactus surviving here. Donkeys trudged slowly along the side of the road, carrying bags of food or pulling carts whose riders relentlessly hit them with sticks. They walked on, heads down, faces stoic, resigned to their miserable lives. It was so hot that even the flies buzzed in slow motion, hovering in the air, making it easy to swat them. But as deserted as it may have felt, I knew Nyala was, in fact, a major Darfurian destination, a historical trade hub with routes to Chad, Central African Republic, Khartoum, and South Sudan.

In Nyala, our offices and residences shared a single compound—a one-story complex made up of five boxy cement buildings, which surrounded an open area where someone had hung a basketball hoop. A lone latrine sat in the middle, encircled by corrugated metal. Next to it was a sink and a small cracked mirror. Whenever I had to go outside, I'd hug the shaded walls, hiding myself from the fierce daylight that reflected off of every surface. *This sun is seriously trying to kill me.*

But it wasn't just the Darfur sun—it was the Darfur dust, which seemed to already have penetrated every orifice. I crunched it in my teeth, tasted it in the back of my throat. After having been there only a few hours the skin on my feet turned a shade darker, and my hairbrush was a dirty brown. In Nyala, the office manager gave me a special handheld dryer for my keyboard that got the dust out of the crevices. As I sat there, blow-drying my computer, I wished that I had a similar device for my skin. I had learned quickly in Darfur that it didn't really matter how many times I showered, since the water coming out of the taps was often dirtier than I was. Some nights as I pulled the fourth brown Q-tip from my ear I'd suspect the dust was mocking my attempts at staying clean. "Nice try, white girl."

❖

The UN was holding a security briefing for all agencies the afternoon Sheila and I arrived. It was nothing more than a small room of twenty or so sweaty and exhausted aid workers sitting around a wobbly plastic table, but this was my first multi-agency meeting, and

I was excited. "It's just a security briefing," Sheila said. "Don't get that psyched."

A man from one agency stood at the front of the room and read out the latest news from the town and camp. "There was an incident yesterday. A fight between the host community and some camp residents broke out. We're still getting details, no one was hurt, but some of the IDPs were taken to jail. We're working on getting them released and will get back to you when we have more information."

Tensions between the displaced people living in the camps and residents of the towns (referred to as the host communities) were common. I tried to imagine the reaction in my hometown if more than one hundred thousand people descended upon it. The displaced were a social and financial burden to areas already strapped for resources. Sometimes the presence of so many new residents decreased wages or increased housing costs. Local businesses could suffer from the stuff aid workers handed out for free: urban water sellers, for example, couldn't compete when people snuck into the camp to get free water and resold it in town, bringing down the price. Or host communities were angered by the free services that IDPs received from aid agencies, the kinds of things they themselves didn't even have access to: the water, for instance, health care or education. Sometimes townspeople rented out their homes and registered as IDPs, taking up residence in the camps. There they were able to receive free goods and avoid paying taxes. The aid community tried to temper such discrepancies and prevent attempts at fraud by providing services to the host community, too. But the limited nature of supplies inevitably created an undercurrent of tension, a strained mood always exacerbated by the apparent endlessness of war and the attendant uncertainty as to when people might be able to return to their homes.

In the meeting room, people had other questions: "When will the evacuation plans be finalized?"

"They're in Khartoum now awaiting approval," someone replied. If severe fighting were to break out, we were all hightailing it out of there on UN helicopters. The problem was that there were more aid workers in Nyala than seats on the helicopters. If push came to shove, UN staff got first priority, NGOs were second. No matter what, though, local staff would be left behind, a sad reality I would come to grapple with soon enough.

"What is the status of the police escorts for women getting firewood?" a blonde woman with a Dutch accent asked. "We've had another rape." I listened intently. I'd heard about rape in Darfur before, but the problem seemed so pervasive and horrendous that from far away it was hard to believe—like reading about American soldiers pissing on dead Iraqi bodies.

One of the greatest needs of the displaced was firewood used to cook food and boil water. Women, who customarily collected these household goods, endured

tremendous risk when venturing beyond camp borders.
To avoid having to stray far from the camp, the new
population cut down surrounding branches, bushes,
and trees, which denuded the landscape, depleted vegetation, and led to rapid deforestation. They even re-
sorted to digging out roots of trees, leaving huge gashes
in the land. When nothing was left, women were forced
to walk even farther outside the protective confines of
the camp to get firewood. These trips could take up
to three or four days. Many women were attacked or
raped by roaming gangs of soldiers, militia members,
or bandits.

Everyone knew rape was a common weapon of war
in Sudan. According to Sharia law, which forbids adul-
tery, it was technically illegal for the women to have in-
tercourse outside of marriage, even if they were raped.
I heard from nurses who had to block the entrances to
their clinics to keep out police officers trying to take
women to jail. No one pursued the rapists. Compound-
ing the problem was "Criminal Form 8," a boilerplate
medical evidence form issued by the Ministry of Justice that victims of violent crimes were required by law
to complete. Women who had been assaulted had to
obtain Form 8 from the police before seeking medical treatment. Since they feared being arrested by the
police, women didn't get the form, which meant they
didn't get treatment. Eventually, after significant advo-
cacy from human rights groups, Criminal Form 8 was
amended. Women no longer had to report to police

prior to receiving medical services, and health providers who did not file the form were no longer subject to punishment for treating rape survivors.

The UN was trying to arrange police or army escorts for women. Their husbands and fathers, their uncles and brothers—they couldn't escort them or go themselves. When asked why, they answered, "Because we will be killed."

As the security briefing wrapped up, a final announcement was made. "Oh, and the party tonight is . . . Where is it again, Mike?"

"UNICEF," Mike shouted from the crowd.

"Right—UNICEF compound. Bring your own JJ." JJ, as I would discover later that night, was the locally brewed alcohol, dubbed Janjaweed Juice.

When we got back to the office, Deddy—a polite young Indonesian logistician with dark hair and a skinny moustache—asked if I wanted to go to the party with him.

"Sure!" Friday was the only day off in Sudan, so Thursday was the night to party.

"You know we have to leave at nine forty-five to get back by curfew at ten," he said, tempering my excitement only the littlest bit.

After dinner, we drove down dark stretches of dirt roads lined by gated compounds and *tukuls*—Sudanese huts made of earth and roofed with thatch—in search of the UNICEF compound. "God, it's hot out here," I said, trying to make chitchat with Deddy. He was a quiet man and not the type to initiate conversation. "What do you think it is?"

"At least 38," he said.

I tried doing the math in my head. "What is that in Fahrenheit?"

"I don't know, but it's hot. The only number you need to really know here is 40. If your temperature is 40, that's 104°F. You probably have malaria, and that's when you go to the hospital."

We continued down the bumpy streets, me gripping the glove compartment to steady myself. "There it is," he said, looking down a narrow path lined with about a dozen parked white Land Cruisers. He slowed and backed into the spot so the car faced outward. "You should always park this way—in case something happens we can get out of here quickly." Deddy had just spent three years working in Iraq, where he picked up these sorts of things.

The party was on the roof. A buffet of neatly prepared dishes graced the tables in the center of the patio. Sitting in a circle in the corner were eight or so expats passing a hookah. I recognized some of them from the meeting earlier that day. One had been on my flight that morning. They were of all ages, from all different parts of the world, but none of them from Sudan.

I made my way over to the table where bottles of liquor had been placed in neat rows. As I was surveying my options, a stocky man in his midfifties approached. "Are you new here?"

"Yeah. I just arrived this morning."

"Ah, a newbie. I'm Bob," he said, holding his hand out to greet me. He was clean-shaven, unlike a lot of the other men I had seen at the meeting this afternoon, and his shirt was tucked smartly into his pleated shorts. He looked like he was going to play golf.

"I'm Jess. I'm leaving for Zalingei tomorrow."

"Oh, Zalingei. You'll like it out there. It's nice."

"That's what I've heard." People described Zalingei as a small, quaint town on a river. "Have you been out here long?"

"I guess so. What has it been . . . Oh, I think I'm on eighteen months now." Bob looked about my dad's age. I found out later that Bob had a wife and three children back in Canada. He saw them over his breaks and R&Rs—the Rest and Relaxation days built into our contracts. Every six or eight weeks, we were given a ticket to Nairobi where we could eat better food, bathe in hot water, sleep in air-conditioning, and watch TV. Some people used Nairobi as a stopover and went even further—to Europe, to beaches on the coast of Kenya or Tanzania, or, if they racked on a few extra vacation days like Bob did, all the way to Canada. R&R was sometimes referred to as "Rest and Reconsideration," because some people never returned after a reminder of what they were missing on the outside.

"So, since you're new to Sudan, you must not have tried Janjaweed Juice yet," he said, pulling out a bottle. I had expected it to look like a Bloody Mary so I was relieved when it came out looking like vodka.

"What is that stuff, anyway?"

"Let's just say, it's what keeps us going out here," he said, pouring me a cup.

"Thanks." I took a sip and coughed. "It tastes like paint thinner." Janjaweed Juice was brewed from fermented sorghum. It may have been urban legend, but I had heard that two men actually went blind from drinking a batch that was prepared incorrectly. I saw some white wine on the table and, trying not to be impolite, switched.

People started dancing to Snoop Dogg. Guys were doing shots. The hookah was relit and passed. I reminded myself that I was in Darfur and not on the roof of the PhiDelt house in college. That a sprawling displaced persons camp was visible from this terrace. That this was no pregame party mixer, but a gathering of aid workers involved in the most massive humanitarian operation in the past decade.

No matter how many of these parties I would attend in my time overseas, there was always something unsettling about our revelry. Years later, one agency responding to the drought in Ethiopia got chided by donors—just ordinary people who had given a hundred bucks to support the response—who saw a photo online of aid workers lounging by a pool. The pool was attached to a guesthouse in nearby Nairobi, where staff went for a short break or stopped off while en route to other assignments. But to anyone looking at the picture, a pool was a pool, and to many people it seemed disgraceful that during a drought, aid workers could luxuriate in the one thing that so many people were dying without. They didn't know that almost all houses in Nairobi had pools, that a refreshing swim was probably just the thing any human working in those conditions would need once in a while, especially in order to return to work more rested and effective. No one was an altruistic robot. Relaxing and finding ways to enjoy ourselves was a way to stay sane, a way to make life a bit more recognizable. But here at this roof party, the proximity to so much suffering—the pronounced imbalance of it all—was hard to ignore, despite the flowing JJ. I looked over the balcony to the dark town below, bathed in foggy yellow moonlight.

Deddy approached me. "You OK?"

"Yeah. This is some scene," I said.

"Welcome to Nyala!" he chuckled. "We've got to get going soon. It's almost nine thirty."

"Do all of these other people just not obey curfew?" I looked around. The party seemed like it was just starting to kick off.

"A lot of people just sleep over and go home in the morning. Do you want to do that?"

"No, no. Let's go."

I said good-bye to Bob, who told me that he was probably heading out to Zalingei in the next few weeks and would see me there. As we hurried down the stairs to the car, I couldn't help feeling like Cinderella about to lose my flip-flop, racing back to the compound before my Land Cruiser turned into a pumpkin.

❖

The Nyala airport where I was dropped off the next morning was surprisingly calm. It didn't have any of Khartoum's chaos—just an open room with plastic chairs and a small café selling sodas, coffee, and some pastries. Even so, and even though I was happy to be rid of Sheila, who would be staying in Nyala, I had been dreading this leg of the trip all week. People joked that the UN helicopters we flew out to remote towns like Zalingei were rickety old Soviet hand-me-downs, sealed shut with a glue gun and tended to by toothless bushmen. I walked outside to see the white helicopter parked on the tarmac; it looked pretty sturdy. But then I recognized the pilot. He had been at the party, doing shots with his friends in the corner. *Please don't tell me he's flying this thing.* He was.

A handful of other aid workers and I climbed up the small steps into the helicopter and took our seats. The hungover pilot started the rotor, turned around, and yelled something about seat belts nobody could hear over the roar of the engine. For a moment, we hung in the air, then rapidly ascended into the cloudless sky. I looked through the little window and watched the veins of the riverbed zigzag across the expanse of coffee-colored terrain below. As we got closer to Za-lingei, signs of life appeared; from the helicopter, goats grazing below looked like white sprinkles on a scoop of caramel ice cream. Before we landed, the helicopter hovered in the air to let a herd of camels pass below.

Their long, clumsy legs kicked up clouds of blurry sand, making the air thick and puffy.

Adam, a driver from my NGO, was waiting with a few other drivers outside the small fence surrounding the airfield. Although we plastered agency stickers onto any moving vehicle in Khartoum, in Darfur discretion was encouraged for security reasons. Here, all the agencies used unmarked Land Cruisers, a policy that made it blatantly obvious who was part of the aid community but at least served to conceal particular agency affiliations.

Adam grabbed my bags and flung them into the back of the pickup. Driving through the small town, we passed men walking slowly alongside the road, their long white *djellabas* and matching turbans glowing against the dry, muted landscape. Some pulled donkey carts or rode on donkeys; others paced the dusty roads with friends, their arms intertwined. Although men and women never showed each other affection in public, it was not uncommon to see men walking through town hand in hand, or with their arms on each other's waists. There weren't many women on the streets, but those who were all wore multicolored *tobes* draped around their bodies. A group of them strolled in sync along the dull horizon, dressed brightly in magentas, limes, golds, aquas. They looked like walking flowers.

The town was centered around a colorful market where vendors came to sell vegetables, meats, grains, and rice. Women sat on the ground or on short stools, adjusting their head scarves, their crops lined up on blankets and in baskets in front of them. Fruit was arranged in miniature pyramids, tomatoes grouped in piles of six, strips of okra stacked delicately. Small shops opened up onto the square, some with freezers containing soda, juice, and water, others with shelves lined with canned goods, biscuits, and cereals. There were designated areas where men parked their donkeys and camels while shopping. Many of the camels were tied with their two front legs folded back at the knee so they couldn't walk anywhere. They seemed confused and helpless, hopping uncomfortably as they tried to stand up.

We drove through the main square slowly. There wasn't a road, just a large open space where cars could pass. In a place like this, where the majority of vehicles were those of aid agencies, roads didn't really exist. Someone told me that you could tell how long a place had had vehicles—and therefore how long aid workers had been around—by looking at the behavior of the animals. If they were oblivious to the sound of a honking horn, you knew cars were new to the scene. In Zalingei, animals strode in and out of traffic, unaware of the potential dangers of high-speed vehicles. Some lounged casually in the middle of the road until drivers got out and physically pushed them aside.

WE PULLED UP TO THE NGO compound and Adam cut the engine. A guard opened the heavy, squeaky gate and we proceeded down a stone path leading to a flowering tree. The complex looked like a low-budget retreat center. To my left was a row of bedrooms and ahead was an open kitchen and dining area, big enough to hold a Ping-Pong table and some sagging hammocks. The workday was over and my new colleagues were already back from the office and sitting around the kitchen table, casually eating and chatting, some with laptops open.

A warm Bangladeshi woman in her early thirties with a round face, deep dimples, and curly hair heard the gate open and skipped over to me as I lugged my suitcase along the pebbly path. She immediately put out a hand to help. "You're Jessica! I've been waiting for you! I'm Amina." After my time with Sheila, I was relieved to be welcomed by such a friendly woman, especially since I knew she would be my direct supervisor. We had exchanged a few e-mails before I arrived but I hadn't guessed she'd be this nice.

Amina introduced me to my new colleagues. Laura, the gender-based violence officer, had already been working in the camps for five months. She was in her early thirties, a hardened rape counselor from Queens who loved the Beastie Boys. She had a thick tattoo around her arm, and spoke with an unsentimental New York accent. Matthew, a shy, sweet Swiss water engineer, oversaw the water and sanitation program, which included everything from basic camp hygiene, to digging wells and designing and constructing latrines. Although he spent his days figuring out how to keep people clean and safe from their own shit, he blushed whenever the word was spoken. "I prefer to call it excrement," he said.

Christine was an adorable blonde Canadian in her early twenties who always seemed to be bouncing. She had been here for more than seven months working as the finance administrator. Like me, this was her first real job in the field. Then there was Jumma, an older Pakistani man in charge of logistics. Jumma was routinely asked to do the impossible, procuring everything from Nescafé to printing paper, from the foam mattresses we slept on to the daily donkey delivery of two barrels of water that we used to shower. He had a head of thick gray hair, stocky legs, and pants with ten pockets. You wanted him on your side because he'd be the one to find a working fan or extra lamp for your bedroom when everyone else said it was out of the question.

Dmitri was the head of the Zalingei office: everyone's boss. A tall, balding, handsome ex-military man from Russia, he was kind and approachable despite his intimidating résumé. He wore a T-shirt which displayed a picture of his wife and son and drank his coffee from a mug with the same photo on it. Dmitri welcomed me warmly and showed me to my room. It was small but had everything I needed: a bed and mosquito net, a lightbulb, a screened window, a fan, and a small dresser. After so much anticipation, I was finally here, and the place didn't seem nearly as rough as I had expected. I unpacked slowly and heard a knock on my door.

Amina popped her head in. "You OK?"

"Yes, yes!" I said. "Here, come in." I didn't have a chair in my room so she sat on the bed.

"It's really great to have you here. I think your study will really help us plan our programs. I have some ideas now and am applying for more funding, but we need to know more about the children and their needs before we can make further plans."

People like Amina ran programs that worked to restore normalcy for children. Experts in child psychology had long understood that children needed structured and stimulating places to go and outlets for play, especially after times of trauma. Usually children were the most resilient people in a population and could rebound easily if given the chance just to be kids. My role was to investigate how the children in the camps were coping with the changes in their lives—to question boys and girls about their feelings of safety, their daily routines, their fears, who they went to for help and support. There were many questions Amina wanted answered. Did girls go to school—or were they too busy with household chores or taking care of their younger siblings? Did boys go to school—or did they try to earn money by making bricks? What did the children here like to do for fun? Had their behavior changed since coming to the camp? Did any show signs of antisocial behavior? What did antisocial behavior even look like in place like Darfur?

"I'm excited, too." Elated was more like it.

"Well, let me know if you need anything and I'll see you out there for dinner. My room is right next door,"

Amina said, getting up to leave. She pulled on her long, yellow blouse so that it hung to mid-thigh.

I changed my clothes for dinner and walked outside. Laura was already there, tucking into a plate of cold lentils, some mushy spinach-like greens, white rice, and chicken. She looked up at me. "Sorry, I couldn't wait. Starving. Plates and forks and stuff are in the cabinet over there," she said, pointing to a tall wooden cabinet, full of all sorts of unmatched utensils, like a rummage bin at a tag sale.

The rest of my new colleagues came out one at a time and I filled my plate with food. It was surprisingly good. I told everyone so.

"Ha," Laura laughed. "That's how you tell the newbies. Give it a few days. We have the same thing every night."

Dmitri came out of his room holding a radio, a satellite phone, and his cell phone, switching among them to get reports of what was going on in the neighboring town of Mukjar. I tried to listen to what he was saying as we ate.

"There's no one in the markets . . . Right. The weapons are facing outward?" Dmitri paced up and down the corridor. "No camels. Yeah, sounds pretty standard. Uh-huh. Right. OK, I'll call back in half an hour." He got off the phone and walked back to where we were sitting.

"So, Alasdair says there's talk of another attack," he announced.

Alasdair was the head of the Mukjar office. Apparently he had information that the Janjaweed would soon be attacking the town. He and Dmitri were discussing whether Alasdair should evacuate the staff and come to Zalingei.

"God, Jessica Simpson has really gained a lot of weight," Christine said, flipping through the *People* magazine I brought from home.

"I'm gonna hop in the shower and then watch the last episode of *West Wing* if anyone wants to join," Laura announced, slapping her thighs before jumping out of her seat.

"Sweet. I'll make some popcorn," Matthew said.

Did no one just hear what Dmitri said? Was I the only one concerned that a neighboring town was being attacked? How far was Mukjar anyway? Was it like Brooklyn to Manhattan or Philadelphia to Manhattan?

"Look, we're not going to take any measures until we get more information," Dmitri tried to reassure me. I must have looked panicked. "But if something should start to go down, you'll get out. Don't worry."

Nothing did go down that night, or any night during my time there. But life was spent in a cloud of looming danger, the prospect that something could kick off at any moment. Just one year later, there were regular attacks in the camp, stories of the Janjaweed setting fire to thirty homes during one raid, a report that a local leader had been murdered. My colleagues were unflinching when faced with rumors of attacks, but I had yet to build up my tolerance for such dangers.

❖

Life on lockdown was pretty straightforward. After 8 p.m. curfew none of us could go anywhere, so we sat around the table talking and smoking. Christine had brought a huge stack of pirated DVDs back from her last trip to Nairobi, and Jumma had sourced an old TV and propped it atop the refrigerator, so sometimes we piled extra mattresses on the floor and watched movies. Other nights we played poker or Ping-Pong on the slanted, rain-damaged table. Or we talked about our lives at home over candlelight in the dining area, licking forkfuls of Nutella and drinking warm, Gatorade-infused water. There wasn't much in the way of privacy and it wasn't long before I'd know when all of my new colleagues were going to the bathroom or to bed, what they looked like first thing waking up or coming out of the shower wrapped in a towel.

Although our compound may have felt like summer camp, on the outskirts of Zalingei were two displaced persons camps—Hassa Hissa and Hamadyia. There were close to one hundred of these camps scattered across the Darfur region, housing villagers who fled violence and came to the closest town, hoping to find safety in numbers and security near an urban center, far from the open stretches of desert where attacks could happen unnoticed. The Janjaweed's tactics were working—their purpose was to terrorize farmers until they ran off their property and were too scared to return. Once a critical mass was reached in these settlements, aid agencies came to provide basic services and ensure humane living conditions.

Camps were never intended to be permanent solutions but their closure and people's safe return hinged on the end of war—requiring delicate political arrangements that might not be reached for years. Suddenly, the very elements that were absent from people's villages were available, free of charge and courtesy of the international community. In the camps, children who had never been to school were now able to access basic education. People who had never seen a doctor received free medical care. Women learned new skills and maybe a new trade. The assistance may have been rudimentary, but it often provided more than many of these people had had back in their villages. Though no one outwardly admitted a preference for the camp over a life at home, the former certainly boasted certain advantages.

The humanitarian community, aware of this discrepancy, struck a fine balance between providing resources in a way that allowed people to live with some semblance of dignity and inadvertently creating permanent slums on the outskirts of urban centers. Some agencies invested back into the community, focusing beyond camp borders in an effort to incentivize people to return to their previous lives when the violence died down. So far, with the ongoing instability of the region, these attempts have not exactly met with marked success: by early 2013 there were still 1.4 million IDPs living in Darfur and 204,000 refugees in Chad.

❖

On my first day inside Hassa Hissa, the bigger of the two camps, I was surprised by how sprawling it felt. Although homes were tightly clustered together, the amount of land the camp took up was massive. Living quarters, built with plastic sheeting, mats, grass, and millet stalks, came in various shapes: circles with sloped roofs, squares with flat roofs. Throughout the camp, men sat on colorful mats, their heads covered by small white caps or loosely tied wraps. A few wore checkered scarves around their necks, the sole splash of color in the sea of white attire. Elderly men sat, holding canes, in the few available chairs. They were sheltered from the sun by threadbare blankets, scrap plastic, or cardboard boxes sewn together and draped over dead tree branches. At prayer time, the men stood in a line, bowing and kneeling in unison.

As in the towns, you didn't see many women out and about. Most were gathered at the water holes or stayed in their homes. One of Laura's projects for the women at the camp was teaching women how to make fuel-efficient stoves out of available materials—donkey dung, dirt, hay. These stoves burned firewood at a rate ten times slower than the traditional method, reducing fuel consumption and making women less vulnerable to attack, since they would spend less time collecting firewood. Laura oversaw the project with local female trainers who taught women how to make the stoves and tasked each of them with teaching ten more women, until the whole camp was covered.

Matthew, our Swiss friend, made sure the population had enough water to drink and places to go to the bathroom. A common form of death for children under five was diarrhea contracted from unclean drinking or bathing water. With such crowded conditions, basic cleanliness was an essential measure to reduce mortality. Matthew trained local hygiene promoters who went door-to-door teaching families about the importance of washing their hands, how to store water safely, or fix the pumps if they broke. Many of the people in the camp were used to walking out to the field somewhere to go to the bathroom. Few had ever seen a latrine or knew its purpose. Many of the latrines that Matthew had carefully and expensively built were going unused because people were afraid of falling in. The hygiene promoters had to teach people how to use them.

Other agencies worked on setting up schools, running clinics, providing food, distributing materials for shelter. I was working on a tiny piece of the whole operation and so my exposure to other branches was limited. My project had a start date and an end date, there were specific pieces of information I was expected to discover and document, my tasks were straightforward. For others, the work never ended. It wasn't until my next assignment in Darfur a few months later that I'd realize how interconnected these programs were, the immense effort that was required to coordinate their projects, and just how messy aid work could become.

❖

I loved my job. I went into the camps every day to play with children, talk to them and learn about their lives. They were so excited to break up the monotony of their days that dozens lined up outside the tent hoping to get in on a piece of the action. Girls, usually tasked with household chores, said that fetching water from the borehole was their favorite time of day. They'd lay their jerry can down, marking their place in line, and braid each other's hair, or play *kebenong qua,* a jumping game where they jumped high, quickly bringing their feet up to their inner thighs and smacking them together before reaching the ground. Some played *Tongag tonga*—a game where they pretended a brick was a toy house. Others sat there chatting and giggling like girls at recess.

Boys' favorite activity was going to religious school, where they were taught to read from the Koran. In the eyes of Sudanese elders, Koranic school was where the boys became men. I'd see boys walking to school, carrying the small wooden boards on which they took notes and learned to read and write. They too collected firewood but didn't share it with girls for cooking— they used it specifically for reading at night.

The children reminisced about the things they

missed in their villages: tending to their gardens, eating mangos, swimming in ponds, sucking on sugarcane. They had beds with sheets there, they said. They missed their good clothing, which they had to leave behind when they fled. Boys missed playing football. Girls missed fetching water from the rivers, where they swam and played. "We moved freely then," they said, looking down at their feet. I asked teachers and parents how their children's behavior had changed since the conflict started. Children showed normal signs of distress, they said: bed-wetting, restlessness, and sadness. Some were easily distracted, angry, and violent. Mothers said a few boys regularly went to the market and pretended to attack it.

Camp life disrupted many social norms of this community. An elderly man wearing a long white *djellaba* told me that, at home, it was customary for boys and girls to sleep opposite one another and for parents to separate themselves from their children by the time they are ten, so they "don't discover the serious relationship between man and wife." He blushed as he told me this, stroking his cane and averting his eyes. Space limitations in the camp rendered such separation impossible. Things were getting awkward.

Other disruptions were due to the arrival of so many foreigners. Whenever a white person entered the camps, children would encircle the car, screaming "*Khawaja! Khawaja!*" in unison. It was like Rwanda, but there we had been *muzungus*. One of my questions to children was who they wanted to be like when they grew up. Many said teachers, parents, or community elders. But some said they wanted to actually become a *khawaja.* To these kids, white people drove fancy cars, helped their parents, and distributed tons of food and goods to them and their families. White people wielded authority.

❖

Most of my interactions with the children were confined to a tent. These makeshift structures may have provided shelter from the sun but offered little relief from the unrelenting heat. In fact, the plastic shell trapped the hot, desert air, turning each tent into a plantless greenhouse. I did my best to stay focused, ignoring the tickling beads of sweat as they trickled down my chest and collected in the folds of my belly. After one of the groups, I stretched my arms and neck, gazing upward at the discolored plastic ceiling that seemed to be melting onto us. As I looked closer, I heard a faint buzzing and noticed a subtle vibration. The roof of the tent was covered with a layer of dank, humming flies. And those brown spots on my notebook? It was fly shit, or fly spit, or whatever it was flies did. I tried not to think about how much of their excrement had fallen onto my skin or gotten absorbed in my hair, and summoned the next group for our meeting.

Haboobs, as the locals called them—I called them mini-tornadoes—swirled through the lanes of the camp, like dust devils in old Westerns. Long skinny lines of dust would scrape the sky, pulling apart any unfortunate structures in their way. One day, while speaking to a group of about fifteen children, I heard an unfamiliar flapping and howling, like a plane passing too low overhead. I peered outside and saw a wall of dust whirling toward our rickety shelter. Parts of roofs from other houses had already been ripped off. Panicked, I huddled the kids together, wishing I could cover them all with my head scarf until it passed. The hut trembled, some straw from the walls tore off, a massive gust of dust and wind burst inside, and it was over. I peered out from my head scarf and looked around to see whether or not we were still in Darfur anymore.

The kids, of course, got an enormous kick out of my alarm. Dust storms were the least of their worries; they dealt with them every day. The only thing new to them was this foreigner whose hysteria over a little bit of dust provided amusement to last a week. They rolled on the floor, laughing and pointing at me. I deserved it.

I couldn't believe how well behaved and obedient the children were after all they'd been through. I remembered substitute teachers back at home coming in to teach fifth-grade math and the ordeal the other students and I would put him through. But the kids in the camps were eager to be there, so enthusiastic to share, staring at me with credulous eyes. I often wondered if they would live in the camp their whole lives, and what their future would be. Whatever program we ended up providing for these children would be such a small offering for a chance at a promising adulthood. What they really needed was structural change, a swift resolution to the conflict so they didn't spend their childhoods languishing in some makeshift camps. But that wasn't really the business we were in. Political negotiations were happening simultaneously to our humanitarian intervention; we just had to wait and see what would happen—and keep working in the meantime.

For the first time in my career, I had my own office, where I'd return at the end of every day to write up my notes and findings. It was a large room, empty save for the desk and a plastic lawn chair. As basic as this room was, having this space all to myself and knowing that after my work was done I was going home to dine and sleep under the same roof as the same seven people every night was a blessing. My agency provided free English lessons to its staff after work hours, so in the evenings the neighboring room was packed with drivers, cooks, and other employees. Curt phrases emanated in staccato unison: "What. time. is. it?" "It. is. noon." "What. have. you. got?" "We. have. got. books." "What. is. your. name?" "My. name. is. Mohamed."

After work, I usually walked back to the compound, this being my only chance to poke around the market and interact with people who lived in the town. Some nights, though, I walked home with Laura, and we'd stop in a shack for a mango juice. This counted as a big night out in Zalingei.

One time, she leaned over to me. "Those guys are Janjaweed."

I turned my head, too obviously. "Who?" No one seemed out of the ordinary to me.

"The ones sitting directly behind you," she said, staring straight ahead, playing it way cooler than I was.

"How do you know?" I asked, whispering loudly.

"The way they are wearing their head scarves."

Their head scarves were hooked around their chins and tucked into the other side of their head wrap. Other men just had their head scarves piled on top of their heads. That was it? If I had been alone, I would have never noticed them.

They wouldn't have done anything to us, but we finished our mango juices and left. There wasn't much else to do, anyway.

❖

One Friday, our only day off in Darfur, we were invited to a party at another agency's compound. There were so few expats in the remote town of Zalingei that it was hard to get a critical mass for an actual party, but either way, it was a chance to just hang out for a few hours, and we didn't pass that up. At the compound, we listened to African music and drank whatever alcohol people could scrounge up—a bottle of rum that someone had brought back from a day trip to Kenya, leftover JJ from the weekend before, some vodka left behind by a UN colleague. It was a small gathering, and it wasn't even that much fun, but it passed the time.

Amina made samosas. "I've never made these with goat before, so no promises that they're edible," she said, walking in with a big tray. Amina cooked food for us on certain occasions—when one of us had a birthday, or if someone was returning from R&R. She said it was her true pleasure, that it reminded her of home. Amina's husband lived and worked in Nairobi, and she had hung photos of him alongside her bed. You could tell that a piece of her was missing. "We met in northern Uganda," she told me once. "We worked for different agencies. It was worse than here, if you can imagine that. But at least there we had each other."

Christine plugged her iPod into small speakers, stopping the African music and turning up A Tribe Called Quest. She started dancing. "Come on guys! Get up!" She bent her knees, put her hands on her lower back and gyrated her hips to the beat in an overtly sexual way that would be inappropriate in any setting, let alone Darfur.

People were starting to worry about Christine. It had been eight weeks since her last R&R, and although everyone apparently got testy right up until the point they got out, her attitude was more toxic. As the finance officer, she had three local staffers working for her. I could sometimes hear her chastising them from my office. "Habiba, is it possible that your English has gotten *worse* since you started this job?" she'd ask. We'd often find her home early from work, sprawled out on a mattress on the floor smoking cigarettes, watching back-to-back-to-back episodes of *Sex and the City*.

Over dinner, she complained about her job. "They just don't understand anything," she'd huff, clanking her plate.

"Christine, you can't talk to them like that," Dmitri told her. "They're trying."

"No they're not, Dmitri! How many times have I told them to turn off the computer when they leave? And what does Yusuf do today when he leaves? He leaves his computer on. I mean, how could he forget again unless he was just doing it to spite me? I end up having to do everything by myself. It's faster if I just do it than explaining to them for the fifth time how to enter the numbers."

"We're here to build their capacity, Christine. You need to work with them and train them. It's part of your job."

"Yeah, well, I also have a job to do and deadlines to meet. And I just have to redo everything that they've done anyway, so I should just do it and let them sit there and play their computer games. That's all they want to do, anyway."

All of us worked with local counterparts who would

take over our responsibilities when we left. The goal was to work ourselves out of a job, to make ourselves redundant, training local people and building up their capacity so that they could manage the program. It was hard to know what to expect from them, regardless of their enthusiasm and desire to learn. Some were using Microsoft for the first time, others had never even placed their hands on a keyboard. When you needed to complete a spreadsheet that was legible, accurate, and presentable to donors, and you were working under a very tight deadline, sometimes it *was* just easier to do it yourself.

That Friday, we were occupied with alcohol and music, and none of us noticed a Sudanese woman walk into the compound. Alison, the gender-based violence advisor whose agency was hosting the party, saw her and rushed to the door. The woman looked frightened. Behind her, a woman lay on her back in a donkey cart. She had been raped. Her friend had pulled her on a cart all the way from the camp to the office.

Alison scolded us. "You guys need to get out of here."

"We know. We're leaving," Laura said.

"I mean, this is really terrible," she said. "No time for a party."

"We know. We're leaving," Amina repeated, carrying her half-eaten tray of samosas.

Alison actually looked excited that there was something she had to tend to. She scurried around, satellite phone pressed to her ear as she called a doctor to come and do a medical exam, her scarf falling off of her head and her bright blue panties showing through her white linen pants.

Laura went into the room where the woman was being treated to see if she could help; as a rape counselor, she had years of experience working in these situations. As Laura spoke to the doctor, Alison hovered behind her, pacing. Finally, she snapped.

"Look, Laura, she came to our agency, not yours. We have it covered."

"Yeah, I can see that. I just . . ."

"It's fine—we can handle it." Alison leaned into the room, turning her back to Laura.

As we left the compound, Laura sighed. "That girl sucks."

In the same way that businesses competed for customers, agencies competed with each other for beneficiaries. All of them wanted to be able to tell donors back home about the good things they were doing. Heroic tales could be converted into more donations. Individuals did it, too: for Alison, this tragedy could represent a huge professional victory for her.

❖

In Sudan, the weather was angry all the time. If it wasn't the drenching rains, it was the thrashing winds, the oppressive heat, or the omnipresent and omni-annoying dust. It was turning to the rainy season now, and each night the wind carried signs of the sky's imminent burst. One night at about 2 a.m. I woke to a drizzle drumming lightly above my head, as if children were running across the tin roof. I guess we all had been longing for rain, because when I left my room Amina was already standing in the middle of the compound, looking up. One by one, everyone joined us there, and together we stood beneath the open sky, soaking it up.

After that night, the rain became a ritual and a nuisance. At around five o'clock each evening, the floodgates opened and the sky dumped buckets of water on the empty, vulnerable land. The rain hit the ground hard, lifting dust into the air, as if a herd of animals had stampeded past moments before. One day, the downpour was stronger than normal. By the time the rain stopped, the compound had turned into a marsh.

This had Matthew, our water and sanitation officer, very worried. One flooded latrine had enough bacteria to cause a serious spike in mortality. He was impatient to check out the damage, so we got in the vehicle and rafted our way through the water, which at that point was up to the middle of the car door. A wide, brown river was raging through the lowest stretch of land in the camp.

"Holy shit," I said.

"That's exactly what it is," Matthew said, blushing.

We walked to the lip of the new river. Hordes of people had already gathered to see the spectacle. The crowd had the awestruck glee of children after a snowstorm, when everyone walks around in a daze, in awe of nature's ability to transform the world so totally and so suddenly. Children were already splashing in the river; donkeys were already drinking from it. On the opposite bank, Laura sat perched on the hood of her car. She had been in the camp for a meeting when the rains started. Now she sat there nonchalantly puffing on a cigarette, waving to us and shrugging. "So now what?"

❖

A few weeks later it was time to leave Zalingei. I submitted my report to a grateful Amina and took the same helicopter through Nyala until I got to Khartoum where I waited for my flight back to New York. As soon as I got back to the States, I started looking for ways to return to Sudan. I couldn't go back to my old job—I had completed my report, and there wasn't enough funding to hire me again—so when I wasn't scouring the newspaper for articles about Darfur, I was filling out applications for jobs there. It felt like the most exciting work in my field was happening there. I got a short glimpse of how this country and the humanitarian operation ran, and I wanted more.

And so when an e-mail came from a colleague from another NGO offering me a job that would allow me to return to Darfur, I jumped on it. I called my dad to break the news.

"You're going BACK? What? But you just came home!"

"I got a job. It's a good job. I'll be in the north this time. In El Fasher."

"El what? Jessica—why do you need to go back?"

"I just do, Dad. I was only there for two months. I need more experience. I want to go back. I want to be there."

And so a few weeks later, I returned to Khartoum. The driver who picked me up at the airport asked if this was my first time in Sudan.

"No, I have been here before," I said.

"Oh!" he laughed. "Then you are Sudanese!"

Center for Survivors of Torture
Fancy Dress Night
NORTH DARFUR, 2005

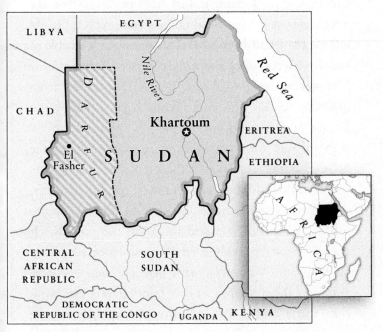

I was happy to be back in Sudan. This time, I would be in El Fasher, the capital of North Darfur, working for a much larger NGO. Instead of simply doing research that would be used to develop future programs, I would actually be helping coordinate projects themselves. But before I could get there, my new employer kept me in Khartoum for two weeks of orientation and security training.

I liked Khartoum: it was the perfect stop between home and Darfur, a chance to readjust to the heat and dust but still revel in the comforts of city life—paved roads, working Internet, dining choices. And for the first time since starting out in aid, I no longer felt like a total novice. I was working for a large NGO; I could tell people I had been to Darfur before; I was able to speak with certainty about the camps in Zalingei.

I spent those weeks with Carla, a friend from graduate school who had already been in Khartoum for six months working for the UN. In some places, the UN had different housing regulations than the NGOs. If the area was considered sufficiently safe, the UN allowed its staff to rent their own apartments, and provided rental subsidies. (NGO staffers, on the other hand, usually stayed in group compounds.) It was a way of providing employees, especially those on long-term contracts, with privacy, independence, and something approaching a familiar domestic routine. Carla rented a two-bedroom apartment on the top floor of a seven-story building downtown. It had air-conditioning in every room, a cold fridge stocked with boxes of smuggled white wine, and a fully loaded bathroom: a hot water tank, Neutrogena skin creams, Kiehl's shampoos. Carla would be living in Khartoum for two years; she came prepared.

There were few luxuries in Khartoum, but we took advantage of what we could find, whether it was a football match at the local stadium or beers at the Chinese restaurant. Smoking cigarettes on Carla's balcony, drinking glasses of pinot grigio in her small kitchen, sending texts to find out where the party was that evening—sometimes, for a second, a night in Khartoum didn't feel so different from a night in New York.

But, of course, it was very different. Khartoum was filled with an incestuous horde of internationals who called this foreign land their home for months, sometimes years. The resulting social climate was a unique combination of surveillance and spontaneity—everybody was, at one speed or another, *just passing through*, which could make interactions feel both urgent and inconsequential. What happened in Sudan, or Chad, or Cambodia certainly did not *stay* in Sudan, or Chad, or Cambodia, and it didn't take me long to realize gossip was the lingua franca of the aid world.

One Friday afternoon, the Sudanese equivalent of Sunday and our only day off, we lounged by a popular pool at a hotel in Khartoum with the other expats in town. It still felt bizarre to be luxuriating like this in Sudan, but I'd come to appreciate these amenities all the more so after going without them in Darfur.

"Did anyone see the new MSF [Médecins Sans Frontières] guy at the meeting?" Carla's friend asked.

"Yeah. Totally cute. Is he married?" another replied, looking up from her book.

"Does it matter?"

"Well, what do we know about him? Where was he last posted?"

"I think he came in from Kabul. I'm going to ask my friend Mark there for the dirt."

That's how it went: your reputation followed you from one country to the next. We all knew someone who had worked with somebody somewhere. "Yeah, I saw him in Liberia in '03." "I lived with her in Timor in '02." "We met in Kosovo during the war." The illusion of this industry was that we worked in the whole, wide world—that the seven continents were just one big office to us. The truth was, our world was tiny, and it got smaller with every job we took.

Although they were still new to me, parties in Khartoum were as regular as UN meetings. Many nights there would be more than one to choose from. Some had themes or required costumes, which tended to be limited by our wardrobes and imaginations: people arrived as human-sized jerry cans, or in togas made of plastic tarps we distributed as shelters; couples came dressed up in pairs—mosquito and mosquito net, for instance, or sugar and salt (the ingredients in oral rehydration solution). So it wasn't out of the ordinary when in any humanitarian setting to get an e-mail with the subject line "War Children Party—Thursday Night—Festive Attire Required!" or "Center for Survivors of Torture—Fancy Dress Night Friday." The expats in town—aid workers, international journalists, diplomats—dressed up and made their way to the Center for Survivors of Torture compound for JJ and rap music, French cheese and Swiss chocolate.

At one of those parties I met Pete, an Australian who

worked for the UN. He was classically handsome—tall, dark hair, olive skin—and he knew it. I would have been attracted to him in any setting and couldn't believe that someone so irrefutably good-looking had walked into a party here. We stood by a table of drinks, chatting about where we were from, our former posts, possible mutual acquaintances.

"How long you in town for?" he asked.

"Not sure. Until my travel authorization gets cleared."

"Oh, so could be a couple of days then."

"Yeah."

"You going to the ICRC party later?"

"Yeah, we're supposed to head over there, I think."

"You should ride with me," he smiled, swirling his tepid vodka soda in his glass. Ice was hard to come by in Sudan.

I wanted to go with him, but I also didn't want to give in that easily. "Oh, thanks, but I'm going with my friends. I'll just see you there?"

We parted ways, and a little bit later Carla waved me over to the door—our ride was leaving. The hot Australian followed us in his car. We navigated down the narrow bumpy Khartoum streets until we got to the large ICRC compound. When I looked back, though, the hot Australian wasn't behind us anymore.

The music was so loud we could hear it from across the street where we parked. The road was clogged with Land Cruisers, and drivers from various agencies congregated outside the party's gates. Some slept inside the vehicles with their seats pushed back and their windows rolled down.

Inside, a dance floor was set up in the middle of the patio. Huge speakers, the kind you'd see at the prom, stood prominently on either side of the room and blared everything from hip-hop and Michael Jackson, to Senegalese bands and bhangra. Bottles of alcohol and flimsy plastic cups cluttered long porch tables. There were more than a hundred people there—some danced, others lounged on chairs, smoking hookahs. A glowing disco ball rotated overhead.

Everyone in the room looked like someone I knew, even though I didn't actually know any of them. By now I was accustomed to the European accents, the ankle tattoos, the Marlboro Reds, the men sporting secondhand T-shirts and five-day stubble, the women in Indian-style three-quarter-length shirt dresses and African bracelets and necklaces. Then I saw Nisha, the kind woman who had invited me to that first dinner party in Rwanda. She was sitting on a low stoop next to her husband.

"Nisha! Tim! I didn't know you guys were in Sudan!" We kissed and hugged, only slightly surprised to see each other again. Nisha hadn't changed; she seemed as comfortable here as she was sitting on her back porch in Kigali. She casually inhaled her cigarette, tilting her head back slightly to exhale. I remembered how timid I was back when I met her in Rwanda; it seemed like ages ago.

Nisha was the one who had the job back in Kigali,

but this time around it was Tim who was working. That's how it went with couples who tried to stay together in the field. It was often hard for both people to land a job in the same place at the same time, but it seemed that Tim and Nisha had made this life work. Their marriage had survived Rwanda and they looked content sitting on that stoop together, carelessly socializing, happy and relaxed. A few years later, I found out that Nisha had an affair with the French procurement officer at work. Tim moved to Kabul. They divorced.

And then the hot Australian walked in and approached me.

"Where were you?" I said.

"Our car got stuck. Someone from UNFPA had a rope and pulled us out. C'mon, I need a drink."

Somehow he'd managed to get even more attractive. His shirt was dirty from pushing the car and it pulled across his shoulders, which now looked broader than before. We got drinks and bypassed the dance floor, which was already hot and crowded. If the hot Australian wanted to join in, he'd have to wait; right then I was too nervous—and too sober—to even tap my foot, never mind actually dance with him. As he went to sit down, he put his hand on my lower back. I hoped he couldn't tell just how excited I was talking to him—a man with an adorable accent, who followed me to this party after pushing his truck out of ditch! I was drunk and, of course, I was smoking and I was just so far from home. At that moment, it felt like I could stay in Sudan, working and living this life for years. There would be endless days and nights like this. We'd work together during the day on serious issues—figuring out how to get health supplies through customs faster, negotiating with the government for access to areas that had been recently attacked, appealing to donors for much-needed funding. But at night we would all act like teenagers. We'd drink and hook up—sometimes on the dance floor, sometimes in the back of a Land Cruiser, or in a sweaty room on a foam mattress under a mosquito net, after driving home drunk through the wobbly streets of Khartoum. I was single and I had no obligations except to my job.

It got late and the crowd was thinning. Carla came over to us. "We're leaving." She turned to me. "You coming?"

I looked at her with begging eyes—*I don't want to go*. She looked at him and then back at me with an expression I recognized immediately—*Don't go home with this guy*. Something about him—possibly just his out-of-place hotness—made it clear to her that he was probably going to turn out to be an asshole.

We exchanged numbers and I went home with Carla. The next day my travel authorization came through and I was put on the next flight to El Fasher. I never got to say good-bye to the hot Australian.

The office in El Fasher was a few minutes' drive from downtown, on the way to the three main IDP camps there—Abu Shouk, Zam Zam, and the recently planned Al Salam. Al Salam was the camp I'd been hired to work as the community officer, which meant I had a budget to oversee, and an important role liaising with community representatives from the camp.

But plans, it quickly emerged, had changed. I hadn't been at the office for two weeks when Mark, the acting head, informed me that the camp coordinator for Al Salam had left, and I was being deputized to replace her. Mark was a small guy, and looked a few years older than me. In one hand, he held a clipboard with papers crinkled brown at the edges, in the other, a VHF radio. I looked at him with his Red Sox baseball cap and his clumsy stance and couldn't believe someone so young was in charge of this entire operation. Maybe he had been hired for a different job, too.

The office was a flurry of activity, with the mostly Sudanese staff hurrying through the hallways or darting in and out of meetings. Our workplace was made up of various interconnected rooms designated as offices with makeshift signs hanging on the doors: Women's Health, Basic Health, Child Protection, Water and Sanitation, Logistics, Finance, IT. Because our agency was one of the largest working in the region, we covered a number of humanitarian sectors. The walls were mostly bare and there were many windows with screens, to get as much of a cross breeze as possible.

Mark led me through a labyrinth of rooms until we reached his office at the end of the corridor.

A beat-up couch and a small coffee table sat on one side of the room, his desk on another. Pale sunlight spilled through a row of uncurtained windows and a floor-to-ceiling map of Darfur hung next to the couch. A large fan swiveled slowly, ruffling a stack of papers held down with a brick on Mark's desk. With each rotation, the papers fluttered softly, as though they were sighing. Mark sat down and took off his baseball hat, combing his hands through his sweaty hair.

Although I had not yet come to realize it, Terms of Reference (TORs) for jobs were so loosely written that sometimes people ended up with completely unexpected responsibilities. As long as the job didn't require technical expertise, like constructing shelters, designing latrines, or delivering health care, there was always the chance you'd be the one to do it. People ended up filling in for their colleagues, as in Mark's case, and also mine. Years later, when I landed a new post, a friend offered the following advice: "Don't let anyone around here see that you're competent. You'll end up doing everyone's job."

When Mark broke the news to me, he tried to put a positive spin on it—"Your first day, and already a promotion!"—but I wasn't persuaded. I was twenty-seven, and had spent only a few months working at a camp before—how would I be able to serve as the primary person overseeing activities in the camp? Mark pulled a thick manual off the wobbly bookshelf behind him: *Camp Management Toolkit*. He plopped it on the desk. I left Mark's office with the handbook and a name: Ishaq. "He's great," Mark promised. "He'll show you around."

❖

When I arrived in El Fasher, aid agencies were in the process of moving twenty-four thousand people—residents of the village Tawila, which the Janjaweed had attacked a few weeks earlier—from one camp, Abu Shouk, across a river to the new one, Al Salam (its name meant "peace"). There was no other option: Abu Shouk already housed fifty thousand people, and couldn't absorb tens of thousands more. The new arrivals huddled around the perimeter of the camp, building shelters with whatever scraps of cloth and sticks they could find. They came inside the camp to use the latrines and get water, already in short supply. But without being officially registered, they didn't have access to the food distributions, and were not permitted to send their children to schools in the camp or receive other basic services. With so much extra use, the pit latrines were filling up fast. Eventually, some had to be sealed shut.

The aid workers who found the land for the new camp hadn't had an easy time of it. It took weeks to negotiate with the government, which had to authorize the use of more land for the displaced; consult with the community leaders to explain the plan; arrange for twenty-four thousand displaced people to move across the dry riverbed, or *wadi*; and finally settle them into the new camp, Al Salam. Busses were provided for elderly and sick but the rest came by foot. It wasn't too long a journey: you could see one camp while standing in the other.

After receiving my "promotion," I followed the advice Mark had given: "Go up to the camp and poke around." I hopped in an agency vehicle that was on its way to the camp, asking the driver to drop me at the registration tent. It took about ten minutes to get from the office to the camp, and the driver sped through the open stretches of desert, lining the tires up with the grooves created by previous cars. All around us was sand, scattered trees, and a few *tukuls*. He turned up the song on the radio—a repetitive, mantra-like Sudanese tune, a male singer's voice ranging all over the scales, the sitar and steady drum beat playing behind him. The hot Darfur air blew in through the open windows, and my hair flitted across my face, strands sticking to damp patches on my skin. I pulled it back in a tight ponytail, using sweat as hair gel.

SOON, I COULD SEE THE new camp—a sweep of sand the size of more football fields than I could count— stretching out before us. Small flags marked its perimeter. A few tents made from plastic sheeting had sprung up near the edges, but most of the wide, dry land was empty. Families were arriving at the registration center, a large domed tent perched at the top of a hill. When I saw the people waiting outside it, the lines curling down the slope, I realized it wouldn't be long at all before all of the land was occupied.

The inside of the registration tent seemed orderly and efficient. About ten desks were lined up in rows, and male and female Sudanese registration officers sat behind each of them, calling families in one at a time. Communities in Sudan are arranged by tribe; there are close to a hundred tribes in all of Darfur. Al Salam held tribes from five regions: Jebel Marra, Tawila, Dar Zaghawa, Jebel Si, and Korma. Each group was headed by a leader, or *omda,* who acted like the governor for that community. The tribes were broken down into smaller groups, and every group was led by a sheikh— the equivalent of a mayor.

To organize the move, sheikhs provided camp workers with lists of families who planned on arriving together. Families presented themselves to the registration officers, who crossed-referenced their names with the lists provided by the sheikhs. The officers carefully entered each family's information into ledgers written by hand. In rows drawn with a ruler, they recorded the number of family members, their ages and genders, and their community of origin. A special note was made if it was a female-headed household. All of this information was copied by hand again onto a wallet-sized card, which was given to the family.

Families were then ushered into an adjacent tent to

receive medical screening. Babies were weighed, children were checked for malnutrition, and any noticeable ailments were referred to the doctor. Next, families were issued a certain number of household supplies based on family size. A distribution team checked the card, stamped it, and dispensed an array of NFIs (non-food items): plastic sheeting (one piece per five people), iron poles (to hold the sheeting up), and rope (to tie them together); as well as jerry cans, soap, kitchen utensils, and a plastic pot for washing.

The camp was divided by region of origin, and each family was given a plot of land, determined by the size of the family, within that division. Families walked to their lots slowly, their new items clanking at their sides, and any personal effects they had brought from their villages strapped to donkeys, or balanced on their heads. Even small children were expected to carry things. Anyone who had arms and legs and could hold something, did.

Unlike most instances of displacement, where communities flee and haphazardly squat on new land, in this case aid agencies had the opportunity to coordinate a more orderly, systematically designed camp, with carefully measured distances between living quarters, latrines, clinics, and schools. It was one of the first times during a humanitarian crisis that a camp was developed this way and so far things seemed to be going according to plan.

Aid agencies need to collaborate to provide people

with material relief—and ideally, help them preserve a sense of human dignity—and there were over twenty such agencies working in Al Salam. A single organization doesn't have the resources or expertise to do it all. If one organization builds a school, another must deliver water and a place for kids to go to the bathroom. If another organization doesn't provide a meal in school, children will typically go hungry and be too exhausted to study. And if yet another organization doesn't come in to assist parents in finding and maintaining their livelihoods, they might not be able to afford to send their kids to school, or pull them out to work instead. If there isn't a clinic nearby where a child can get treated if he gets sick—well, then he wasn't going to be coming to school anyway. People didn't need just one kind of intervention. They needed a package of services, and agencies had to come together to provide comprehensive support. It's like building a house: you need a contractor to pour the foundation and erect the walls, an electrician to install the lights and outlets, a plumber to put in the sinks and toilets.

❖

Unlike Zalingei, where the expat staff lived in one compound, in El Fasher we were spread across guesthouses within a quarter of a mile radius of the office. Since El Fasher was a larger town, there were plenty of these small homes to rent. My agency had leased five of them, and I was assigned a room in Guesthouse Three with Lila, a tall, thin Kenyan woman who had a six-year-old daughter back in Nairobi. Many Kenyans were in Sudan working for aid agencies. For most expats, going home meant traveling for at least two days. But for Kenyans, getting from Khartoum to Nairobi was an easy two-hour flight.

"I'm setting up a women's center," Lila told me. "It will be a place where women can come to learn a new trade, where we teach them about women's health, give them a space to go to just relax." Her eyes opened widely as she spoke about the center, her smooth, cropped hair (that I later learned was a wig) shining in the sunlight. She had built one with success in Congo the year before with the same agency, but here they were having trouble procuring some of the necessary supplies.

Agencies that wanted to erect permanent structures in camps had to get permission from the government. Since the displaced communities were only supposed to be there temporarily, neither the agencies nor the government wanted to create the impression that IDPs could—or would—stay indefinitely. But a balance had to be struck, as temporary facilities were often unable to withstand strong winds and heavy rains. Restoring them constantly cost time and money, and oftentimes they went unrepaired. We all knew that the IDPs would be here a long time, so Lila had gotten permission to build a semipermanent structure on the agreement that the host community would get to use it when the camp's current occupants returned to their homes, if they returned to their homes. Years later, a friend would give me this advice: if you're planning camps in a place like Darfur, "plan the camps as though they'll be there forever."

The guesthouse Lila and I shared was small and bare; it would be just the two of us living here. Everything was made of the same rust-colored cement: the floors, the walls, even the inside of the bathrooms. Like most of the compound interiors I saw in Darfur, it seemed hastily put together—the walls were lumpy, the floors were slanted, and the entrances to rooms looked accidental, as if someone had run out of cement and simply wandered away, leaving a few vaguely rectangular holes behind. Lila and I shared a bathroom and a modest screened-in living area that had two wooden couches covered by faded yellow foam cushions. Our kitchen was in a separate hut.

That first night, I walked around the compound aimlessly, still overwhelmed by the news from Mark. I pulled out the *Camp Management Toolkit,* its weight on my lap like a phone book. I started flipping through it, but became overwhelmed and decided to unpack instead. I carried my bag to my room, and had to heave my shoulder against the door to open it. No one had been in there in a while. The air was stale and smelled like my grandmother's attic. Light poured in through the one window, illuminating a trickle of dust. A patchwork of colorful prayer mats was spread over the floor. The bed looked like a bottom bunk without a top. Metal poles stuck up around the frame, over which someone had draped a mosquito net, now covered in dust.

As I was surveying my new home, my phone beeped. It was a text message from the hot Australian: "Hey, you want to get dinner tonight?"

The night before felt like a lifetime ago. How I wished I were back there now, or with Carla, a friend to talk to. "Would love to but already in Fasher," I texted back.

"☹" he wrote.

It was so nice to hear from someone even remotely familiar that I ignored his lame emoticon. I could already tell it would be harder to make friends here. The agency I worked for now was not only more prestigious than the one in Zalingei, but also much larger. The operation felt so big that it would take a while before I knew everyone.

Still holding my phone, I pushed the bed net aside and sat on the foam mattress. It sagged under my weight. I felt like I had just been dropped off on my first day of college. I wanted to go back to high school where the halls and teachers were familiar and welcoming, where the expectations were not as great—where I was neither alone, nor terrified of failing.

The next morning a lanky man was waiting for me at the office gate. "Jessica!" he called, bounding over to me. "I'm Ishaq!" he said, proudly. I couldn't tell how old Ishaq was, but I guessed early forties. "Yesterday when you arrived I was busy at the Ministry. Mark told me you were here." He held a large blue notebook to his chest. "Welcome to El Fasher. How are you settling in?"

"Oh, it's OK!" I said.

"Not too hot in this Darfur heat?" he asked.

"No, no. It's fine."

I was lying. El Fasher was hotter than Zalingei, even hotter than Khartoum. I was already a sweaty, wrinkled mess, whereas Ishaq was dressed immaculately in a collared polyester shirt and bell-bottom pants perfectly altered to fit his tall, slim frame. It turned out, no one could figure out where he got these clothes, what inspired his decidedly unique fashion sense, or who his tailor was.

I followed him inside the compound and he led me to our office. It looked like all the others and held a small metal desk, two plastic chairs and two windows on opposite walls for ventilation. I put my bag down. "So you've been to Al Salam already, yes?"

"Yes, I went to the registration yesterday."

"Good, good," Ishaq nodded. "I've been working on getting that set up. Yesterday we had a slight problem with the Ministry, but it seems to be OK now." He nodded again, as if reassuring himself that things would work out. The Humanitarian Aid Commission (HAC) was a government agency, and it wielded strict authority over all our actions. Before aid agencies could do anything in the camps—erect a tent for a meeting space or provide hygiene training—the project had to be approved by the Sudanese government. Which was perfectly reasonable—this was their country after all; we were their guests, working with the Sudanese population. They had every right to be involved in and informed of the work we were doing there. But introducing them into the process slowed everything down—they took their time green-lighting plans, usually because their own bureaucracy was so inefficient that whatever petition needed to be approved—be it a request to lead a seminar on sanitary practices, or install a dozen latrines—had to pass through many hands before it reached the official authorized to endorse it. Some aid workers were also suspicious of HAC's motives—they were indeed an office of the government, the same government that was killing and driving these people off their land in the first place.

THERE WAS NO TIME TO worry about whether or not I was qualified to do this job. With my *Camp Management Toolkit* under my arm and Ishaq by my side, I jumped in. The first thing we had to do in Al Salam was set up a committee that would represent the twenty-four thousand residents of the camp, and which would be the group I would meet with regularly. The *Camp Management Toolkit* advised setting up fair elections, but I was already coming to realize that the manual's rules didn't always account for reality. The *omdas* and sheikhs were the ones who presented themselves for the jobs, which made sense: these were the traditional leaders of the community, they had always spoken on its behalf.

At my first meeting with the committee, Ishaq introduced me. The men nodded respectfully as I started speaking to them in English. Ishaq translated.

"My name is Jessica," I said. "I'm from the US, and I'm here to work with you in the camp." The whole thing felt ridiculous. Some of these men were old enough to be my father. I wondered what they thought of me, a naive twenty-seven-year-old American girl, clutching her camp management toolkit like a life vest. How strange it must have been for these men, after all they had been through and all they were still grappling with, to have me there to discuss and negotiate their living conditions. Over time, though, I realized that my naïveté and humility actually worked to my advantage. I listened to the men on the committee and constantly asked for their input. They desperately wanted to participate in the decisions that were affecting the lives of their community members and families. Being there every day, listening to their concerns, and relaying those concerns back to other aid workers was the best way I could do my job.

The committee assumed considerable responsibility for day-to-day camp management and would eventually come to help distribute food, report on any Janjaweed activity spotted in the camp, and assist in the planning of NGO activities like where new water points would be constructed, or what other NFIs were needed. In the coming months, I would rely on these men for everything, but I knew they didn't represent everyone in the camp—such as the women and the youth. I set up separate smaller committees with representatives from these groups as well.

THE FIRST THING THE CAMP committee requested were name badges, to distinguish themselves as leaders of the community and to show the aid agencies working in the camp that they also had a say in its administration. The issue of the name badges was very important to them; they asked me about it each time we met. I told them we could make name cards back at the office, but they insisted on real badges, with a photo and a stamp. Nothing in Sudan felt legitimate unless it had an official seal: when you bought a soda, the shopkeeper wrote up your purchase on a small piece of paper, which he carefully blotted with a red rubber stamp.

I was sure that El Fasher wouldn't have a photo lab, but Ishaq knew of one downtown. It looked like one of those low-budget Glamour Shots portrait studios you'd find at a mall. There was nobody inside except the shopkeeper. I asked him when I could bring twenty-seven people in to have their photos taken. Anytime was fine, the excited shopkeeper said, as long as there was power in town.

We only had two vehicles to move everyone, but before I could even explain that we'd have to make a few trips, the Land Cruisers were filled: some people sat on the floor, others on laps; a few men stood and held onto the back of the vehicle. This was certainly against agency regulations, but I wasn't going to make a fuss. I felt as if I were chaperoning a class field trip—I had only worked with these men inside the camp so it was fun to see them out and about in town.

Sometimes I'd found the photos of other African residents deceiving; even the silliest of people came out looking stoic and serious. I realized that the images we saw didn't always look like life—they didn't capture the character of the person they depicted, or the true spirit of the place he or she came from. Out in the field, you saw children playing, doing backflips, running around wildly—and then as soon as you whipped out your camera, they froze like deer. Their bodies became stiff, their faces drawn, their eyes wide, focused and solemn. Nobody had ever taught them how to project an image of themselves, or told them to say "Cheese!" and smile for the camera.

When we arrived at the studio, the committee members waited in line to get their passport-sized photos taken. Whenever someone's turn came, he would stand in front of the light blue background, look intently at the camera until it flashed, and then melt into giggles. After each of them had gone through, they wanted one last photo of all of us together. I was working on a very tight budget, and we had already maxed it out. I told them so.

"They want to pay for it themselves," Ishaq told me.

"Oh, that's ridiculous. They're not paying for it." I couldn't imagine why they would want to spend whatever little money they had on a photo. But they insisted.

The leader of the group, Ahmed, waved me over. "Come, come!" he said. I had never heard him speak in English before. "Jessica, come!" The photographer organized us in front of the safari backdrop, as though we were in a large wedding party. I knelt down with some of the shorter men, smiled, and waited for the click.

❖

Days in Darfur usually went by too quickly for me to feel I'd accomplished anything. I was essentially a messenger between the people in the camp and the aid community. With various agencies running three clinics, five schools, biweekly food and non-food distributions, hundreds of latrines and water pumps, someone had to be the go-between, and that person was me.

It was silly being Ishaq's "boss"—we both knew that I was dependent on him for everything. He grew up in El Fasher and had been working for our agency long before I arrived. At meetings with the committee, he'd translate for me, but I thought it would be such a better use of time if he just led the sessions himself. However, I soon realized that I was technically the one in charge not only because I could use Excel and read and write in English. I noticed how differently both Sudanese and expats treated us. People perked up when I entered the room—my skin color afforded me this undeserved authority. If Ishaq was going to a meeting alone, he'd sometimes ask me to come with him.

"Ishaq, why? You can do it—you know it better than I do!"

"I know," he said. "But believe me, they'll listen more if you are there."

Despite the fact that I was probably twenty years his junior, that he knew the IDPs and had been to all of the towns they came from, that he spoke their language and shared their religion—despite all this, I was the one everyone deferred to. But the truth was, I yielded to Ishaq's judgment on pretty much everything, from which government minister we needed to see to where we should eat lunch.

Over time, Ishaq and I became close. Some nights we had dinner together at the local restaurant in town, where we'd drag our sticky bodies up to the roof, order mango juices and goat and onion sandwiches, and collapse on the unsteady plastic lawn chairs. It was nice up there, one of the only places in town where you could get a steady breeze. A flurry of people bartered in the market below, carrying their vegetables home in flimsy blue-and-white-striped plastic bags. Camels were herded through the streets, their steps deliberate and slow, making puffs of sand with each clop. Soft music, the impatient honks of car horns, and the roar of diesel engines wafted up to where we sat. The sky stretched as far as the dusty dunes, and at sunset it matched the orange earth.

Ishaq's compound was a short walk from Guest-house Three. The first time I visited, his younger daughter, a four-year-old, was standing naked in a big metal bucket, lathered in soap, as her older sister poured a pail of water over her head. They both froze, startled. Ishaq heard the creak of the gate and rushed out to greet me.

The boxy furniture inside his house looked the same as what Lila and I had in our living quarters. But Ishaq's home was decorated with personal effects—a photograph of what looked like his parents hung on the wall; faded green hand-sewn curtains draped the windows. A drawing by his daughter was displayed next to a large shelf that held books in Arabic. The living area was crammed with furnishings: bulky wooden chairs with the familiar foam cushions, a well-polished wooden table.

To have this compound—to dress as he did, to be as educated as he was—Ishaq had to be wealthier than most Sudanese, and he was. Having a senior position at an NGO was a good job, one that he took pride in. If the war hadn't broken out, if the NGOs weren't there providing services to IDPs and salaries to men like Ishaq, he might not have had a career. A gig at an NGO paid more than a government assignment, which was hard to get anyway, usually requiring a family member on the inside. If the war stopped and all the agencies left, I wondered what Ishaq and the rest of the local staff—the drivers, the maids, the guards—would do. Aid agencies were the biggest employer around, and without a war to keep us here, Ishaq and many others would be out of work. With the existence of a parallel economy fueled by international agencies, local aid workers didn't really have an incentive to discourage its continuation—or, by extension, to solve the problems that kept us here and kept them employed.

At dinner that night, Ishaq's silent wife served piles of mushy vegetable stews from a big round silver tray, which she carried into the dining room on her head. *Ful,* the hearty bean soup that I tried with my colleagues that first day in Khartoum, was a staple in Sudan and eaten by dipping *kissra,* a flat bread made of millet, into it. Ishaq's older daughter brought out a large portion in a tin bowl, along with boiled cassava, a tomato salad, and a plate of goat meat. I was touched and humbled by how much trouble they went through to prepare the meal. We sat around the small table, Ishaq, his bathed daughter and her older sister, his wife, and I, the plates of food taking up most of the space. They sat in silence, the two girls staring at me. I realized they were all waiting for me to start. I took a piece of the *kissra* and dipped into the *ful.*

"This is delicious," I said.

Ishaq smiled and translated for his wife, but I

understood her response. "*Shukran,*" she said quietly—
thank you.

I'D MEET ISHAQ AT THE OFFICE each morning, and
over two little plastic cups of Nescafé we'd lay out the
plan for the day. The first thing we usually did was ride
to the camp to see if anything had happened overnight
that we needed to address. Whether it was a collapsed
latrine or a water container that looked low, Ishaq
spotted problems way before I did.

"Stop," he instructed the driver one morning, pointing out the window. "Those tents aren't occupied."

"How do you know?" I asked.

"Look at how the dust has gathered around the
opening of the tent. No one's been in there."

We stopped and walked over, Ishaq trudging
through the sand in his polished brown shoes. I could
see large drifts of sand had pushed up against the opening of the tent, pinning the bottom down. We peered
in. Ishaq was right. The tent was empty.

As we feared, people who weren't really IDPs had
been registering as IDPs, receiving a card to get rations,
pitching a tent, and then going back to their real homes
either in Abu Shouk or in town. Once, Ishaq told me,
he had even recognized his neighbor in the registration line. He laughed and escorted her away gently, but
he knew there were more like her in line and that we
had already accepted other hopeful imposters who had
managed to slip through the cracks.

It's well understood that some percentage of aid goes to people for whom it's not really intended. People who aren't the "target" population—IDPs from a neighboring camp, for instance—show up and try to get in on the action. I had seen this in Rwanda, when Charles plucked people who had forged their ration cards out of the distribution line. Agencies try to limit this by making the registration process as efficient and accurate as possible, and the cards themselves difficult to duplicate. But when twenty-four thousand people need to be registered, their names are some version of Ishaq Adam Yusuf, or Adam Hassan Mohammed, and the staff is keeping records by hand, someone's bound to slip through.

It wasn't just poor record keeping that allowed for the errors. The sheikhs whose lists we took to cross-check the family names were in on the game, too. Often people who weren't eligible for aid bribed sheikhs to get on the list, or the displaced paid to get on the list twice, under two different names. I met someone who had worked on distributions in West Africa and made people dip their fingers in blue ink to indicate they had already received their shares. Kids came back hours later with their fingers scrubbed raw in hopes of getting more supplies. I had heard that in some camps, agencies went so far as to eye-scan the beneficiaries to keep track of them.

Years later, my British friend Lewis helped me put the situation in perspective. "When I was in my twenties, I applied for welfare. I wasn't really eligible, but

I got it anyway because I took the time to fill out all those damn forms, stand in lines, make those calls, and deal with those thick bureaucrats. But at that time, I really needed that hundred extra pounds a week. Later, the hundred pounds weren't worth all the hassle. So I didn't bother applying. You have to think—those guys who are from town or the next camp standing in these lines for two days, dealing with the forms and the shit we put them through—they must really need those jerry cans. So we gave ten percent of our supply to people who technically aren't IDPs? So what? Those people need the stuff just as badly."

I didn't really mind. As far as I was concerned, as long as we had this stuff in warehouses we *should* be giving it all out. But after we pulled up to see the tent that Ishaq had spotted, we soon found another. And then another. It was happening all over. "This is bullshit," I said.

Ishaq never swore, but he nodded his head in agreement. "Yes, yes. It most certainly is."

I called a meeting with the committee to get to the bottom of it. "We cannot keep giving things out to people who aren't IDPs. Because if we do, there won't be enough for people who really need it. We plan everything around the population of the camp—how many latrines to dig, how big schools should be, how many beds we need in the clinics. We need accurate numbers for this. We can't be using these inflated lists." At these meetings, the committee members sat in rows of chairs, looking at me intently and furrowing their brows. Even though they nodded in agreement, I knew that the problem would continue. This was a market like any other, and if people could game the system, they would. It was nothing personal. Everyone needed a little extra to get by.

LATER THAT MORNING, WE MET with teachers in an empty classroom of one of the schools, a large tent with a few benches and many rolled-up prayer mats, which the children sat on during lessons. A lone chalkboard stood at the front of the tent with a faded math problem written across it.

One at a time, the teachers stood up and informed us of the issues.

"The children don't have enough notebooks. They're sharing three children to each notebook."

"We haven't been paid in two months."

"The classes are so overcrowded that some children are sitting outside." At one point there were one hundred and fifty children to a teacher. Up to eight children were sharing one lesson book. The UNICEF school being built at the edge of the camp would alleviate some of this overcrowding, but it still hadn't been completed because the brick was stuck somewhere on its way from Khartoum. This was to be one of the only permanent structures created in the camp, and it would be used as a school for the host community when the IDPs returned home. *If* they returned home. In the meantime, we erected extra classrooms for the other children with leftover plastic sheeting.

A woman in the back stood up. "The school is too far from where we are living." It was about a ten-minute walk away. "We want to move it," she declared. Ishaq translated her request to me and then continued in English: "OK," he said, shaking his head. "Now they're just playing games." A few weeks later, at a similar meeting, there were requests for us to build a mosque and a movie theater.

At 11 a.m., after the meeting, Ishaq needed a place where he could wash his hands and pray. At that time we were usually at the registration tent, which was now functioning as our camp office. He'd duck around the back, find a mat, a place to wash his hands and face, and pray. Other men were back there doing the same.

At 1 p.m., we had a health meeting with an agency that ran one of the three clinics in the camp. Apparently, someone had dropped one of the bottles of medicine we had received from an American NGO in the water. The label peeled off, and the original sticker underneath showed an expiration date that had already passed. It was rumored that the US military, and other groups, sometimes relabeled old medicines, then dumped them onto camps as "charity." Were these still OK to use?, the health workers wanted to know. I had no idea. To be safe, the agency ordered new medicines, but in the meantime, the clinics would have to make do with an even more limited supply.

An hour later I was meeting with the camp committee to designate a plot of land where people could be buried. I never imagined I'd be mapping out a cemetery.

At 4 p.m., we stopped by a water and sanitation workshop where an agency was training people how to wash their hands properly, how long to boil water before drinking it, how to clean their children thoroughly. Half an hour later, I met with the water engineers to find a place in the camp where the ground was solid enough to support what was called a water bladder or a pillow tank because it basically looked like a giant pillow filled with water.

These meetings were scheduled with precision in my date book, but nothing ever went according to schedule. Time was a flexible concept: there were the numbers on watches and clocks, and then there was the actual pace of camp life. People showed up when they could, closest to the time they said they would; but if things came up, which they always did, time, appointments, and schedules were just ignored.

For my job I didn't actually *do* or *build* anything. I just made sure the people responsible for doing and building things did what they said they would. If the water pump in block A17 was broken, leaving two hundred people without water, I got the news from Ahmed or another member of the committee. I'd go to Oxfam and see when they could fix it. When the roof blew off the school in block C23, I waited at the Save the Children office for the person who was responsible for replacing it to give me a timetable for getting it done.

A latrine collapsed in block F3? I went to check it out, made sure no kids were inside, and told Islamic Relief to fix it. I was the shock absorber for everyone's frustration—the camp residents, who were upset because things weren't moving fast enough, and the people from other agencies, who bristled at my requests because I wasn't actually their boss, and couldn't I just leave them alone? But I found that if no one was pushing, if no one was showing up every day to make sure the roof was being patched or the water pump repaired, it would be days or weeks before the roof or the pump actually got fixed. It still may have taken days or weeks to get things done anyway, but at least people knew that someone was there paying attention and holding everyone to account.

Once a week, the aid agencies convened around a table to make sure that camp needs were covered and that people in one part of the camp weren't getting more assistance than another. It was important to make sure that we were all providing equitable services—that the clinic serving blocks A–F had the same quality materials as the one for people in blocks W–Z, for instance, or that if Refugees International hired people in the camp to serve as hygiene promoters, they were paying their workers the same amount that NRC (Norwegian Refugee Council) was paying their promoters. If this wasn't coordinated, the camp population would find out about the disparity and become angry.

The agenda for these meetings was always the same.

I'd start by apprising everyone of the latest reports from the camp's committee members, and then each agency would go around and give updates on their projects.

"We've seen a rise in malaria in under fives around blocks A12 through B14. We think it's because the covers for the latrines still have not arrived," the health coordinator explained. Without the covers, mosquitoes could get inside the pit latrines and use them as breeding grounds.

We all looked at the representative from Oxfam, which was responsible for getting the covers.

"They're coming. They're still in Khartoum."

"And people are defecating everywhere. There are piles of crap all over the place," the health coordinator continued.

The heat baked a bubbling poop stew in the enclosed latrines, so you couldn't blame anyone for not wanting to go inside them. I knew this from personal experience: one time I was in the camp with a colleague and had to pee so badly that if our Land Cruiser went over one more bump I was certain I was going to burst.

"Hey, can we stop at one of the latrines?" I asked.

"You're gonna go in there? You can't wait until we get back to the office?" Lindsay, my colleague, a Brit in her midtwenties, asked.

"Yes!" I cried, and she pulled over.

Inside the latrine—a box-like structure, made of blue plastic sheeting held up by four sticks—mounds of crap were piled around the hole—as if it were there just for decoration. The putrid stench made my eyes water. I found a safe place to park my feet around the hole, pulled down my pants, and squatted. Then I got it, why people crapped around the hole, not in it. As soon as I started peeing, dozens of flies swooshed up from inside the foul pit. I stood up quickly and came out with a wet spot on my leg.

"Don't say anything," I said to Lindsay, getting back in the car. She laughed and pulled away.

Back at the meeting I asked, "What can we do to speed this up? You've been saying this for three weeks. Can we procure any of this locally?"

"We'll see, but I've gotten assurance from Khartoum that they should be here this week. They're on the truck."

Someone from the IRC clinic chimed in: "We've been seeing a number of kids with cuts on their hands from the unfinished hand pumps. This is mainly in the northern part of the camp."

All eyes went to the representative from the agency responsible for drilling the boreholes where women and children pumped water to fill their jerry cans.

"The protective covers have arrived and we are going to be attaching them starting tomorrow."

As the discussion turned to the delivery of medicines, my cell phone buzzed. The hot Australian and I had maintained an increasingly flirtatious text correspondence since Khartoum, and contacted each other as often as the network actually worked. At night, with my other entertainment options consisting mainly of computer solitaire and a dwindling stack of paperbacks, our flirtation felt like a lifeline. But it was unusual to get a text from him while the sun was still up; intrigued, I clicked it open. "I want you sitting on my face ☺."

❖

A few weeks later I had my first day off since arriving in Sudan. It was scheduled for my birthday: I would be turning twenty-eight. As exhausted as I was from work, I decided to go to Khartoum for the night. Days before, the president of South Sudan's plane had mysteriously crashed, an event eerily similar to the one that had sparked the Rwandan genocide. The North and South of Sudan had been in conflict for decades, and it was only in January of 2005 that the government and rebel leadership in the south had signed a peace agreement, ending the twenty-two-year-long Second Sudanese Civil War—a war largely independent of the crisis in Darfur. After the crash, southern Sudanese thought that the northern troops were to blame for the president's death and riots erupted on the streets of Khartoum. A colleague in Khartoum happened to be walking down the street when the riots turned particularly violent and a spear landed in his back. He survived, but was sent back to America on the first flight out. Aid workers were advised not to leave their homes, and all flights from Darfur to Khartoum were cancelled.

While my friends in New York were checking Hop-Stop to see if the L train was running, I was checking

Al Jazeera to see if people had stopped burning tires and throwing rocks into windows long enough for me to get to Khartoum and get laid. When the normal flight schedule had resumed, I packed my most enticing outfit (baggy jeans and a tight-ish long-sleeved shirt that revealed a silhouette of just enough cleavage) and hopped on the next plane to Khartoum.

Years later, preparing to depart for an assignment in Juba, South Sudan's capital, I decided enough was enough: I wasn't going to spend the whole time looking like a frumpy librarian. I packed a few nice outfits, makeup, and even fancy face cream, and I was so determined to have them with me that when the security guard at Heathrow told me my suitcase weighed too much I bought another one. Approximately five minutes after disembarking in Juba, I watched that very suitcase fall off a baggage cart and land in the middle of the runway, where it was promptly run over by a truck. Its contents—including the toiletries I'd carried for thousands of miles—went spilling all over the tarmac. The world was getting its point across to me, loud and clear: fancy face creams weren't meant for places like Sudan.

Even if such things did make it into the country, they rarely made it out, for one reason or another. We washed whatever we had in our suitcases so frequently with dirty water and harsh soaps that even a new shirt would be faded and threadbare by the time we were packing to go home. Once, when one of my friends was preparing to leave, she packed two bags, one full of the clothes she wanted to take with her, which included a Donna Karan dress she had worn to a friend's wedding in Europe. The other she filled with everything she planned to leave behind. She gave both bags to her maid, asking her please to ship the former and keep whatever she wanted from the latter. The next day, my friend's coworkers—locals, and apparently friends with her maid—showed up at the office, one wearing her silk scarf, another her fitted blouse: the maid had gotten the bags mixed up. What was I supposed to do, my friend said when she told me what happened, Ask them to take off their shirts in the middle of the conference room? So my friend left, and her clothes stayed, and somewhere in Sudan her maid's sister is wearing that Donna Karan dress.

WHEN I LANDED IN KHARTOUM, Carla picked me up at the airport and we drove to a small party, where I knew the hot Australian would be. This time I went home with him. At that point, it didn't even matter who he was. After so many long, hot days made worse by lonely nights, just touching another human being felt incredible. I had one night with him, and we stayed up until the sun rose, me savoring every affectionate hour knowing I'd soon be returning to nights of eating tuna stew and playing Marco Polo with a mosquito humming inside my bed net.

The next morning he drove me to the airport and waited as I checked in. It turned out my authorization to go back to Darfur had expired, and I would have to wait in Khartoum for a few days while it got renewed. I was ecstatic—another meal or two at the Italian restaurant, a few more warm showers, good cell phone coverage, and sex! I came out of the terminal bouncing. The hot Australian looked pleased, but also panicked.

"So how long you think it will be until you get the visa sorted?" he asked.

"Depends how long it takes our visa section to process it—and you know they're about as efficient as the Nigerian postal service," I joked.

He chuckled, but seemed distracted.

The next morning the hot Australian was up before me. When I opened my eyes, he was already showered and dressed, sitting on the side of the bed.

"I need to tell you something," he said.

"What," I said, edging back, pulling the sheet up to my chin.

Oh, please don't tell me you're HIV positive.

"The thing is," he said slowly, "I have a girlfriend. And, well, she's arriving tonight. So, you can't stay here."

Carla was right. This guy had turned out to be an asshole. Although the hot Australian was just a cheating jerk, and I passed it off as such, eventually I realized that he was my first encounter with how hollow this work could make you—how easy it was to shirk attachments, when you are always leaving one place for another, and how hard it was to build anything resembling a sustainable relationship.

❖

Darfur was a lonely time. I developed rituals: on the way back from the office, I'd stop at the small shop that had a freezer full of cold drinks. The shopkeeper knew me and after a few days had my plastic bottle of mango juice waiting when I arrived. It wasn't every day that the juice was cold—it depended on whether the shop had power to keep the freezer on. It didn't matter; cold or not, I'd take it back to the compound, drag one of the kitchen chairs outside, and drink the juice slowly. It came out thick like a sweet sauce and I sat there, savoring each gulp.

Our compound was within walking distance of the market, where I'd go to purchase tomatoes and other vegetables, or just to have something to do. One time, I went with Lila to buy a chicken.

"Which one do you want?" she asked, pointing to a fenced area where more than a dozen chickens pecked at the ground.

The only chicken I had ever bought before was wrapped in cellophane. I wasn't sure how to choose. "I don't know. Which one looks good to you?"

She scanned the chickens running around and pointed to one with black feathers. "That one."

"OK, that one then," I said, gesturing at the little old woman sitting on the ground, surrounded by her chickens, to show her which bird I meant. She grabbed the one we wanted violently, the bird's wings flapping hysterically. She held the chicken upside down, wrapped its feet in straw, and handed it to me.

"Wait, now what?" I said.

Lila started to laugh. "You silly *muzungu*. You want her to kill it for you?"

Was that even a question? Of course I wanted her to kill it for me.

"It will cost extra, you know."

"I don't care. *I'm* not killing that chicken!"

By now the chicken vendor could tell what we were discussing and started laughing, too. She was still holding the chicken upside down, but it had stopped flapping.

"You want it feathered, too?" Lila asked.

Of course, I wanted it feathered. "Uh-huh."

"It's also going to cost you more."

"I just want a dead, featherless chicken."

Most nights though I cooked pasta with tuna or egg on the tiny gas stove in the kitchen. The Internet didn't work at the residences and I plowed through my books so quickly that I had to space out my reading. There were occasional parties on Thursday nights, but most of the time people were just too exhausted to do anything. I made up an exercise routine that I did around the compound, using water bottles as arm weights and a piece of rope from the NFI package as a jump rope. Lila would just sit there, looking at me. I could hear her voice in my head as she rolled her eyes: *You silly* muzungu.

THE GEOGRAPHIC SPAN OF DARFUR was massive—the region is roughly the size of France—and the problems were always changing. I never felt I got a grasp on the overall situation, but in this small part of North Darfur, I understood the challenges, the context, and for the first time since I started doing this work, I felt I played a big part in it. Even so, the job was hard and frustrating and many of us often felt we weren't doing enough. Every time things seemed to be on track, there would be another setback. A village was attacked; another rainstorm flooded the camp; a key staff member got malaria and was out for two weeks; a car was ambushed and all movement stopped until it was safe again to drive the streets.

If fighting should break out nearby, there were sketchy evacuation plans for internationals, but none whatsoever for local staff. And they were the ones who were more vulnerable to attack—after all, there were more of them, so the odds that they would be on a road that was ambushed were higher. Before militias discovered there was a high price tag for expat releases, kidnapping or harming foreigners was considered a political risk not often worth taking.

Our Sudanese colleagues had to sit in security briefings as Mark explained the evacuation procedures. I knew this was the norm for agencies that operated in insecure areas, and we couldn't evacuate them. This was, after all, their country. Every expat worker was just an individual; a national came with his whole family. We couldn't be responsible for getting entire families out, and staff wouldn't leave without them. Even if we wanted to shoulder that obligation, the logistical hurdles would be too great. Oftentimes expats were evacuated across borders; with Western passports, they could easily get a visa. Some of our national staff didn't even have passports, and probably wouldn't be eligible for visas. When expats left the country, they were simply in transit; when nationals left the country, they were making an escape.

I had spoken to expat aid workers who still felt guilty after being evacuated in Rwanda and having to leave their Tutsi friends and colleagues behind. I couldn't imagine having to tell Ishaq that I was leaving him in a war zone after his family had shown me such kindness. I looked over at him; he sat with his legs and arms folded, his head cocked to one side. I was sure he had heard this speech dozens of times by now. This was what he had come to expect. I just hoped that it would never come to that in El Fasher.

Years later, I knew that many aid workers were being kidnapped and abducted in retaliation for the International Criminal Court's warrant for President Omar al-Bashir's arrest. But at the time, it wasn't that dangerous in Darfur. Petty theft was the biggest risk then. Often we'd have to pull off the streets in downtown El Fasher and wait until a convoy of twenty or so military trucks filled with Sudanese soldiers passed. They'd be sitting on the backs, all in Rambo-style camouflage uniforms. Some of them left their weapons resting on the floor. Others held their guns pointing outward, at the road—at us.

"This scares the shit out of me," said Mark, as we sat in the car on our way to the camp.

"Why? They're not going to shoot us," I said.

"No, not intentionally. But how many of those guys thought to put the safeties on those guns? How many of them even know *how* to put their safeties on? A wrong bump and one of those AK-47s goes spraying." That was the fear. Not that we would be directly targeted—at least not during the time I was there—but that if fighting broke out between militias, we would be caught in the cross fire.

Mark instructed us to drive with the windows up.

"I thought we were supposed to drive with the windows down?" I asked. Back in Zalingei, Dmitri made sure we always kept the windows down. He and Laura had been driving home one night after curfew. They didn't see any guards, and no one told them to stop. Then Laura heard the cock of a gun.

"Dmitri, stop!" she shouted.

Three guards, all armed, jumped out of the bush. Maybe the guard would have shot if they kept driving, maybe not. But if her window had been up, Laura wouldn't have heard the gun.

After that, Dmitri scolded us, "I swear, I see another person driving with the windows up, I'm going to smash them all."

Mark had a different position, though. "No, you drive with them up. In case people throw things at the car."

❖

Not long after I arrived, Hurricane Katrina struck New Orleans. We all gathered around a small radio and listened to the reports coming out of the United States. CNN and the *New York Times* website had plenty of images of the flooded streets, makeshift shelters, and Red Cross volunteers running around handing things out.

"This looks just like Africa, except the people are too fat," my American colleague said.

Later that day, I spoke to my dad. "This is our tsunami, Jay," he said somberly. It had been eight months since the Indian Ocean tsunami of December 2004.

It was the first time I felt that my father understood what I did. But I wanted to correct him: Katrina was not nearly as devastating as the tsunami. Suddenly, Americans were grappling with things that were familiar elements of daily life in other parts of the world: plastic tarps, outbreaks of disease, former-football-stadiums-turned-displaced-person camps, theft—and the endless search for places for people to defecate. No longer could Americans sit in judgment of the rest of the world when violence and disease erupted during times of crisis, or criticize from their couches the length of time it took for a proper response to start. This was happening in a country with money, a federal agency specifically tasked with on-the-ground disaster relief (FEMA), rule of law, and a functional government. But all over the world, even in America, people were people, desperate and ready to do what it took to feed themselves and their families.

❖

After months of weekly camp meetings, Ahmed, the camp committee leader, and I were friends. It was hard to know how old Ahmed was—his head was always wrapped in a white turban and his body cloaked in a matching *djellaba*. A soft-spoken gentleman with subtle mannerisms, Ahmed carried himself with the wisdom and authority of an elder, and the other committee members and I treated him as one. Even though we communicated through Ishaq, he and I had an unspoken understanding; sometimes I knew what he was saying just by the tone of his voice. Regardless of the scams going on in the camp—the forgery of food cards, the regular theft of materials, the bribery and internal politics—I felt that Ahmed was always straight with me.

One day after a camp meeting with the usual agenda—overcrowding in the schools, the broken latrines in block A13, the food distribution disputes from the week before—Ahmed approached Ishaq and me.

"My niece is sick. Can you come see her?"

"Ahmed, I'm not a doctor," I said.

"I know. She needs help. I don't know what else to do."

I suggested he take her to the clinic, and he looked down. "I already have."

"OK. I'll come tomorrow. I promise, Ahmed. I have to go now."

The next morning I was back in the camp to meet with an agency about where camp residents' cattle could graze. They had started developing a pasture on a parcel of land that the residents had already cleared to build a prayer space. We needed to find an alternative.

Ahmed was waiting for me at the registration center. As soon as I saw him, I remembered. "Your niece," I said. "I'll come after this meeting." He waited patiently in the corner until we finished.

"OK. Let's go." Ishaq came with us to interpret, and we piled into the vehicle and drove to Ahmed's tent. His plot of land was larger than that of many other families. He planted shrubs around the periphery to make a gate and I almost tripped as the cuff of my pants got stuck on one of the twiggy branches.

Ahmed pulled back one of the plastic sheets to his tent, and we slipped inside. His sister, meek and soft, sat on the floor with a large pillow covered by a towel on her lap. She looked up as we walked in, but her face was stoic and expressionless. Ahmed said something quietly to her. She slowly pulled back the towel covering the pillow.

Underneath lay her infant daughter. Her malnourished body was tiny and frail; her head twice its size, swollen and puffy. It looked like a balloon floating on top of a skeleton. The child's nose was distorted, her eye sockets sunken in, her cheeks and forehead bags of fluid. When she moved her head, her neck twisted awkwardly, too weak to support the bloated mass. She let out muffled gasps of discomfort.

"Oh," Ishaq sighed.

I felt queasy. I had never seen anything like this.

"Have you taken her to the hospital?" I asked.

"Yes," Ahmed said, crouching down to touch her.

"What did they say?"

"They can't do anything for her. There is surgery she can get, but it's only in Khartoum." He covered her head again and stood up.

"OK, well, she has to get to Khartoum then," I said. sternly.

"Yes. We have to get her to Khartoum," Ishaq repeated to me in English.

"We'll get her to Khartoum, Ahmed," I said to him. "We'll get her to Khartoum," I said again, looking at his sister, who was still sitting on the floor.

I went back to the office but none of the doctors were there. So I called the only doctor I knew I could reach—Dad.

"She has hydrocephalus. Swelling in the head. It's a congenital condition. They usually catch it in utero in the States," my father said, when I'd finished describing what I'd seen. He was sitting in a lounge chair on the beach in Fire Island.

"Will she die?" I asked.

"If she's not treated, yes. She needs to be shunted. They drain the fluid from her head and she can be OK."

"Her head's already huge, Dad. How much time?"

"It's hard to know from here. But she needs to get treatment soon."

THERE WAS AN URGENCY about this situation that felt new. Perhaps it was the personal relationship I had with Ahmed, but whatever it was jolted me into action. The attacks in Tawila, the Janjaweed raping women, the rainstorms—these were all out of my control. But a sick child? That I could actually do something about.

I went to Mark.

"There's a girl in the camp. She has hydrocephalus."

"What's that?" he said, looking up from his laptop.

"It's swelling in the brain or something. Her head is huge, Mark. She needs treatment. The family has exhausted all their options here. We've got to get her on a plane to Khartoum and soon."

He leaned back in his chair, sighed, and combed his fingers through his hair. "WFP won't let IDPs on the flights. You know that." The World Food Programme was the UN agency that transported aid workers in and out of Darfur by plane.

"Yeah, I know. But can't we pay for her and her family to get on a commercial flight out there?"

"We can't do that. We can't pick and choose IDPs to fly to Khartoum for medical treatment."

"OK, well, then I'm going to pay for their flights," I informed him.

"I don't think you can do that, either. It will be seen as coming from our agency even if you are paying out of your own pocket because you're employed by us."

I called the Khartoum office and asked them. But I got the same response. "Last month there were a few IDPs with heart conditions who needed to be sent to Khartoum," the emergency coordinator told me. "We couldn't do it. We can't send some people to Khartoum and not others. It would just be chaos."

I talked to the health coordinator in one of the clinics who said the same thing. "There were people with lung issues in the camp a month ago," she told me. "We couldn't take them all to Khartoum."

"So what happened?" I asked.

"Two of them have died already," she said.

With every rejection, my resolve intensified. I hadn't been confronted with this degree of clinical detachment before. How could I go back to Ahmed and tell him that there was nothing I could do, nothing that the humanitarian community could do, to help? That I was sorry, but he would have to watch his niece die. For the next week, I spent my nights dreaming of exploding heads, and my days negotiating with WFP, UNICEF, UNDP, none of which would agree to help get the girl on the flight because it wasn't "in their mandate"—it wasn't, in other words what they had come to Darfur to do and, therefore, they weren't responsible for it. Large aid agencies like these developed programs for tens of thousands of people—large-scale operations that provided a little to many. But working at an individual level—a case-by-case basis—wasn't what we were in the business of doing.

I sat across from Wilbens, the logistics officer from the United Nations' World Health Organization (WHO), which oversees health care in emergencies. Certainly it had to be in their mandate.

"Look," he started. "We have requests from IDPs to go to Khartoum every day. If we took up every request, we could not operate. It's sad, I know." Wilbens smiled.

"We can't set this precedent. If we fly this girl and her family to Khartoum for free, how do we tell the next sick person that we can't fly them?"

"*Shouldn't* we be flying sick people to Khartoum for treatment? I mean, shouldn't that be part of our job? We're here to save lives and reduce suffering, aren't we?"

"We can't save everyone, my dear," Wilbens said.

Wilbens had a point, as did everyone else, and I may have been wildly naive. I could understand their arguments in the abstract. My personal relationship with Ahmed was clearly blurring my logic. But giving shelter, some measly food items, a few bars of soap, and providing overcrowded schools and medical care that wouldn't stand up to malpractice lawsuits at home—this was the sum total of the humanitarian operation? This was the best we could do? With all the resources spent on getting us here, trucking us around this foreign land to "help," was this it?

"Don't even bother. Let this one go," Lila instructed me over dinner one night. "It's not going to happen, so you shouldn't worry your head about it anymore." Others weren't as sympathetic. "All the time you're spending on this girl, you could be helping a lot of other people. Get back to your job," Mark told me over a smoke in the office a few days after our initial meeting, when he knew I was still obsessing about it.

But I refused to rationalize the path of least resistance. I was determined to get this girl to Khartoum, no matter what logistical challenges I had to overcome, no matter what arcane UN bureaucracy I had to navigate, no matter the number of people sitting behind desks who politely said, "No, I can't help." I had heard "no" many times before as camp coordinator: when we didn't have the funds to purchase crucial sanitation equipment; when we weren't able to transport rice to a sister camp because of an impassable road. "No, it is not possible" was the uncomplicated way out, but I often found that bending rules and mandates here and there, and a bit of creativity were the only ingredients required to turn the allegedly impossible into reality.

I had learned this persistence from Mom. She was the woman who always asked—politely, yet sternly—if she could "speak to a supervisor" when things weren't going her way. One time, our family was taking a vacation to Block Island and we were late for the ferry. We sat in the car as a crewmember gestured for my father to roll down the window and then proceeded to inform us that there was no room for our bulky Buick station wagon. We'd have to wait for the next ferry—which wouldn't depart until the following day. Mom leaned over my father from the passenger seat to speak to the deckhand. "What about there?" she said, pointing to a spot at the edge of the boat. She unbuckled her seat belt and got out of the car to show him.

"Ma'am," he said, "the boat is about to leave, there is no room for your car." Dad turned around to address my brothers and me. "Watch your mother, kids. Just watch."

I peeled my skinny legs off the sticky plastic seats and leaned forward. Through the windshield, I saw Mom *sit down* on the divider between the boat and land. "We have a reservation for this ferry. There is one more spot left and my family is getting on it. I'd like to speak to the captain!" People on the upper deck were dangling over the railing to see what was going on below. Finally, the man pleading with her gave up. He opened Dad's door, told him to slide over, and drove the car onto the boat. The back wheels grazed the edge.

"Thank you," Mom said, wiping her hands on her shorts as she stood up. "Come on, kids!"

WHILE I WAS TRYING TO talk my way onto a ferry—so to speak—Ahmed was making plans to help his sister, her husband, and their daughter get to Khartoum through the desert on the back of a donkey cart. I found him in the camp that morning.

"Ahmed—I'm trying. I really am." He looked at me with confusion. What could I tell this man? That there is not one agency here that is willing to pay for him?

"They're leaving by donkey tomorrow," he said.

"Give me one more day, OK?" I pleaded. "And then they go."

A few days into my quest, I learned that a prominent agency in Darfur regularly flew planes filled with supplies back and forth from El Fasher to Khartoum. Most of the time, though, the planes were half empty. That night, I approached Jean-Pierre, the agency's logistics officer, and told him my story.

"I think we can probably manage this," he said.

"Really?" I couldn't believe it.

"I mean, we've never done it before, but I don't see why not."

"That would be so great. What do I need to do?"

"Why don't you come to my office in the morning and we'll figure it out. It may be a bit tricky, but we'll see."

He seemed genuinely interested in helping Ahmed's niece, and I was so grateful to have met him. As we continued talking, I learned Jean-Pierre was in his midforties and had worked in Kabul and Peshawar; he had a sophisticated European accent that suggested a peripatetic childhood and degrees taken at various continental universities.

It turned out that when Jean-Pierre called the operation "tricky" he actually meant necessitating nothing short of a minor miracle. Jean-Pierre laid out the requirements the next morning: Ahmed's family had to sign a waiver stating that they would not seek help from the agency once they landed in Khartoum and that they had no expectations that they would fly them back to Darfur; a doctor had to accompany them on the flight; they had to have all of the proper identification and travel authorizations in order; and an ambulance had to meet them at the airport. And all of this would have to be arranged before the girl's condition got worse. I left his office deflated and angry at myself for having been hopeful the night before, knowing by now that nothing came that easy in Darfur.

But somehow, it all came together. By now, everyone in town knew about this case and the crazy girl who thought she could rustle up an airplane. A doctor that I had worked with previously happened to be going to Khartoum in two days and agreed to fly with the girl. A friend of mine in Khartoum, a nurse, agreed to pick the family up at the hospital and say that her vehicle was an "ambulance." Ahmed would sign whatever piece of paper I put in front of his face and happily took a pen to the dotted line when I rushed back to the camp to explain the situation to him.

The only thing left was the travel authorization. Ahmed had no identification, no birth certificate for himself, let alone his sister or her daughter. But Ishaq's cousin worked at the Ministry of Social Welfare and was able to pull together a special transit pass that would satisfy the airport guards. Breathless, I returned to Jean-Pierre's office with all of the required documentation. He seemed surprised, but dutifully inspected the paperwork nonetheless. When he reached the bottom of the final sheet, he looked up and said, "OK. They go."

I dashed back to Ishaq's office.

"They're going!"

He stood up. "Really?"

"Yes, the authorization came through just now!"

He leaped over to me, and I swear he was about to hug me. He got a hold of himself—a Muslim man cannot embrace a woman unless she is his wife—and just touched my shoulder. I touched his, and for a few minutes we bounced around like that, giddy and laughing. When I told Mark that everything had worked out, he seemed impressed. Coincidentally, I ended up having to be in Khartoum for a meeting on the same day that Ahmed's niece arrived. That morning, I met with the Sudanese doctor who would see her at the hospital and told him I would cover any medical costs. He smiled. "I will not charge these people anything."

I went with my friend in our makeshift ambulance to pick up Ahmed's sister and child from the airport. She carried the little girl through the terminal on the same large pillow she had been clutching when I met her. She covered her baby with a towel that both protected her and shielded her from the stares of strangers. I showed them to my friend's "ambulance" and we embarked down the crooked Khartoum streets.

When we reached the hospital, the doctor was already waiting outside. Ahmed's sister took my hands in hers and held them for a few moments before she scooped up her heavy baby, and carried her through the hospital gates.

❖

Back in Darfur, my situation was getting harder and harder to bear. I dreaded going back to the compound, unsure if we'd have power, but certain I would be facing another empty night. I met a German guy who was in town for a few weeks doing a water assessment. We had nothing in common. In fact, I found him pretty annoying. But I hooked up with him anyway. In the field, age and nationality really didn't matter. You mingled with people much older, or much younger, from dozens of different countries. As long as you shared some common pop culture references, had traveled to the same parts of the world, and could basically speak the same language, you'd get along just fine.

Being with the German temporarily alleviated the boredom and the monotony of my nights. He had a car, so sometimes we drove through town just to break up the scenery. But we couldn't go past a certain checkpoint. It felt like we were on *The Truman Show*—the invisible borders of our world as rigid and impassable as actual walls.

But after five months and the onset of Ramadan, everyone seemed to unravel at once. The Sudanese, who fasted all day, walked around in a trance. Ishaq was still usually full of energy, but most of our other colleagues gave up. Some pulled mattresses out of storage, laid them in the halls, and napped. Those of us who were eating didn't bother trying to rouse them. It seemed cruel and dangerous, in this heat, to have to work without water. And when they spoke, the Ramadan-induced halitosis was so putrid you couldn't help thinking it'd be better if they didn't.

Lindsay was in charge of the NFI allocations. It wasn't a fun job—she had to manage the safe arrival of tons of goods, and very often the trucks delivering them were looted along the way. If they did arrive, Lindsay then had to organize and oversee their distribution. Once, Lindsay was on her way to the dispensary, where residents had been lined up for hours waiting to receive hygiene kits—soap, buckets, jerry cans, Dettol. Outside the distribution tent, a few women had placed their goods in the path designated for cars. Lindsay needed to get into the tent and honked her horn. The women didn't know what she wanted. The ordinarily calm and competent Lindsay sat there with her elbow on the horn, her eyebrows raised, and her free hand gesturing for them to move their things. When they still didn't understand what she meant, she drove ahead, flattening the jerry cans and ripping through the buckets.

"What is she doing?" shouted our coworker Chris, who was supervising distributions that day.

She pulled up to where we were standing.

"What the hell was that?!" he yelled.

"Chris, they have to learn that they cannot block the entrance. I gave them a warning. I told them to get out of the way."

"You need a serious vacation," he said and walked away.

She looked back at the women scurrying to get their things. "I guess I do." She tried to explain to them what was wrong, making sweeping motions with her arms. But the women just threw the broken items at her feet. She walked into the supplies tent, cutting the line that curled around the entrance, and emerged with four new jerry cans and a few buckets. "Here," she said, apologetically.

I STARTED TO QUESTION THOSE of us who made the choice again and again to come to places like this. What kind of expectations did we have for each other? Sometimes it felt as if we were giving ourselves a pass: because we were all making sacrifices to be here, because we were "giving" of ourselves, maybe it was OK when we acted badly. It was how we psychologically managed what we were doing. We were frustrated, we were tired, we were lonely, we were hot, but we were here! So maybe we got pissed off and yelled at drivers and ran over people's possessions, but we were just human, we were good people, some of us too young to know how to deal with what was going on around us.

My own stress was starting to show, too. The loneliness of the place was what really had started to strip me of my sanity. By this time, the communication networks were down so often that we started calling them "the notwork." No network, no Internet. No network, no phone. I could feel myself slipping, my irritation mounting, my mental strength withering. I hadn't actually thrown rocks at children that one morning walking to the office, but that seemed like a trivial distinction: just wanting to was bad enough. I was on the edge of—something—and for what? I knew the services in the camp were keeping people alive for the time being, but alive with what standard of living? Was that enough? Should I feel guilty for what I did, or for not doing more of it? Or should I be angry at the circumstances—the government, the weather, the whole indifferent world—that contrived to make any victory feel fleeting and insubstantial?

One afternoon after returning from a meeting at the camp, a guard knocked on my door.

"Ms. Jessica. There are some people from the camp here to see you."

People from the camp never came to the office—I always went to them. I assumed something must have gone wrong and hurried to the gate.

Outside, three of the men from the camp committee sat waiting.

"We came to see if you were OK," one of them began.

"What? You walked all the way here?"

"Well, we wanted to make sure you were feeling OK."

Was it that obvious? Was it my tone of voice? My growing impatience with how slowly things were going? My restlessness at meetings over the general lack of progress? It never seemed as if things moved or improved here. In fact, a lot of the time it felt like things got worse. Another attack, or even just a rainstorm, could undo whatever headway we had made overnight. The setbacks just kept coming: the colleague on leave deciding not to return, HAC rejecting our project proposal, staff members stealing from the agency. It was like those trick birthday candles we had at birthday parties as kids. No matter how many times you thought you'd blown them out, the flame would still maddeningly reappear.

"Thank you. I'm really OK. I'm sorry if I wasn't earlier," I said. "I can't believe you walked all the way here to see if I was OK!"

I gave them a ride back to the camp, still thanking them, touched that they had come to check on me, but embarrassed that my mental frailty was so obvious.

THERE WERE THREE THINGS I could rely on—my bed, having water in the house, and knowing that the power would be on until 10 p.m. But then one night the rains were so bad that water seeped through the walls and drenched my bed. Next, our water pump broke and the man who was supposed to fix it never showed up. But it wouldn't have mattered if he had, since the generator was busted, too. No power, no pump, no shower. I felt bad for complaining and for being annoyed. And, of course, aside from the pressure not to grumble about these things, there was an underlying pressure not to go on R&R. "Who would go on vacation when all of this is going on?" some colleagues would say. The martyr complex permeated my psyche, and although I desperately needed a break, I felt negligent when I left. But people who skipped R&R to tough it out were the ones who kicked something if it didn't work. They were the ones who beeped at women for not moving their stuff fast enough. They shouted at drivers for being late and cursed at staff for not turning off their computers. They retaliated when children threw rocks at them, or wanted to retaliate.

Still, sometimes it didn't matter if we were at our best or at our worst. It didn't matter if we did everything we could or if we didn't. Darfur wasn't a test, and there was no such thing as a perfect score. If one thing didn't go wrong, another would. In the end, all you could really say was there were just things we didn't anticipate. And so one morning I woke up and learned that children in the camp had drowned.

Back in their villages, women dug holes far from their homes where they buried trash. Things were different in the camp, where women couldn't stray far from their plots of land and living quarters were much tighter. It became my responsibility to organize a waste disposal system. We distributed small red tin barrels throughout the camp for people to dump their trash and hired a local company to cart away the garbage once a week. And that was pretty much that, for a while. After we'd gotten the system set up, I didn't think too much about it. I was busy making sure that the drugs for the clinics were delivered. I was negotiating protests from teachers who hadn't been paid in months. The trash wasn't at the top of my to-do list—until it started raining.

Sudan's weather patterns are extreme. When it's dry, it feels as though a giant straw has sucked the moisture from every molecule. There just isn't enough water to ever make you feel clean or refreshed. Then, suddenly, the skies open and the rains start. It's a binary situation: there's no trickle, there's no drizzle, when the rain comes, it comes with a fury. The clouds clap and throw down everything they can without mercy. As I had seen in Zalingei, roads turn to rivers in minutes.

After one night of heavy rain, a few dozen pit latrines collapsed. NFIs in the lower part of the camp washed into the river. We mapped the most vulnerable areas, drafted contingency plans for moving people to higher ground, and distributed supplies to anyone whose belongings had washed away. We delivered burlap bags to camp residents to fill with sand and protect their shelters from the flooding waters. But we didn't think about the holes.

It turned out that the trucks that came to take away the trash every other week weren't doing much because people weren't using the bins. They didn't even know what the bins *were,* so they just went about things as they always had, digging holes and depositing their garbage there, meanwhile, filling the bins with the sand and twigs they dug up. When the storms came, the rainwater filled the deep holes and left stagnant pools of water—a breeding ground for mosquitoes. And then there were the drownings.

"How? Where?" I asked.

"They fell into the holes. And they drowned," Ishaq told me. He scratched his head and looked down at the ground.

"Oh my God. How many?"

"Three."

This was now an emergency. We hired people to fill the holes and canvassed every tent telling women to use the bins. We made posters showing the danger of the holes and hung them all over the camp. We tried our best to get the message out quickly, but how do you change behaviors that have existed forever? At home, how long did it take people to start wearing seat belts, or for the "Give a Hoot, Don't Pollute" campaign to catch on? How could we expect to change these long-held habits before the next big storm?

Regardless of what I told myself, I couldn't help

feeling that I had been somehow responsible for the drownings—that the cause of death, for each of these children, had been my neglect. If I had known what to look out for, if I had more experience, maybe I could have anticipated this. But others were dealing with the unexpected, too. The heat in the camp was so intense that any relief—whether it was walking in a donkey's shadow, or just sitting under a sheet held up by two poles—helped. So when vehicles were parked for hours in the camp, children crawled under them to get some shade. Two children were almost run over this way, but scrambled out from under the car just in time. Ian, our British logistician, called an emergency meeting for the drivers and ordered them to check under their vehicles before even starting their engines.

Soon, Tawila got attacked again and the camp was flooded with more people waiting to get in. More and more of them appeared every day, and one morning when Ishaq and I pulled up to the registration tent we were swarmed by so many people that I couldn't even open the car door. Women and men pleaded for attention, for their dignity, for someone to listen to and look at them as individuals and not lump them in with the morass of people, all desperate, all needing, all with their own stories of loss. They shoved papers in my face, showing they had come from Chad and shouting in Arabic. I walked ahead, trying to make it to the registration tent, but I was surrounded by a dizzying whir of people tapping on my shoulder, tugging the back of my shirt, grabbing my hands. Women swirled around me, clutching babies shrilling with snot bubbling out of their little noses, their crusted upper lips trembling.

"I know," my friend Ben would say years later, when we talked about these moments. He told me a story.

"When I was in Cambodia we were registering people for a food distribution. This tiny old woman kept coming up to me begging for more food. There were hundreds of people on line getting what we could give and this lady wanted more. I turned to her and said, 'Why should I give you more food? Why are *you* more deserving than any of these other people?' But she just kept pleading, telling me that her daughter was sick and she needed more food. All of these people's kids were sick. Everyone was hungry. I just walked away, but she kept appearing, begging for more food. I kept trying to ignore her.

"She finally left and I sort of forgot about her. Until I saw her in the distance walking toward the camp. This little old woman, carrying her daughter, literally a sack of bones, in her arms. All she wanted was to get my attention. She pushed her way to the front of the line again and handed me her daughter. I've never seen someone dying of starvation, let alone held one in my arms. Ugh," he sighed. "I still think about that and feel awful."

Eventually there were so many people flocking to the camp that we had to build a fence around the registration tent to keep order. The African Union Peacekeepers came in to do crowd control; two unarmed men stood at the gates of the fence so it wasn't mauled. Still, people pushed up against the barriers, desperate to get in and register. I was afraid there would be a stampede, the children sitting on the ground next to the fence would be trampled, and the whole place would implode. Everyone there, the mothers carrying babies, the worried men with their donkeys, the children whose little faces poked through the fence, they all expected me to have an answer. I wondered what Charles would have done in this moment, remembering his coolness under the same chaos at the distribution in Rwanda. I wished I had that kind of calm, but I was in over my head. I was never trained to deal with riots. I didn't know what to do except to call on the camp committee members and have them quell the mayhem.

AT A CERTAIN POINT I FOUND myself teetering on a meltdown. I'd wake up to the call of prayer every morning at 5:30 a.m. and trudge to the office, almost in a coma. One day, Abdullah, the driver who was supposed to take me to the camp, was late. I was scheduled to meet with Ahmed and the rest of the committee to discuss registering the new arrivals. I waited outside the office under the shade of a tree, cursing.

"Where the hell is he?" I said. "Has anyone seen Abdullah?" I demanded, addressing some local staff standing by the gate. They all shook their heads.

"*Goddamnit,*" I muttered as I walked away. I'm sure they could hear me.

About twenty minutes later, Abdullah pulled up in the vehicle. I got in and slammed the door. "Where *were* you?" I asked.

"*Malesh,*" Abdullah said—*sorry*. "My daughter had to go to school and my wife is sick and so I had to take her." I didn't respond.

We got to the registration tent and Ishaq and I sat with the camp committee members to plan the registration that day.

"Jessica, can I go pray?" Ishaq asked.

"Really? Now?" I responded.

"Yes, I was here early this morning and missed the morning prayer."

"Can't it wait?" I needed his help.

He gave me a look. It was a familiar one. One that I had seen my first time in Sudan, on the faces of staff when Sheila left the room after an outburst back in Khartoum. And then it hit me. I was becoming the very person I had despised.

"I'm sorry, Ishaq," I said. "Go pray."

He walked away slowly. I knew I needed a time-out. But there was no time.

❖

And then, out of nowhere, I was offered an escape—a permanent one. I was sitting in my office when an e-mail popped up, offering me a job in tsunami-affected Sri Lanka and Indonesia. I would be working with a team, evaluating how a large agency had responded to children's needs in the wake of the disaster. It was a three-month consultancy, and it would certainly be easier than what I was doing in Darfur.

I sat in my office reading and rereading the e-mail, expecting it to end with: "Just kidding!" I didn't even remember applying to this job; it must have been months ago, when the tsunami hit and I started sending off résumés. I had already been in Darfur for seven months, which made me a novice. Sure, for people not in this line of work seven months living and working in Darfur was forever. But I was surrounded by colleagues who had spent years here, who extended contract after contract, choosing again and again to stay. How could I face them and admit that I was even considering leaving? I imagined they'd be angry, suspicious, peg me as a sellout and a phony.

"Leave!" Lila commanded me over breakfast. "Are you some crazy *muzungu*? If I had a chance like that, you think I would stick it out here like a fool? Do what you need to do, girl. And leave me your DVDs."

I confided in another Kenyan friend, Joseph. He was one of Lila's best friends. "I just don't know what to do. It's fine here. I could stay—of course, I could stay. But this is a really great opportunity. What do you think?"

"You've been here how long? Five months? And you were here for two before that? That's enough. You should go."

"But what about the camp?"

"What *about* the camp?!" He laughed. "You think being here is going to change that camp? I'm sorry, my dear, but that camp will be here no matter if you are or aren't. Seven months is plenty. I'm jealous—get out of this shit hole. People leave jobs all the time. Don't feel badly about it."

Again and again, it was my African expat friends who sanctioned my leaving. They had a seemingly sensible take on the whole thing. We were here doing a job; this whole thing we whites thought of as philanthropy was irrelevant. Sure, they cared, but their reason for being here was straightforward: they came in order to be able to leave—to return home, eventually, and have an easy life. These jobs allowed them to save more money than they ever would in Kenya or Uganda. For them, being in Sudan was just a means to an end. There was no ego involved. For the Western expats it felt different, like we were here proving something. Our self-worth was wrapped up in this life.

While my Kenyan colleagues may have let me get off easily, I couldn't bear facing the camp committee. At the end of the next meeting, I found the courage to tell them the news.

"I'll be leaving in three weeks," I said, almost in a

whisper. Ishaq translated my message. I had told him earlier that day. He had looked at me blankly, but could sense how distraught I was and didn't want to torture me. "OK, then," he said. "Let's work until you leave!"

The group sat silently, staring at me.

"Where are you going? Why?" Ahmed asked.

What was I going to say? *Sorry, but I'm leaving to go to Sri Lanka and Indonesia, to work there. It's not that I don't really care about you all, it's just, well, I got a better job.* So I lied. I said I was going home for my family.

"But we *are* your family," Ahmed protested.

"I know you are." My hands were shaking. I could barely speak, I was so ashamed. "I need to go home, though," I said softly, my voice quivering.

Two of the members spoke at the same time. "They want to know when you are coming back," Ishaq translated.

The truth was, I wasn't coming back. I was just one of many camp coordinators who would fill this role. Just like the person who would replace me, I came in for a few months, did what I could to make life a bit more pleasant. But I could leave, and would; I had options, and at any point I might get on a plane and go home or on to a better job. These people were left in their broken country, ruled by a relentlessly corrupt government that often seemed to do more to fracture the nation than rebuild it. Most of them would remain in these—or similar—conditions for the rest of their lives.

Ishaq started laughing. He knew the score; he had worked with countless foreigners before. They had come and gone—in and out. Transience was the defining nature of this work. Sure, we all exchanged e-mail addresses, promising to stay in touch. But he knew that once I left, I would be gone.

"What are they saying?" I asked Ishaq.

He chuckled. "They want to speak to your father and tell him that you must stay."

Ahmed pulled out his mobile phone.

"He's asking for your father's number," Ishaq said.

"What, he's going to call my Dad?"

"Yes. He wants to tell him to make you stay here."

"This is ridiculous. Does he even know what time it is there? My Dad's sleeping!"

But Ahmed was serious and the rest of the group insisted. He didn't realize that he couldn't possibly have enough credit on his phone to call the United States.

"Tell him to use mine. This is insane." I gave my phone to Ahmed. I told them my home phone number and Ahmed dialed.

All of the committee members leaned in, some of them giggling like children. I could hear the distant, tinny buzz as the phone rang, and then my father's voice. Excited, Ahmed started speaking very quickly, and in Arabic—to my dad, who definitely does not understand Arabic. I took the phone from him.

"Jay?" my weary father said. It was the middle of the night for him. "Is everything OK? What's going on?"

"Hi, Dad. Sorry for calling this late. My friends here in the camp insisted that I call you. They don't want me to leave."

Ishaq took the phone from me.

"Hello, sir." I couldn't imagine what Dad must have thought on the other end of that phone line. "We do not want Jessica to leave. We are her family here. She needs to stay." My dad was clearly saying something because Ishaq kept nodding and saying "Yes, sir." He passed the phone back to me.

"Jay? What . . . ? Who was that?"

"Dad—I'll call you back. Go back to bed. Sorry."

The committee waited for Ishaq's verdict, leaning in and looking at him with anticipation. He said something to the committee in Arabic. They leaned back in their chairs and grinned. They knew I was going.

I WAS SITTING ON MY bed back in the room where I had lived for the past five months when I called my dad back. I was crying. "Dad, how can I leave? I can't go."

"Jessica—this is not your war," he said. "You are one stick in a river of shit. Nothing you are doing will solve this problem. I know you want to stay, I know you're doing important work for today, but come on, get out of there. Don't look back."

"But I want to feel like I've finished something. *Anything!*" Each day I won small battles, lost others, but I didn't ever feel like I had done anything substantial. I'd come to learn that this feeling of powerlessness, this recognition of the insignificance of your own work beneath the overwhelming, endless avalanche of problems, is what aid workers face every day. We worked so hard, put in exhausting effort to move the bar a mere two inches. Such little progress after so much exertion—it was psychologically demoralizing.

"Look, I know you are committed to your work, but how long will you have to stay to feel that sense of completion? It could be years. And what are you willing to sacrifice to feel it? What does achievement in a place like Darfur look like, anyway?"

Maybe Dad was right. The fate of Darfur wasn't resting on whether I stayed or went. Even Ahmed's niece, whom I had managed to get out—who had been, briefly, my one shining achievement—had died after medical complications.

❖

Three weeks later, Ishaq brought me to the small airport in El Fasher. He sat next to me as we waited until I boarded the little plane to Khartoum, where I would get my connecting flight to Colombo, Sri Lanka. I knew I would never see him again and he knew it, too.

When it was time to board we walked slowly to the security area. I wanted to hug Ishaq tightly. But we couldn't—and so he shook my hand and leaned in so that our shoulders grazed. "I'm sorry, Ishaq."

"You must be strong," he said. *How ridiculous,* I thought. *Him telling me to be strong.*

The little plane lifted up and I looked down on Al Salam, with its ordered rows of tents that we had worked so hard to plan. As we ascended higher, the landscape transformed into a miniature map—tiny blue tents pitted onto pale graph paper.

A FEW WEEKS LATER, the agency did hire another camp coordinator to replace me. Six months after I left my friends still in El Fasher told me that Al Salam had virtually doubled in size—to forty-five thousand people. How were they living, where were they bathing or disposing of their trash? We tried so hard to keep the place orderly, with enough space for everyone to live without being on top of each other. I couldn't imagine cramming twice as many people into the carefully planned plots of land inside the camp borders. But I didn't have to. Doing the unimaginable was someone else's responsibility now.

Four years later, the government kicked out thirteen Western aid groups in retaliation for the International Criminal Court's decision to issue a warrant for the arrest of President Al-Bashir on charges of war crimes. Did the roof that we fixed on the school in block D16 even matter now? Did the covers we put on the latrines to stop the flies mean anything anymore? They were fine solutions to stop the immediate problems, but this war was much bigger than me, than the agency that I worked for, than the countless humanitarian workers running around providing bars of soap. The country needed a government that didn't terrorize its own population, one that was committed to peace and didn't back a militia that ran people off of their land. And without this, without a government that worked with the aid community, not against it, our programs could only be short-term solutions.

More Money, More Problems

SRI LANKA AND INDONESIA, 2005

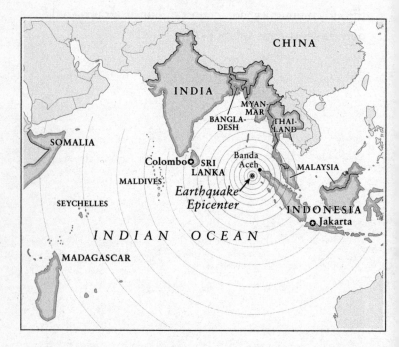

The first day on the job I was greeted by sliding glass doors, marble floors, and enormous flower arrangements in the lobby of the Colombo Hyatt. Tourists roamed the atrium, gripping maps and guidebooks, with cameras dangling from their necks. In one corner, a small café sold croissants and cookies; in another, a man played Barry Manilow songs on a polished grand piano.

Businessmen sat on the cushy couches, reading the newspaper or talking on the phone. I was given a note at check-in: *"Welcome to Sri Lanka. We have a meeting with Save the Children at 10 a.m. See you then."*

I had been hired by one of the largest agencies responding to the emergency to assess their response to the tsunami. As the aid world became more professionalized—establishing minimum standards by which to operate, requiring master's degrees to enter the field, developing codes of conduct and measures to increase accountability—evaluations like the one I was doing were now common practice. I would be traveling throughout tsunami-affected areas in Sri Lanka and Indonesia examining programs for children while the rest of the team covered education, health, nutrition, and water and sanitation. We weren't there to build the toilets, run the clinics, or reconstruct schools; we were examining the agency to determine whether the toilets *they* built, the clinics *they* ran, and the schools *they* reconstructed were working and were working well. I was an outsider—or independent evaluator, as industry jargon put it—looking in on this operation.

I had never worked in a sudden-onset emergency operation before. The humanitarian relief I had seen was in times of conflict, prolonged crisis, chronic distress. At that time, the tsunami was considered the biggest natural disaster the humanitarian community had ever responded to. The event killed more than 220,000 people across fourteen countries and displaced 1.7 million more. I was curious to see a relief response to a natural disaster in countries with stable governments and functioning civil sectors. The reconstruction would take years, but here you could work toward such a goal with some hope, feel you were genuinely building momentum and traction. Although both countries had preexisting challenges, especially in their education and health infrastructures, neither Sri Lanka nor Indonesia were failed states. And if we ever forgot or made comparisons to where we had come from, the local staff and government were there to remind us, "This is no sub-Saharan Africa."

By the time I arrived, nine months after the tsunami hit in December of 2004, the event had faded from the nightly news and the front pages. As the crisis became less acute, the media's interest waned. Once the first bottles of water and bags of rice were delivered and interviews with English-speaking tourists were wrapped up, the cameras stopped rolling. The reporters—with a few exceptions—filed their last stories, and moved on to the next assignment. But the long-term tragedy for the survivors had really just begun.

The Sri Lankan coast was a tropical paradise by any standard. Men walked along the side of the road wearing colorful sarongs, which they tied like skirts around their waists. Women strolled together draped in bright, glittering saris. People on bikes casually rode through

lush hills past endless rows of palm trees. But reminders of the tsunami's devastation were everywhere.
Dotting the otherwise tranquil horizon were the brick
foundations where buildings had once stood. Bridges
were crooked and collapsing, their roadways dangling
just feet above the water; roads were cracked, slabs of
concrete smashed up against each other, resembling
the shifting tectonic plates that caused this ruin. The
water had pulled everything in its reach back out to
sea, like a windshield wiper clearing a soaked window.
Much of the remaining debris had been removed by the
time I arrived and it wasn't until I saw a barge that the
sea had carried one mile inland that I could understand
the magnitude of the wave.

Many children were orphaned, but many more
died. As witnesses explained, the tsunami first pulled
the sea back, away from the shore, exposing hundreds
of fish flopping on the naked sand. Children raced in to
catch them. They were jumping around with the fish
when the first wave, like a boomerang, swept back in.
"It's strange," a professor from graduate school said
to me before I left. He had worked in Indonesia during the early days of the emergency, and I called him
for advice. "You walk into these villages, and there are
just no children." I was used to children shouting "*Muzungu*" and "*Khawaja*"—white person—whenever our
Land Cruiser entered a rural area. But for my professor, what he remembered from the days after the tsunami was the silence.

More men survived than women, not only because

they were more likely to know how to swim, or because they were stronger and could hold onto stationary objects—trees, roofs—tighter, but because the clothing women wore (saris in Sri Lanka, head scarves in Indonesia) got caught on floating debris and sucked them underwater. Some fishermen were far enough away from shore that they only felt the sea swell, their boats rising and falling with the current. They couldn't know the destruction happening on land.

MAYBE IT WAS THE DUSTY Darfur smell and the sand tucked into every crevice of my clothes or my notebooks filled with to-do lists from Al Salam that reminded me I had abandoned the camp. Maybe it was the constant travel along the coast of Sri Lanka and Indonesia—packing and unpacking, dragging bags down hotel hallways, lugging them into the backs of the vehicles. Mental checks: Do I have my wallet? Where's my passport? Shit, I left my toothbrush. Or maybe it was walking along the remains of what was left after the tsunami raced onto the coast and swept back out to sea carrying children, women, men, houses, roads, schools, anything that its foamy fingers could reach. It must have been all of those things because the months I spent in Sri Lanka and Indonesia were hell.

I spent most of my time there in a daze. Even a nightly dose of Ambien couldn't get me to sleep. Every morning, my eyes throbbed with exhaustion. I'd look

into the bathroom mirror at my pale face, raccoon circles around my eyes, the edges of my lips drawn down,
my hair overgrown and knotted. *I don't look like this.
This isn't me.* Only days ago, in Darfur, I had been
dodging hedgehogs and using bottled water to bathe.
In the capitals, I was now staying at five-star resorts
with lavish buffets, poolside bars, overstuffed pillows,
hundreds of television channels, and steaming showers with pressure that drilled into my neck and back. I
should have enjoyed it, but the lingering shame of leaving Darfur still clung closely. Being pampered in my
new surroundings only made it worse.

At the time, the tsunami response was the most generous and rapidly funded international humanitarian operation in history. By December 2005, a year
after the tsunami struck, a total of $14 billion had
been pledged or donated for emergency relief and reconstruction. About 40 percent, or $5.5 billion, came
from the general public. For most humanitarian crises, that figure is usually around 15 percent. The out-
pouring of donations from the public was due to a
number of circumstances: an enormous and blame-
less natural disaster, its timing (right after the Christmas holiday), the number of Western tourists who
had been present, and the extensive media coverage.

The influx of money, of human resources, of gifts in kind—they were on a scale the aid world had never seen before.

And with hundreds of agencies running around trying to "build back better," there was also an increased interest in analyzing what the aid community was doing. I had read plenty of background reports about the tsunami; they could be easily downloaded online. Hundreds of evaluations were going on, so many it sometimes seemed as if there were more evaluators *examining* the response to the tsunami than there were people actually *responding* to it. To me, all the ground appeared to be covered: how efficient agencies were, how effective their response was, and how well organizations coordinated and worked with local actors. Other evaluators had already scrutinized the response from a gender perspective, an environmental perspective, and inspected the financing instruments used, and whether the money got where it needed to be fast enough.

"This may be totally naive of me, but what else is there to say?" I asked our team leader, Toby, a chain-smoking chubby Brit in his midforties, as we rode together in the back of a rickshaw. It was my second day in Sri Lanka and we were on our way to speak with people from the Ministry of Education. We sat close together to avoid the raindrops seeping through the sides of the plastic panels that hung over the scooter.

"It's a question I've asked, too," he said. "This thing has been analyzed to death."

I found myself comparing everything about the tsunami response to our work in Darfur. What would an evaluator say about Al Salam? There were agreed upon international standards and benchmarks: twenty people to a latrine, 15 liters of water per person per day, minimum surface area of 45 square meters (or about 484 square feet) for each person in the camp. Our initial plans for Al Salam followed the standards closely. But nothing about aid really ever went according to design. With new people coming each day, the pace at which we could get in materials, the unexpected rainstorm or militia attack, these standards became more aspirational than realistic. I reasoned that here, hopefully, with seemingly fewer constraints and so much more money, the aid community could do more.

I shuffled through meetings with government ministers, UN and NGO staff, police, community leaders, mothers, and teachers, all along the coast of Sri Lanka. We then flew to Banda Aceh, Indonesia, to do the same. I asked a lot of questions about the agency's work: How fast did they react? What did their programs do? What was the quality of their response? Were the affected populations consulted in the process? The final report would be read by not only the responding agencies but also people at headquarters and large government donors who paid for multimillion-dollar programs and who wanted to see how their dollars were spent.

I also interviewed people from other agencies to hear what they had to say about the overall response. People kept complaining: "There's actually too much money." At first, I dismissed this kind of statement; it seemed like an aberration. But after six weeks of countless interviews, I realized that I hadn't just heard it once, but again and again.

In Darfur, we stretched our budget to the limit. We turned the generator off at 10 p.m. every night and suffered through the immovable heat to cut fuel costs. The office I wanted to build for the committee, with multiple meeting rooms, had to be scaled back to a single room because we didn't have the budget to build extra walls. But aid money is lumpy. People are mesmerized by the images of suffering that come out of a disaster like the tsunami. The chronic emergencies—the northern Ugandas, the Darfurs, the Congos, and the Somalias—don't have simple, iconic images and can't be summarized in easy-to-digest sound bites. Yet those crises slowly kill as many people or more than the tsunami did. Estimates put the number of people displaced as a result of violence in northern Uganda at 2 million, and the International Rescue Committee has calculated that roughly 5.4 million people died in the Congo between the time war broke out in 1998 and 2007. But these tragedies never get the same kind of attention or funding. Still, I didn't understand. How could too much money ever be a problem?

Aid funding after an emergency like the tsunami is one big feeding frenzy. To stay in business, agencies must appeal to funders. The largest donations to the UN and NGOs are from Western governments' foreign assistance budgets (USAID, for example, is the

US government's international assistance branch that doles out millions of dollars each year to aid organizations, the Brits have their own federal aid branch, as do most other wealthy nations), large foundations (such as the Ford Foundation and the Bill and Melinda Gates Foundation), and more recently, private companies (such as Google or Ikea) and the foundations they endow. Agencies compete with each other for this money. Their employees write proposals about projects they envision—how many tents they can distribute, how many clinics they will set up, how many schools they're going to rebuild—and how efficiently they'll execute these plans. The donors award grants to the most persuasive agencies, the ones best at convincing benefactors they can deliver. With this influx of cash, agencies get to work. Humanitarian responders gear up, parachute in, and provide lifesaving assistance— water, food, and rudimentary shelter—as quickly as possible.

Over the years, I'd learn that disasters are actually good for aid organizations. They present opportunities for agencies to attract more funds, garner greater publicity, and essentially grow global empires. After any emergency, I'd imagine PR teams giving each other the thumbs-up after presenting colorful spreadsheets showcasing the number of times the agency was named in the press, or the number of new hits to the agency's website—because that's when the money starts pouring in. Sure, the UN and NGOs use those contributions to respond to emergencies, and they need the funding to do their work, but this good-hearted profession is an industry just like any other. It needs dollars, and lots of them, to survive. With such huge surpluses coming into post-tsunami Asia, no agency was going to struggle to survive.

Only MSF stopped collecting donations once they'd received as much money as they thought they could use. They did so less than a week after the tsunami hit, that's how fast the money was coming. The other ones just let the tap run on full blast, accepting check after check, until they realized that there was no way that they could actually spend the tens of millions of dollars in the six-month time frames demanded. Getting necessary materials into the country, reaching affected areas and finding out what they needed, working on construction plans, and hiring people to see them through—it took time to do it all right.

BUT NOBODY HAD THE TIME. With so much funding, so much media attention, organizations were under extreme pressure to get things done quickly. Why hasn't the money been spent yet? Why hasn't rebuilding started yet? This was the resounding cry from donors and the general public. They wanted to see their funds going to use; they wanted an immediate response to the dreadful images they were seeing on TV. Get it out and get it done fast became the operating mantra from inside the agencies. Those who got their tents up the quickest or were the first to have their pictures in the

press were the successes. They'd take a photo to accompany the reports, whose breathless text revealed
a measure of relief, at having gotten the thing done:
"Here! Phew! We got the center up. We distributed the
supplies. We set up a clinic, a school, a child-friendly
space." Check. Check. Check. And if tents went unused, because people knew they would blow over if you
sneezed on them, or a newly built community didn't
have a water source or connection to electricity—well,
at least you could tick the box that you had built the
damn things. But the quality of these items, and the
consequences for beneficiaries—for actual human
beings—seemed like afterthoughts. I had read somewhere in graduate school that aid was the world's largest unregulated industry. Here it was clear: NGOs
were implementing their programs but there were few
mechanisms in place to measure program effectiveness that would enable donors to hold actors accountable for their successes and failures. This was where
our team came in: we were there to assess how things
had gone, this time around, and draw lessons for the
future—and hope that someone listened to them.

TOO MUCH MONEY ALSO MEANT hundreds of organizations had the funds to come into the countries, set
up shop, and offer assistance. The space became so
congested that people were literally scrambling to put a
stake in the ground before someone else did. Once, my
team and I passed a flattened area where a school would

be built. Flagpoles with banners reading "GOAL" marked the area. Construction hadn't begun and nobody knew when it would, but this was GOAL's territory, and other relief providers had better stay away. It was like watching a dog pee to mark his territory. Benefactors made sure that their logos were stamped onto everything they funded, and before a donor visit, agency employees would scurry around making sure that all the distributed tents had the donor's logo on it, too. Both the agencies and their patrons wanted credit and they needed something visible—some easy photo to deliver to the press and the people back home.

This pointless and petty competition was often counterproductive in terms of the welfare of the people these efforts were meant to serve. For example, so many child centers were popping up, there weren't actually enough children to fill them. One afternoon, a woman who ran one of the facilities for children explained the problem. She folded her bright red sari under her legs as we sat on one of the mats under the tent, watching the children. Some were drawing or skipping rope; others were kicking a ball around outside and chasing each other to catch it. The woman pointed to the group of kids. "These children, they have been through so much. The child spaces, they are good, but there are so many of them. Save the Children has one there," she said, pointing down the road. "IRC has one there." She pointed the other direction. "And they all are trying to lure children to come to their space. They give them sweets and balls and games. The children are confused. They don't know who to choose, and there is pressure to go to one over the other."

❖

The amount of money donated to the tsunami was also disproportionate to what the rest of the country had. The needs outside of the affected areas were great, too; in both Indonesia and Sri Lanka, conflicts had been brewing long before December 26, 2004. In Sri Lanka, the Tamil Tigers (or LTTE), a rebel movement, and the government of Sri Lanka engaged in a decades-long civil war. It is estimated that up to 100,000 civilians were killed in the war, with the forced displacement of hundreds of thousands more. Indonesia witnessed similar years of political instability and conflict, first in the region of East Timor, which became its own independent nation in 2002, and later with the Free Aceh Movement (GAM), a separatist movement seeking the independence of the Aceh region. Serious international political motivation to respond to these crises had been lacking, and aid agencies were responding to the humanitarian fallout on comparatively shoestring budgets.

After the tsunami, donors earmarked funding specifically for tsunami programming. Some of the camps for tsunami victims that I visited were replete with flushing toilets, regular electricity, and hardwood floors. A few meters away were the camps where people displaced by the enduring domestic conflicts had been living. Their age showed: the tents were tattered, the alleyways lined with sewage, the latrines daunting, od-iferous cesspools.

"We've been getting complaints. It's really causing a lot of problems," one of the local leaders explained to me. He stood in the middle of the newer camp in flip-flops, a white button-down shirt tucked into a checkered sarong covering his legs, and a mop of black hair on his head. "People from the conflict camp are asking, 'Why can't we have what they are getting? Because we didn't lose our house in the tsunami? Well we lost our house long ago! Why are they being rewarded and not us?'" No one was saying that the victims of the tsunami should get run-down equipment, but their relatively well-appointed shelters, and the quality and quantity of the supplies devoted to their care, struck many around them as disproportionate. This inequity was causing tension and people worried that it could lead to civil unrest. Even within the new encampments, people could recite the type and amount of goods their neighbors in distant camps had received. Some de-manded to know why they weren't receiving the same benefits.

The economic distortions that aid caused went be-yond the discrepancy in living conditions. Suddenly, productive and educated members of the workforce were being snatched up by NGOs. I met a local judge who was now working as a driver for an NGO because his new job paid him twice what his old one did. School principals worked as administrative assistants for international agencies. One day in Sri Lanka, I arrived at a temporary school to monitor a teacher training session with Arjun, my translator, a slight man with a thick moustache. As soon as they spotted us, the students spilled out of the classroom and flocked to greet him. "I used to teach at this school," he explained.

As a translator, Arjun made three times what he would as a teacher. Instead of participating in the training, Arjun came to work as a translator for *us*, translating our presentations for his former coworkers in the school. We needed people like Arjun, people who could read and write in English, people with enough skills to manage projects. A job at an NGO—almost always the biggest employer in town—was a lucrative position for a person who lived there, and we poached some of the best and brightest right out of the very civil society we were trying to support, luring them into what were essentially temporary positions. We weren't going to be here forever, and when we were gone the jobs would be, too.

After the training, as we got in the car to go, Arjun turned to me and said, "The other teachers want to know whether you have any jobs for them."

Money also equated stuff. Tons of stuff, which poured in from well-intentioned people all over the world. Ports were flooded with boxes of clothes, toys, and books, none of which had a place in these countries. Women who only wore saris and had never exposed their legs to slacks, let alone ripped jeans, were now being sent someone's old dungarees. People who had worn only sandals were being handed four-inch heels. They didn't *want* the inappropriate hand-me-downs that were sent from people's basements or closets. Much of the clothing sat on the sides of the roads, where cattle started chewing on it and getting sick. Basketballs and American footballs were sent to kids who played cricket and soccer. Shipments contained children's books written in English, medicine bottles with labels printed in languages nobody in these communities could read, open tubes of Preparation H and Neosporin, even Viagra. These items had to go through customs, just like the life-saving supplies. Civil servants had to divert time from other projects to get rid of it all.

"We're not beggars," one told me as he pointed out the window of our vehicle as we made our way to a government building. Outside we passed large piles of unwanted stuff rotting on the side of the road. "We don't want people's junk."

I could imagine the church fund-raiser or the elementary school benefit where these contributions came from. People were good-hearted and only wanted to help. What they didn't realize was that there was a cost to transporting and ultimately disposing of unused donations. It was a waste of everyone's time and money.

"If you knew the time it took to sort through this shit and figure out what was garbage and what was actually useful, you'd be amazed," Mike, a stocky British logistician who looked as if he was right out of the army, told me inside a large warehouse that held everything from fuel-efficient stoves to blankets. He was walking briskly through the aisles, supplies stacked in tall piles on either side of him. I felt as though I was following him through Costco. He had a clipboard in one hand, a pen tucked behind his ear, and a radio attached to his belt. "I've got my logs guys up to their ears in tents and tarps and the other items that people actually need. And then I have some guy from America sending me a box of teddy bears for kids. OK, thanks mate, but what do I do with them? Who do I give them to? It's not enough for all of the children we work with, and giving this stuff to just a few leaves the others out. Some of this stuff is ridiculous. Yesterday I sat here sorting through Santa costumes." In some cases, logisticians such as Mike delivered the excess to the easiest neighborhood they could reach. This caused further distortions: some people received three bikes, while others got none.

Four years later, on an assignment after Cyclone Nargis in Myanmar, I heard of donated plastic sheeting for tents that was of such low quality the aid community didn't know what to do with them. "They looked like tablecloths that you'd use on your back porch," someone recalled. There was no way this material would stand up to the next rains or heavy winds, and it certainly wasn't anything you'd want to live under. But the aid workers there were inventive. They didn't distribute the sheeting as material for shelter. Instead, they hired local tailors and turned thousands of sheets into rain ponchos for kids.

ONE DAY IN BANDA ACEH, Indonesia, I interviewed a local man who worked for one of the shelter agencies. We were sitting in the remains of a café that had been demolished and was now covered by plastic tarps. The waiters, grateful for our patronage, constantly refilled our small cups of tea. He told me about *gotong royong,* or mutual aid, a local tradition that had characterized the response in the early days. I had read numerous reports that described the impressive lifesaving action and early emergency support shown by survivors themselves.

"People were so helpful to each other. They're the first responders. The survivors are the people who are doing things—feeding each other, pulling each other out of debris, rebuilding what they can."

Maybe it has something to do with how the media portrays people who have just suffered a serious disaster, but the public usually thinks that affected populations are more helpless and less resilient than they really are. In Myanmar, I would learn this firsthand. In the days immediately following Cyclone Nargis—

and the deaths of more than 130,000 people—the ruling junta closed the borders to foreigners and forbade aid workers from entering the country and providing relief. International agencies panicked, forecasting further devastation if the hundreds of aid workers currently swarming around Bangkok waiting for their entry visas weren't granted immediate access. Without them, disease, starvation, and widespread homelessness were all but guaranteed.

As it turned out, although the ruling junta provided almost nothing, the immediate relief operation carried out by concerned citizens and monks was nothing short of extraordinary. When at last the foreign relief workers were allowed access, and saw how the affected populations were getting on with things, they nodded and scratched their heads. Things weren't nearly as hopeless—people not nearly so helpless—as they'd predicted. No one was sitting around waiting for the expats to swoop in and save the day. They were too busy rebuilding their homes and picking up the pieces of what was left of their lives. It seemed the doomsayers had been wrong.

Back in the tsunami, though, with so much aid, the self-help mentality had shifted. "Now, they have become used to us giving them things and paying them for their help," my colleague told me.

"What do you mean?" I asked. Although paying people to assist with distributions wasn't something agencies usually did, they did provide small stipends to community members who helped them dig latrines or construct buildings. The community should be involved in this reconstruction, the thinking went, and compensating people was a way to remunerate them for labor and to ensure they were part of that rebuilding effort. But paying people to help with distributions or other tasks could potentially change community members' expectations about what aid agencies were there to do.

"The other day I packed up a truck full of items to send to a village. When the truck got there, one of my drivers got out and asked people to help him off-load the materials—hygiene kits, I think it was. But the men just sat there. They demanded that he pay them to help. And when he refused and said that he would just off-load it himself with his team, they said they would not allow it. They wanted a payment and weren't going to let him deliver these items without one."

"So what did he do?"

"He called me to ask what he should do. I told him to get back in the truck, turn around, and tell the community that he would go distribute somewhere else," he replied, chuckling. "The next day the community leaders came to my office apologizing."

THE EVALUATION WAS A REVELATION—BUT something about it made me uneasy. I felt like a voyeur, peering in on the suffering of others and taking notes, as if I were on tour. After so many evaluations, I got the sense that people were sick of talking to us foreigners. I couldn't blame them—I'd wonder, even if they were polite and forthcoming, how many before me had stomped into their communities with clipboards and surveys, asking questions but not giving anything in return. People didn't know how the information they provided was used and didn't understand the decision-making processes behind the delivery of aid. I had heard of a community in Congo being asked so many times the same questions by aid agencies without receiving assistance that someone in the village finally wrote down the usual answers and tacked it to a tree. When the next inquiring aid worker drove in, the community just pointed.

❖

Good work was being done—there was a significant reduction in morbidity for treatable diseases such as malaria, children returned to school, and temporary shelters were housing thousands. I met dozens of smart and committed people who worked in exceptionally challenging conditions to improve the situation for the affected population. Although I knew genuine progress had been made, the critical lens through which I was seeing these things made me question some of the most fundamental assumptions I had about aid. One night when I was even more overwhelmed than usual, trying to make sense of things that didn't make sense, I did what I always did when I needed a sounding board: I called my dad.

"Hello?"

"Dad?"

"Jay? Where are you? Are you OK?"

"Yeah, I'm OK." We caught up for a few minutes—and then I couldn't help diving into everything I was seeing. "Dad," I said, "what if there were a tsunami at home? Just imagine it."

"What do you mean?"

"Well, imagine if everyone in Ridgefield died."

"That's what, around 22,000 people?"

"Yeah. Now imagine ten times that many people died—that's—"

"220,000."

"That's how many people died here, from the tsunami." I didn't know how to make my father feel exactly how enormous a figure 220,000 was—I didn't know how to translate these numbers into words. So I stuck with numbers, ones he'd know: "They read all 3,000 names of the people who died in 9/11 every year, right? Imagine how long it'd take to read 220,000 names."

My dad was quiet for a moment. "Yeah," he finally said and sighed.

"But from a humanitarian perspective, in a way, we don't have to worry about those people. We have to worry about the hundreds of thousands of survivors. I mean, if it happened at home, where do you think you would you go?"

"I'd go to Jeff and Molly's and would stay there and figure it out," he said. Jeff and Molly were some of our oldest friends who lived nearby.

"Well, Jeff and Molly don't have a house now, either. No one you know has a house anymore. Jeff and Molly may not even be alive," I told him.

"Everything is gone—your car, phone, computer, bed. *Whoosh!* And I may be dead, too. You also have no money—because all of the banks are destroyed. And there's no electronic version of any records. So you can't get money out of your account, any cash you had is gone because your wallet is somewhere floating in the ocean. And you're walking around, in the rubble that once was your house, trying to figure out what the hell just happened to your life.

"Everyone around you is in the same position," I continued, unable to stop. It was the first chance I'd had to vent, and Dad patiently let me. I paced around my hotel room, twirling the phone cord around my fingers. "Everyone's trying to put the pieces together. You're feeding each other with whatever you can find. You're living in a tent on your property to watch over it. All the roads are washed away and whatever transportation that used to exist doesn't anymore. Americans from the South and West are coming in to bring you clothes, water, food, and some shelters." I was barely taking breaths between sentences. The phone cord had twisted tight around my knuckles. "Someone's telling you that the government will be moving you and all of your neighbors to another part of the country. Far from the sea. Far from your livelihood. Far from everything you've ever known. But you don't know if that's going to happen or when."

Finally, my father cut me off. "God, it's terrifying not to be in control of your life," he said, his voice calm and thoughtful.

"Well, also not to have any information about what is going on or what will happen. Then the international aid workers come in. By the hundreds. The thousands, it feels like." I lay down on the bed and stared up at the ceiling still holding the phone tightly to my ear.

"People come up to you on the street asking you what you need and what you want. But, you know, they don't speak your language—they don't really listen. They have their surveys and their translators and they ask you for your input but where do you even start? You need everything back! Your house, your land, your children, your job, your life! They take pictures of you while you're sitting by your house, as you're sorting through the remains. You don't know these people, they don't know you, but they want your picture. Your loss and suffering is going to end up as part of a marketing campaign somewhere, on a website or brochure. You know, those shiny reports we get at home don't talk about these people as people, but as this mass of poor things that need help. If it were you, wouldn't you want to scream?!"

"Yeah," Dad said.

"And then some people come and bring saris or burkas, and you're like, 'Thanks, but I don't wear burkas! I wear jeans and T-shirts.' And they just look at you when you don't want these things and think— *But you're getting something! Why aren't you more grateful?* And you're hearing that there is trouble at the port—that shelter and other relief items can't get through because they're letting these things you can't use through first." I stared out the window onto the busy Colombo street below, watching the steady flow of traffic, the cars starting and stopping and starting again. I knew I was getting carried away, but my father was waiting quietly on the other end of the line, and so I let myself keep going.

"Then medicines come and are dumped in your village. The local doctor—who may or may not be alive anymore—can't read the Japanese or French labels that are on these medicine bottles. The meds for your blood pressure are obviously gone. Where are you going to get these drugs now? It's not like the drugstore is open. So you ask one of the foreigners with a clipboard how you can get medicine. He looks at you and says he deals with shelter, not health, sorry. He says he'll ask a colleague. You never see him again."

"The reports we get here never mention that kind of stuff," Dad said.

I felt sad for talking so angrily to my father. I can only imagine how startled he must have been. *What happened to my daughter? Where did the energy, the optimism, the excitement go?* I couldn't stop myself, though. Suddenly, seemingly out of nowhere, everything I'd seen and felt was crystallizing inside me. And I still had more to say: "Can your friends please stop e-mailing me telling me what amazing work I'm doing?"

"Jess, what is the first thing you will do when you get home?" Dad asked brightly, trying to redirect the conversation.

"Sleep."

I Make a Living
Off the Suffering of Strangers
NEW YORK CITY, 2006

I returned home three days before the wedding shower of one of my best friends from high school. Although I had looked forward to the party, coordinating my flight connections so I could make it, by the time I got home I was dreading it. All I wanted to do was lie in bed and watch television. *Law & Order* reruns were particularly good at making the time pass. I wasn't at all prepared to put on a dress or make small talk. But I was a bridesmaid and had a line to read in the singsong poem her sister wrote, so I took the train from Connecticut to Washington, DC, where she lived now.

When I arrived at the shower, I followed the female chatter up a long staircase to a room decorated in pristine pinks and whites. Flower petals were sprinkled on the tables. Everyone was perfectly dressed, and I was wearing the only pair of shoes I had been able to find that morning, an ugly pair of flats I'd worn to an eighth-grade piano recital.

This was the first time I had seen Rebecca since

her engagement party eight months before. She had clearly lost weight, and her small body seemed overwhelmed by all the attention. I approached her and we hugged.

"It's so good to see you," she said, touching my hair. I hadn't had the chance to get a haircut, and in my opinion I looked like I was wearing a witch wig.

"You, too. You look amazing."

"Thank you. How are you?" she asked.

"Honestly? Not so OK. I'm having a really hard time," I said, surprised to find I was tearing up.

"I'm sure. We'll get into it later. But just not here," she said, still stroking my unruly hair. I wished she would stop.

"I know. God, I'm sorry," I said quickly, embarrassed.

"Thanks, Jess. I'm so glad you're here." She turned away to greet an aunt or cousin behind me, patiently perched on tiptoe, waiting to dote on her.

Around me, women were mingling near the bar. A long bench was stacked high with gifts wrapped in delicate paper and textured ribbons. Waiters in tuxedos passed colorful hors d'oeuvres and glasses of champagne. I grabbed one.

I couldn't remember the last time I had seen most of these women. I spotted an old classmate with whom I kept in occasional touch and made my way toward her. "Oh my God! Jess! How are you?!" She hugged me, trying not to spill the Bloody Mary she held in one hand or drop the potato puff clutched in the other.

I responded cautiously. "I'm good. I mean, I'm OK. How are you?"

"Whatever, I'm fine. I want to hear about *you*! What was it like?!"

"Um, it was . . . hot."

"Right, I'm sure!"

"And hard. It was really hard. Darfur is in really bad shape. And the tsunami response is so complicated."

She was nodding thoughtfully but her eyes were already wandering. While she might have been interested in where I'd been and the work I'd done, my friend Jenn didn't have the words to talk about it. And the truth was, neither did I. Jenn just wanted to know how I was doing; I was the one struggling to put sentences together. I didn't have party-appropriate anecdotes I could rattle off or dramatic stories that would cause a crowd to gather around us. Most mornings, I had trouble even bringing myself to get out of my pajamas.

I deflected the conversation back to her. "But how are things with you?"

"Good. I mean, but it's nothing compared to what you do."

A school acquaintance overheard our conversation and came to greet me. "Hey, Jess! I heard you were away—Rebecca told me Sri Lanka and Indonesia? For the tsunami?"

"Yeah."

"Oh my God. So how was it? Was it, like, fun, or devastating?"

When a question like that, about one of the most

publicized natural disasters in the world, came from a graduate of Yale Law School, I wasn't quite sure what to say. These were mostly private school–educated women, wealthy women, women who ate at fancy restaurants, went to art openings, and belonged to book clubs. So these conversations always caught me off guard, and I didn't have the slightest clue how to respond to her question.

Rebecca opened gifts and we "oohed" and "ahed" on cue—gasps of delight for cutlery and crockery, linens and lingerie. After lunch, we ordered coffees and cappuccinos and nibbled on caramel-drizzled brownie sundaes. Julie, another classmate, wasn't touching her dessert. She looked over at me gobbling mine—I hadn't eaten anything this tasty in months.

"How do you stay so thin, Jess?" she asked.

Jenn answered for me. "She lives in Ethiopia, that's how!"

I laughed politely. I didn't bother telling them I had never visited Ethiopia.

❖

In retrospect, I came into the wedding shower too raw. These friends meant well, and I could have easily slipped into this setting only a few years before. But now the fantasies that people had about the places I worked somehow disturbed the fabric of these social gatherings. In most people's imaginations, I was a million miles away from what they knew, what they could relate to, so of course their awe—their curiosity, their self-consciousness—came out sounding shallow. My friends wanted desperately to relate to me and what I was doing; they were seeing a person who, in a way, they didn't recognize anymore. But they didn't know how to integrate me back into their world as much as I didn't know how to integrate myself. Despite my new worldliness, I felt annoyed and disconnected—I couldn't extend the same sympathy to these people that I could to people in Darfur. In some ways, my dumb-founded reactions were just as shallow as theirs.

I see now that I had begun to lose it long before I touched down in New York. It was foolish to think I could go straight from Darfur to Sri Lanka and then to Indonesia without a break. The tension had been building for months, and by the time I finally landed at home I was unhinged. It wasn't just the lingering guilt of abandoning the camp; after these two consecutive assignments, my idealism seemed to have vanished. I felt lost, betrayed. With such high ambitions for this industry, the flaws seemed overwhelming. And—while I was questioning the extent to which aid had positive outcomes—what did this commitment even mean any-more? Did my endless fatigue mean I wasn't cut out for the physical rigors of this job? It was disorienting to suddenly doubt the profession that I had spent years trying to break into. Was I still willing to throw my life into chaos for an industry that I now questioned? And if the answer was "no," then what *would* I do?

Unpacking, I couldn't find bracelets—silly, inexpensive bracelets—that I had carried with me all this way. I hurled a shoe at my bedroom wall and slammed a cabinet.

"Where the hell are they? I know I packed them!" I was yelling and stomping like a child.

My father looked at me as though he didn't recognize me anymore. "What's wrong with you, Jess?" he said, and walked away. I looked out the door of my bedroom and saw him, still in his pajamas, perched at the edge of the stairs, holding his head in his hands and shaking it.

Reintegrating into my life at home was hard, but a lot of my anxiety was attached to a decision I knew I had to make, and soon. In Darfur, I learned that I had been awarded a Fulbright Grant to study child soldiers in Sierra Leone. I'd applied for the Fulbright when I graduated from my master's program, before I'd gone to Sudan. Now I only had two months to decide whether or not I was going to go. As the deadline approached, my anxiety intensified. I pulled my hair and bit my cuticles until my fingertips were red, raw stumps. I was prescribed Xanax. I took long baths. I got a massage and went to the gym. I did yoga, Pilates, meditation. Nothing worked. But after two weeks, my friend Joanna called. I hadn't seen her since we parted ways outside her office before my first assignment to Darfur.

"Enough of this. When are you coming to New York?" she asked.

"I'm not."

"What do you mean you're not? I want to see you."

"I'm not going into the city. I don't want to. I just want to stay here."

"Stay there and do what?"

"Not leave bed. I don't know. Jo, I look like shit. I don't want to talk to anyone. I just don't want to do any of it."

"Whatever." She let me off the hook for a few days. And then she called me back. "If you don't come in this weekend, I'm coming out there and dragging your ass back here."

So I went. I stayed in her Brooklyn apartment and the first night we drank beers and ordered Chinese food and huddled around her space heater because her heat wasn't working.

"I don't know why I feel so lost. I kept thinking that home was going to be so great. I couldn't wait to get back where things seemed to make sense. Back to what was normal. But everything feels different. I don't even know what normal is anymore."

"It'll probably take some time, but you'll be OK," she reassured me.

"Will I? And what will OK look like, anyway? I'm

supposed to go on this Fulbright to Sierra Leone and I don't even want to. The thought of leaving again, of going to another unfamiliar place, of being so far away, again, so soon, I don't know if I can do it."

"Then don't," she said matter-of-factly.

We finished one six-pack, then another. We opened a bottle of wine and finished that, too.

"There's a party in Fort Greene. You want to go?"

"Not really."

"Come on. Let's get you out. It will be fun. And if it sucks, we can leave."

At the party, dozens of people my age were crammed into the living room. Pounding music came from one of the bedrooms, now a dance floor. I met a guy in the kitchen while pouring myself a vodka soda.

"What do you do?" he asked.

I didn't want to get into it. "I'm a middle-school teacher." Admitting to running a camp in Darfur would make me stand out as much as being the only white face in a sea of Sudanese.

"That's cool." We chatted for a few more minutes and parted. Later, he found me in the living room.

"Your friend just told me you were in Darfur! That's amazing! You should be telling everyone. You're like a good person! The world needs more people like you!"

By now I was used to this kind of reaction but I still didn't know what to say. It wasn't false modesty; I really couldn't point to what I had done to warrant such praise. *I abandoned the camp. I almost lost my mind*

out there. I almost threw rocks at children. I make my
living off of the suffering of strangers.

By virtue of our chosen profession, aid workers
are automatically ascribed certain qualities: bravery,
righteousness, badass-ness. We never had to actually
prove that we possessed these attributes—the job title
spoke for itself. And if that didn't convince people, all
we had to do was drop the name of a country where we
had worked, a war or natural disaster we had been on
the ground responding to, and the assumptions were
confirmed. "I feel better about myself just hanging out
with you!" a friend in finance once told me.

But people didn't understand that this work hadn't
turned me into a saint. People like me, out there "doing
God's work" and "saving the world," wanted to get
drunk and laid, too. We have the same concerns—
ageing, putting on weight—as anyone else. It just so
happened that the dull, daily work of caring—the familiar task of living our lives—was played out against
a backdrop of humanitarian catastrophe.

People asked me how long I could afford to volunteer. What no one seemed to understand was that I
was paid to do this work, just like they were paid to do
their jobs. Yes, I was committed to aid work and the
difference I still believed it could make, but I went to
these places not only out of philanthropy. Like other
aid workers, I had plenty of selfish motives as well: the
building of a career, the adventure of travel, the excitement of meeting different people. Except unless people

were fleeing, dying, ailing, or starving, I wouldn't have a job. "See you in the next one," people said at their farewell parties in the field. We'd all be reunited at the following war, flood, or earthquake.

"YOU MUST HAVE SEEN SOME horrible things," people would say to me, but I hadn't seen death the way they imagined. Yes, suffering was all around me, but people coped. They were strong and alive and doing their best to rebuild their lives. I grew accustomed to impoverished surroundings in a clinical way, like an ER doctor getting used to seeing multiple gunshot wounds. But the cumulative effect of those months had eroded me. My depression wasn't just about feeling out of place at home, but the sense of disorientation I felt in all worlds. I certainly couldn't live in a place like Darfur for the long term, but living in New York now felt just as strange.

I had heard that at some point many people in the aid industry continue to return to the field because they drift so far from home they no longer recognize themselves in it, just as a soldier might keep signing up for duty because the chaos of war feels more comforting than the banality of paying electric bills, fixing the dishwasher, and picking the kids up from soccer practice. I had been warned about the disaster addicts, the emergency enthusiasts, the aid junkies—and now I was worried I had become one of them. The world I came from told me that by the time I was twenty-eight I should be making money, getting an apartment, thinking about establishing roots somewhere. But I didn't have a boyfriend, I wasn't dating anyone, the last person I had slept with was somewhere in Bangladesh now. At least in Africa, as an expat, I may not have been part of the culture, but I was part of a subculture. I knew where I stood. It wasn't the novelty pushing me to these places anymore. Now I kept going because I saw myself as someone who kept going, and so did other people. It was how they defined me, and it was how I defined myself. As much as I may have wanted to slow down, I couldn't. If I wasn't the person pushing herself to the next scary place, then who was I?

After a few weeks of being unable to shake the grim mood that had clung to me since my return, I decided to see a therapist in Connecticut. He had come highly recommended, and I hoped for some relief.

"Do you think I understand where you're coming from?" he asked, stroking his tie.

"I don't know. I guess so."

"I think I do. And you know what I think you could use? A spa retreat. Just a few days away at a spa. A patient came in here a few months ago—she was going through something similar—and I recommended she go to a spa for a few days. She came back refreshed and so much more relaxed. It'll take the edge off."

He didn't understand where I was coming from at all. The last thing I wanted to do was to pack another suitcase and be alone at a spa, getting pampered by strangers. Other therapists were worse.

"You were where? Darfur?" one said, leaning back in her chair, looking at me over her little glasses, pencil poised to take notes.

"Yeah."

"Interesting . . ." She started jotting something down. I have no idea what since I hadn't even started talking yet. I looked around at the fancy degrees, matted and framed, hanging on her wall. On the table between us was a box of tissues, perfectly centered.

"What do you think that says about your family life? Your relationship with your father? It sounds to me like you're looking for an escape."

I looked for an escape from her office and left.

War Don Don, Peace Don Cam

I had delayed starting my Fulbright for so long that if I didn't arrive in Sierra Leone by the end of March, I'd lose the grant. But I still wasn't sure whether I wanted to go. One cold night in January, I sat with my father in front of our roaring fireplace. Since Mom died, Dad kept a running tally of which of his three children he had to worry about the most. "You came home, and just slid right into first place," he joked. I laughed with him.

"Look, I know it's hard to think about leaving again," Dad began, in his cool, reassuring voice, "but it's a great opportunity. I think you will regret passing this up."

I didn't want to lose the opportunity either, but I just wanted to sit still for a bit longer—sit here, in my father's house, where a fire kept me warm during the bitter New England winter. I didn't have the desire or energy to pack my suitcase, leave for another country, meet new people and start all over again. But the research project I had proposed still interested me and I really wanted to see it through.

During a summer internship in graduate school I had worked with a research team in Mozambique, investigating what happened to boys who fought in the civil war. The organization wanted to know what kind of adults these children had become. Did they turn out to be the lost generation, the future barbarians, as everyone had assumed? Or were they integrated into their communities as fathers, husbands, men with jobs and social connections? It turned out that—although their ability to reintegrate largely depended on how long they were in conflict, the role assigned to them by the rebels, and the circumstances under which they were recruited—for the most part, the boys, now men, were working members of their communities and contributing members of society. I was so inspired by the research that while searching for jobs for after graduation, I applied for a Fulbright to repeat the same study in Sierra Leone, where children had been abducted by the fighting forces, as they had in Mozambique. By now, four years after Sierra Leone's war ended, the people said, "*War don don, peace don cam*"—The war is done, peace has come.

"How about this," Dad said. "We'll go for a week. I'll come with you; if you hate it, you don't stay." Although the offer was sweet, it seemed a bit too Mom-holding-my-hand-into-class-on-the-first-day-of-kindergarten. He offered another idea that made more sense. I'd buy a round-trip ticket that brought me back to New York after six weeks. Technically, I couldn't leave the Fulbright grant that early, but it was an out, and it was a way to break up the ten-month commitment into something I could handle.

❖

I arrived in Sierra Leone the same day that Charles Taylor, the former President of Liberia, was brought there to stand trial at the Special Court (SCSL), an international criminal tribunal. A few days later, Taylor appeared for the first time at the courthouse in Freetown, where he was charged with five counts of crimes against humanity and five counts of war crimes. He was also accused of one additional violation of international humanitarian law: the recruitment and employment of child soldiers. I hadn't even unpacked my suitcase, but I knew I couldn't miss Taylor's trial: this was an event that would be recorded and remembered, this was a moment in time that would harden into a *fact,* the kind you learned in school—this, in other words, was what it felt like to live history. At the court-house, I stood with the swarms of sweaty journalists in the security line and lied to the guard, telling him I was one of them. He was easily convinced. We walked in unison, press passes dangling around our necks, to the back of the courtroom, where the reporters frantically scribbled notes and elbowed their way in for a clear view of Taylor. High glass walls separated the observa-tion gallery from the well of the courtroom, where the judges and lawyers sat dressed in their long black and red robes.

I stood in the back of the observation gallery and watched Taylor's face, which remained expressionless as the judges read aloud the crimes for which he had been indicted: rape, murder, abduction of children, maiming, looting, theft. Cloaked in a suit, Taylor stood up and defiantly refuted the charges. "Most defi-nitely, Your Honour, I did not and could not have com-mitted these acts against the sister Republic of Sierra Leone. . . . Most definitely I'm not guilty."

Indeed, Taylor was in Liberia during the eleven-year Sierra Leonean war, during which a rebel movement attempted to overthrow the government. However, the rebels were heavily supported by Taylor, who had an interest in the diamond-rich eastern part of the country.

According to Sierra Leone's Truth and Reconciliation Commission, the years leading up to the war were characterized by endemic corruption, and the denial of basic human rights—schooling, health care, water—which led to a frustrated and angry population ready for revolt. Youth formed the Revolutionary United Front (RUF) with the intent to overthrow the government to create a fair and just society. But their initial quest for justice quickly turned into a ruthless conquest, as the RUF began slaughtering and maiming innocent civilians who were thought to have sided with the government. The RUF specifically targeted young children for recruitment, abducting them from their homes and forcing them into battle. During the 1996 elections, when citizens voted by thumbprint, the RUF amputated people's hands as a tactic to prevent civilians from voting or to punish those who had. Amputation also prevented people from farming their land, which the RUF then seized. Thousands of people, including children, survived having their limbs amputated by the RUF. It is unknown how many died after amputation.

THE RUF'S ASSAULT ON THE country was aided primarily by Charles Taylor's National Patriotic Front of Liberia. The RUF took control of the diamond-rich areas of eastern Sierra Leone, harvesting the diamonds in order to purchase weapons—from Taylor in particular—

and enter the global arms trade. Taylor was found to also have personally planned attacks in parts of Sierra Leone, including Freetown. Finally, in 2002, the RUF was defeated and the country could slowly begin to rebuild.

WHEN THE INDICTMENTS BROUGHT BY the chief prosecutor of the Special Court for Sierra Leone against Taylor were made public in June 2003, Taylor resigned as president of Liberia and sought refuge in Nigeria. Three years later, Ellen Johnson Sirleaf, the new president of Liberia (and first female African president), requested his extradition to the Special Court. Taylor attempted to escape but was arrested by border guards when trying to cross into Cameroon and was immediately handed over to the Court.

The Special Court was much like the war crimes tribunals of Iraq, Yugoslavia, and Rwanda, which prosecuted Saddam Hussein, Slobodan Milošević, and Jean Kambanda, a former prime minister of Rwanda. But Taylor's was a special case: unlike the other trials, which happened outside of the country involved, Sierra Leoneans could bear witness to Taylor's prosecution. Another difference was that unlike the other international tribunals, which were mainly staffed by expats, the Special Court also included Sierra Leonean judges and lawyers. Although I didn't know it then, the trial would come to play a larger role in my own life, too.

The name Sierra Leone comes from Portuguese *Serra de Leão,* which means "Mountains with Lions." (*Sierra Leone* is the Italian translation.) There are no lions in Sierra Leone; the phrase, coined by Portuguese explorers in the fifteenth century, refers to the lion-shaped mountains on the peninsula beyond Freetown. The capital city, Freetown, was established as a settlement for freed slaves in the final years of the eighteenth century. Over the next few decades, thousands of former slaves from the United States and the West Indies came to make Freetown their home.

Sierra Leoneans speak Krio, an English-based creole whose lexicon includes words from a number of African languages. They shorten the name of their country to Salone, and the rest of the language is hilariously literal. A popular local baked biscuit got its name after a man stopped his car at a market, bought a bag full of them, and pulled out into the street. Moments later he was killed in an accident. From then on the biscuit was called "*Kill Driva.*" Once, when a friend locked her keys in her car, children from town surrounded it, telling her she needed a "sardine key." One of the children returned a few minutes later holding the top of a sardine can, which he skillfully used to jimmy the lock open. Instead of saying "How are you?" people asked each other "*Ow di bodi*" (literally, "How the body?"). The standard response is "*I tell God tankey, di bodi fine,*" which means, "I thank God, the body is fine." (I was told that this saying came from the slave era when blacks were regularly beaten by their masters. So they would ask each other, how's your body, or have you been flogged?) Sierra Leoneans' take on John F. Kennedy's famous speech is rearticulated as: "*No ask watin Mama Salone don de for yo, but ask watin yo don do for Mama Salone.*" In Sierra Leone, diabetes is "the sweet piss"; someone who's peeing is "easing themselves." A thin woman is referred to as "straight cut," a plumper one as "bum cut." There are no other sizes.

The names that commanders chose for themselves during the war were no different: Captain Blood, Major Bomb Blast, Colonel Bullet, Sergeant Cut Head, Colonel Dead Squad, Colonel Butt Naked, Major Kill Man, Colonel Long Life, Commander Man Suffer, Colonel No Joke, Colonel Park a Man in a Vehicle, Captain Poison, Captain Rambo, Colonel Road Block, Captain Sucking Blood, Brigadier Superman, Colonel 31 Rounds. And during the war, even the most horrific of acts were spoken of in classically Sierra Leonean terms. When people's arms were amputated, some were given a choice. Either "long-sleeved"—a chop below the elbow—or "short-sleeved"—a chop above.

Maybe it was the excitement of the Taylor trial, but my anxiety about leaving home disappeared immediately. In Sierra Leone, time passed quickly, and my return ticket—the one Dad had encouraged me to buy, which would have taken me back to New York after six weeks—languished somewhere in my suitcase. I'd forgotten about it entirely. I found a place to live in an apartment overlooking the city and the sea, in a building filled with people who worked at the Special Court as lawyers, human rights monitors, reporters. Some of my new housemates had come from other tribunals, like International Criminal Tribunal for Rwanda in Arusha, Tanzania. Years later, when many of the Sierra Leone trials ended, some moved to Phnom Penh to work for the Criminal Court trying the remaining members of the Pol Pot regime.

When I returned home from Sierra Leone, some people said they couldn't believe I'd "made it out of there alive" because—"Well," they'd ask me, "did you see *Blood Diamond*?" But Sierra Leone was no longer the country that was portrayed in that movie. The war had stripped the small West African country of its natural resources, leaving the cities and countryside shrouded in poverty. The combination of malnutrition and the absence of even the most basic preventative care—vaccines, vitamins, mosquito nets—made Sierra Leone's infant and maternal mortality rates among the highest in the world. Almost one out of three children born in Sierra Leone died before reaching the age of five. In 2007 Sierra Leone ranked the least developed country in the world according to the UN's Human Development Report. Yet Sierra Leone seemed to defy hardship. Freetown was a Matisse-colored world, bursting with traffic jams and street music on every corner. Unlike the barren landscape of Sudan, Sierra Leone was a tangled, hilly green. A large cotton tree sat in the center of town, its branches reaching higher than the surrounding buildings and its flowering leaves bending toward the frenetic traffic below. In a place such as Freetown, where the war was over and people were motivated to recover, normalcy came quickly, or quicker than it might have elsewhere. Sierra Leoneans seemed almost to will it into existence, they were so in love with life. You saw them celebrate it every day, dancing, singing, shouting in the streets.

That isn't to say Sierra Leoneans no longer faced significant hardships. Like drought. When it stopped raining for a few weeks in a row during what had traditionally been the rainy season, the dry earth seemed to cast the country's scars into relief. Because the reservoir was drying up, the government rationed the water and only turned on the pipes to Freetown a few times a day. Toilets started backing up in our home; the taps in our offices ran dry. Overnight, the cost of bottled water tripled. We, the rich foreigners, would be fine, and continued buying bottles of water, which we used to cook, bathe, and flush our toilets. But people living in town were so desperate that they overturned a water lorry coming to refill a well.

It's one thing to ignore requests for money, even for food. But when people come to you begging for water—that's an entirely different story, one I wouldn't have predicted but will never forget. The words just hit your body in another way. Before leaving home I often filled a few large water bottles from the coolers we had at our apartment and stuffed them in my bag. Only a few meters out of our gate, however, I had already poured all their contents into empty cups that people thrust at me.

Children, whose role it was to collect water for their families every morning before school, now had to walk three miles farther to get it from the closest working well or water pump. To make matters worse, the water shortage happened to occur right at the time of school exams. Because children now had to fetch water so much farther away, many of them missed their exams and could not pass to the next class level. Children's agencies were lobbying with the Ministry of Education to let the students take the tests at a later date, but it wasn't clear whether they would. These were the decisions that families and children had to make: pass to the next class in school or go without water.

When the Sierra Leonean conflict finally ended, 45,000 fighters were disarmed and demobilized by UN peacekeepers. Men put down their guns in fields and the international community, along with the Sierra Leone National Commission for Disarmament, Demobilization, and Reintegration (NCDDR), tried to facilitate their return to something like their normal lives. Aid organizations and the local government distributed starter money, provided transportation home, and helped people as they tried to find work.

For children, the process was different. Between 1998 and 2002, nearly seven thousand children who had been forcibly conscripted to join the war were demobilized. Many had been transported far from their homes and the NCDDR and the international agencies were attempting to reunify them with their families. These children were placed in Interim Care Centers (ICCs) until someone could track down their families and return them to their homes.

I came into my research project with a lot of questions. What was the reunification process like? What strategies were most effective? What were these children doing now, and how had they fared since returning home? Being free to formulate these questions on my own also meant traveling the country and making connections at my own discretion and pace. At times, the autonomy that came with being on a Fulbright could feel overwhelming. But eventually, I began to get my bearings, and found plenty of organizations that had worked with children after they were demobilized, and it turned out they were asking the very same questions I was. They were happy to collaborate and provided transportation, accommodations, and the names and contact information of people I ought to meet along the way. With two assistants, one translator and one driver, a backpack filled with notepads, and the necessary toilet supplies for living in the bush for a few weeks, I went to the field to track down and interview former child soldiers, social workers, and reunification officers about the demobilization process.

On these trips I learned more than I had set out to. Children were an uncomplicated target for the rebel groups—they were easy to manipulate, their minds malleable and their bodies quick. They did as they were told, their innate obedience heightened by the drugs the rebels administered through injections or by cutting a child's skin and rubbing the chemicals directly into the wound. In order to extinguish any family ties, rebels would force children to kill or rape their relatives. This was torture, and a kind of insurance policy: now, even if they wanted to escape, the children would have no home to return to. The rebels also branded children as a way to keep them close. If they ran away and were captured by another one of the factions, children with markings from the rebels would immediately be killed.

After a visit to a community where I met a few former child soldiers, one of the boys followed me to the car and asked if he could speak with me in private. We walked behind his school and he lifted up his shirt. Carved across his chest were the letters "RUF": the Revolutionary United Front.

A medical agency came right after the war and performed plastic surgery on some of the boys to remove the scars. They'd missed this one.

"Can you help me get these letters off?" he asked, looking away, too embarrassed to even make eye contact. I didn't know any agency that was doing these procedures anymore. But I told him that I would ask around.

"*Tankey,*" he said, as he pulled his shirt down and tucked it tightly into his pants. I was never able to find an agency to help him.

Many boys were taken deep into the bush where they were trained to shoot and fight. Older boys were forced to steal, kill, rape, and maim. The younger ones, too small to carry guns, were used by the militias as porters, cooks, messengers, and servants. Many were sent on spying missions to see what was available to loot in neighboring villages. Girls as young as seven were taken as bush wives. Some of the older ones became pregnant, and some of the younger ones bled to death after sex. Often, girls needed surgery to repair the damage to their bodies caused by rape and early pregnancy. Those who gave birth had their children labeled *rebel pikin*—rebel children—and were rejected back at home.

Meeting the children now, it was hard to believe the trials they endured. But as I learned from my first assignment in Darfur, children are usually the most resilient of all. For the most part, they were reintegrated into their communities and seemed happy going to school and getting their lives back on track.

Occasionally, I was joined on my travels by Claudetta, my Sierra Leonean friend and colleague, who had worked with one of the agencies that helped demobilize children. "Jessica, *yu ma nehba taya*," she'd say to me, which literally meant, "*You never tire*," or, "*You are always on the go*," because I'd wake up early to get on the road or keep working into the night. Claudetta was definitely bum cut, and flaunted her full figure with sexy tank tops in aquas and pinks and tight jeans. Her smile was sly and playful and when she laughed her head fell back, as did her bright, dangly earrings. We had a fun time on the road together, playing music and stopping for fruit or snacks at every stall we passed. Sometimes when I ate too much she'd jokingly pinch my stomach and exclaim, "Oh, Jessica, *yu don fat-o*!'—Jessica, you've gotten fat! On our long trips we'd talk about our lives, but mostly about boys. She had a boyfriend and couldn't believe I was single. "*Yu noh geht man?*" (You don't have a man?) "No, I don't!" "*Yu noh mared?*" (You're not married?) "No!" Then we'd go through the whole routine again.

Claudetta survived the rebel attack in Freetown in 2002 but her father was killed. Half of her family's house had burned down and they still did not have enough money to repair it. Once, when we were in the process of interviewing a group of children, one of them described marching into the capital, drugged up and leading the way. Claudetta's face went gray. To her, this was the scariest part. "They don't have a sense of right or wrong yet. They don't yet understand what it means. It's a game for them at that age. There is no hesitation for them to just shoot!"

FIELD RESEARCH PROVIDED A VIVID counterpoint to desk work. Leaving the city, we'd drive deep into the countryside—rows of shell-colored buildings giving way to open fields and damp woodlands, the roar of traffic fading into the dense silence of the forest. Walls of trees, tangled and lush, surrounded us; in the distance, hills floated against the blue sky like pale, mossy stones in a pond.

But there were also plenty of times we'd drive at night down unlit streets, with only one of our headlights working. Trucks, cars, and motorcycles—none of which had headlights, either—flew by in the opposite direction. It was impossible to tell how close they were until the driver had just enough time to swerve away. Some trucks didn't even have taillights, and I'd heard of motorcyclists fatally crashing right into the backs of them.

Other times, the rain fell so thick and so fast the sole working windshield wiper couldn't keep up, and all I could see was wet, gray fog. And I would sit there, with my seat belt fastened, thinking: *If I can't see anything, I can be pretty sure that the driver can't, either, and this Land Cruiser doesn't have an air bag, there is nothing but a piece of metal about as sturdy as a cookie sheet between me and the tree we almost just smashed into.* Sometimes I'd try to talk myself down, tell myself we wouldn't be doing it if it weren't safe, but eventually I didn't bother. These were the risks I had to take if I wanted to work in these places, and I did, so there was no point in dwelling on them. I just had to ride the fear through, until I didn't notice it anymore. First, I stopped being pricked by dread each time I spotted a potential danger, then all the dangers—the collisions, the slippery roads—blurred together. They were just part of the landscape, like the trees along the road.

❖

In most cases those research missions took us to former Interim Care Centers (ICCs), where demobilized children received assistance from local social workers while waiting to be reunified with their families. While in Bo, a city in southern Sierra Leone, I met a social worker named Francis. A tall, thin man, Francis was in his forties but looked twenty years younger. We sat on a wooden school bench outside a classroom as he recounted the children's temperament when they first arrived at the ICCs. "They were so stubborn when they came. Troublesome. They picked fights. They stole," he recalled, shaking his head. "Some of the older ones who rose to certain levels wanted us to call them 'Sir.' These *pikin,* ugh! They were so aggressive." He looked ahead as he remembered more. "They were boastful about their exploits. One boy, he came up to me and said, 'Do you know how many arms I've cut off? Two boxes of arms and I will soon be a second lieutenant.' They didn't think they had even done anything wrong."

Other children, he said, were sullen; many had trouble sleeping and kept to themselves. Francis and his colleagues didn't do clinical interventions but used drama, song, sports, and drawing to help the children. "Through these things they can regain themselves," Francis explained.

Some children were so young when they were taken from their villages they could no longer remember where they were from, or what their mothers looked like. Francis recalled a girl who "no longer understood her own language. She was only four when they took her." As far back as they could remember there had only been war. "Some said they wanted to be reunified with their warlords. There was a strong attachment to commanders, thinking that he was a savior, a protector," Francis said. It wasn't easy for people like Francis to break these links. "Some of the children had risen from the junior ranks and the younger children continued to salute them in the ICCs."

Family tracing programs began. Social workers took pictures of the kids, displaying hundreds of faces on large posters that were circulated across the country. Parents scoured the images for their children.

When one was found, social workers informed the appropriate ICC and a tape recording of the child's voice was prepared for the parents. When—if—the parents confirmed that this was their child, the social workers scheduled a reunion.

Many of these reunions were joyous, but some were not. "Children themselves were scared about how they would be received when they went home." And for good reason. "Sometimes when we took children back home, the community threw rocks at the car," Musa, a social worker from Makeni, told me. "We were in serious danger. 'That boy was one of them who led the RUF to our village and burned our homes! These children destroyed a nation' the community would say." Musa still worked with foster children, and I interviewed him in a café near the school where he was now employed. To our meeting, he wore a bright red collared shirt, which had been tucked in tightly enough to reveal the outline of his belly button.

Musa recalled the months he and other social workers spent preparing communities for these returns, explaining that everyone was a victim of the war, even the children. "It's not a day's work," he said laughing. "Some people said they would not associate with these children. Others said they were bush people and not fit for the community. They didn't want the kids to even sit down in their houses." Musa and other social workers visited villages, spoke to local leaders, and developed radio programs that instructed people to "stop provoking these kids."

IT'S NO WONDER THAT MANY children tried to leave home as soon as they had returned. Even if families did accept the children, Musa explained, they couldn't provide three meals a day, or the toys and regular educational opportunities that the children got at the ICCs. "We would reunify a child with his family or a foster family and think that everything was OK. A month later we would find out that the same child left that family and enrolled in a different ICC where he wouldn't be recognized," Musa recalled. And this time they were smart—they told lies about where they were from, delaying the process of getting "reunified" in order to extend their stays at the center for as long as possible.

The school Musa now worked at was one that had accepted former child soldiers when they were reintegrated. One of the ways the aid groups tried to persuade the children and the communities to accept each other was by covering the children's school fees for five years. But even this was complicated. Some children had missed too many years of school to enroll in grades appropriate for their ages. They needed to catch up somehow, and a rapid education program that condensed six years of schooling into three was launched. But why should the children who participated in the war be rewarded, community members protested, when those who weren't taken, who stayed home or fled alone, got nothing? The community called the support "blood books, blood materials." To mitigate some of the resentment, the aid community provided school supplies—desks, pens, pencils, bags—to all of the students at schools where children were reintegrated.

One afternoon, I spoke with a group of teenage girls who had participated in a vocational-training program when they were returned. They had just left class and were still dressed in their brown uniforms. We sat together on a picnic bench outside their school. "No one would talk to us. The boys all thought that we had sex with our captors. They said we were damaged goods," one girl explained. They giggled together as they recounted the story. A small NGO had come in and created a microcredit program for girls. Soon they were earning not only enough to pay back their loans, but to be the breadwinners of their homes. "After that, the boys all wanted to be with us. We told them, 'But I thought we were "damaged." Why do you want to be with us now!?'" They laughed and slapped their thighs.

AFTER HEARING SO MANY STORIES of pain and anguish from civilians, I didn't understand how people—my friends—could defend the perpetrators. "Look, this whole international criminal tribunal thing would be a circus if there wasn't a good defense," my American friend Scott said. He was in his thirties and had worked in corporate law back in New York, but was taking two years out of the grind to do something more interesting. I was back in Freetown, and he had come over to my apartment for a typical meal of rice and chicken. We were sitting on my terrace, eating and drinking as the sky began to turn soft and dark above the city.

"Everyone—even a war criminal, Jess—has a right to a fair trial. The prosecution would have a field day with these guys if we didn't hold them to some standard. They might very well have been war criminals, but it was for particular acts at particular times. They didn't do everything in all places at all times, which is what the prosecution is throwing at them." With so many warring factions, all of which had members who had committed grave human-rights violations, culpability wasn't just in the hands of a few people or even one fighting party. Everyone, regardless of which side they'd been on, had to be brought to justice for the country to recover.

Sierra Leone was in what the aid industry referred to as a post-conflict development stage. Now that peace had come, international aid workers and local civil society groups were undertaking longer-term projects. When the political climate has stabilized and the first, frenzied stage of emergency has passed, humanitarian actors generally exit the picture and development folks enter. Development agency staffers typically stay in countries for longer periods of time, trying to restore the country's infrastructure and create a stable, sustainable foundation for civic life and economic health, which would hopefully be resilient enough to endure future crises.

Some of my friends worked for the ministries, advising them on policy formulation on everything from economic growth to improving health systems. A couple of Brits started a development fund with money raised back home and invested it in local businesses in Sierra Leone. Others founded an organization that provided legal aid for women who were being held in prison for petty crimes or serving sentences on behalf of their husbands, who were nowhere to be found. One friend capitalized on the rich music scene in Sierra Leone and arranged concerts across the country to promote safe sex and HIV/AIDS awareness.

The expat community was as active as anywhere else, but in Sierra Leone, so were the Sierra Leoneans. They were confident and loud; they had attitude and flaunted it. Our lives intermingled at work and outside of it—they came to our parties and we went to their bars. Many of my expat friends, both men and women, were dating Sierra Leoneans.

Regardless of how integrated we were, we would always be reminded that we were first-world people in a foreign land. One night, for instance, Amy, an American friend who worked as a reproductive health nurse, sat down at dinner and lit a smoke. "Well ladies," she said exhaling, "some days you are just a white lady explaining genital discharge to Muslim primary-school students in West Africa."

We laughed. All of us had been in some situation like that at one point or another. "How about going through customs in Somalia and having the male inspectors pass around your tampons, thinking they were biological weapons? I had to explain—pantomime and all—what they are used for," another friend, Claire, recalled.

Stories like this could go on all night. My contribution was a story about something that had happened just a few days before, while I was away on a trip doing research.

"You know when I was in Kailahun last week?" I began. They nodded. "I was staying in a container and stupidly left my light on when I went to dinner." (A lot of times agencies used prefab containers as bedrooms; a group of them together looked like a trailer park.) "Well, when I got back, I thought the door to my container was moving. I got closer and realized that the entire thing was covered with slithering bugs."

"Ew!" my friends screamed in unison.

"No, you guys, it gets worse, seriously," I promised, as I went on to tell them the rest of the story. Eventually, I found the bug spray and hosed down the door, sending bugs everywhere. Some of the ones that died were so big they actually hit the ground with a *thud*. When the coast was clear, I ran into my container and killed the bugs that followed me with my flip-flop.

I considered the problem solved until I woke up a few hours later, having to pee. My neighbor had left his light on and another ecosystem of bugs was now flying around his door, which I'd have to walk past to get to the bathroom. I decided that instead I would pee in a small bucket I had in my room and then empty it out the window. I completed the first part of the mission and was carrying the bucket to the window when I slipped—banana-peel style—on the giant, wet corpse of one of the bugs I'd murdered earlier. The bucket jolted in my arms, and I drenched myself with my own fresh urine.

Occasionally I'd think about that night and wonder if it weren't an apt allegory for working abroad, for the particular stance you had to take toward the unexpected and uncontrollable. Living in Sierra Leone meant practicing radical acceptance: sometimes, you just had to stand there in your own piss. That's what one of my trips to Liberia felt like, when I had a ticket on a flight scheduled to depart at noon. Noon came and went, and we hadn't even boarded the plane. There was no sign or announcement saying that the flight would be delayed. You have to make a conscious decision to embrace patience in Africa, but I had a meeting that I couldn't miss. I got up to ask the woman at the counter when we would be taking off. She checked her watch. "Noon."

I looked down at my own watch. It was half past twelve. I told her it was half past twelve.

Her face remained expressionless. "The flight," she repeated, "will take off at noon."

I stood there, unsure whether she had understood what I was saying. Should I even try to engage with this woman or just sit back down and wait? I decided to return to my seat, because essentially she was saying, *Look, white lady, I don't know what to tell you. Deal with it.*

Eventually, I went through security with the rest of the passengers and more incompetence ensued. We took off our belts and shoes, placed our bags in trays, and walked through the metal detector. None of the security guards were paying attention. As I waited to retrieve my bag from its tray, I turned back and noticed that the monitor was blank. The security men were looking at a blank screen. And the metal detector? It wasn't plugged in. The airport had no power. But they put on a good show anyway, as if to say, *Maybe if we pretend it's working, it will.*

Making friends in Freetown was easy. Perched on one of the many hills in Freetown, near the US embassy, sat IMATT—the International Military Advisory and Training Team—a compound of mostly British soldiers who were deployed to Sierra Leone to train the fledgling Sierra Leonean army. On the weekends, they drove around Freetown in their 4x4s with the windows rolled down, Bon Jovi blasting from their radios, wearing wifebeaters and sporting cute buzz cuts. Most had come back from tours in Iraq and Afghanistan. This was a vacation for them, and they paraded their freedom.

I started dating one of the British soldiers—Sam, a six-foot-five human G.I. Joe.

On weekends, with surfboards strapped to the top of the car, coolers filled with beer and soda, a bunch of us sped through the bumpy back roads to the beach where we'd camp for the night. For supplies, we had military equipment—sleeping bags, netting, tents, and fluorescent glow sticks, which we'd hang from the branches of trees, and would light up our campsite all night. On our way to the beach one afternoon, we passed a man fixing the holes in the road. He used a shovel to dig up the rocks and then smoothed the craters with his hands. He toiled in the thick jungle air. Sam stopped the car.

"Hey, can you grab a soda from the cooler?"

I handed him a can of Sprite.

Sam rolled down the window and offered it to the man who put down his shovel and took the can. Sam shook his dusty and calloused hand and said, "Here you go, buddy. Thanks for the work." The old man smiled and nodded. I think he was hoping for money.

Sam rolled up the window and sped off. He took out a small bottle of antibacterial gel and wiped some on his hands. "Hearts and minds, Jess. Hearts and minds."

We continued the drive and passed a bridge that looked over a river where people always gathered to bathe. Men swam wearing only underwear; children went naked, splashing and jumping off rocks. The women, whether they were cleaning themselves or their clothes and dishes, usually went topless. The IMATT boys called it "Titty Bridge."

They frequented the nightclubs in town. Most were teeming with prostitutes. Usually the boys took multiple women home at once, their Land Cruisers brimming with eager, scantily dressed women. Others stayed at the bar drinking and dancing. Dancing inevitably led to one guy taking off his shirt. Then another would take off *his* shirt. Before you knew it, all of the big white guys were shirtless, dancing, flexing their pecs, and drinking vodka straight from the bottle. Then one of them would up the ante and pull down his pants. Another would follow. And you'd look up and there'd be a group of boys—some in boxers, some with just cowboy hats on—swinging their cocks around to the beat and shouting, "Jim's got the biggest schlong I've ever seen!"

I had never met people like this at home. No one I knew joined the Army. Yet, as wild and rowdy as they were, I could relate—they were like fraternity boys you'd see on spring break. Amidst everything else I was doing in Sierra Leone, meeting people like the IMATT boys reminded me of part of what I loved about this work: the preposterous range of people who you not only meet, but who you end up going surfing and spear fishing with on weekends.

We spent lots of time talking about their experiences in Iraq and Afghanistan. I wanted to know what it had been like for them. It was hard to believe that these young, silly boys were the same people carrying out air raids while wearing night goggles, jumping out of helicopters with AK-47s, fighting Al Qaeda and searching for Osama bin Laden. One soldier, Mike, tall and quiet, drunkenly told me about a night in Afghanistan that still clearly shook him. He had a slightly overgrown buzz cut and one of his front teeth tilted back, pressing behind the others.

"It was dark, and there was a guy who was speeding toward base camp. There were lots of signs along the way to slow down, checkpoints, warning shots fired, the whole thing, but the guy just kept coming. He was driving really fast. It was a quick decision, and I didn't know what else to do. We fired at the car and killed the driver."

"Why didn't you shoot at the tires? Why did you have to kill him?" I asked.

"That is stuff you only see in movies, Jess. Do you know how hard it is to hit a moving tire? It just doesn't work like that."

"Who was the guy?"

He sighed. "It turned out he was coming to fix our air conditioner," he said, turning away. "I was the one who hired him to come to fix the damn thing."

Three years later, I learned that Mike was killed by an IED in Afghanistan. I read it online and saw his picture next to the article. He was the first person I knew who died in the war.

❖

Sierra Leone was the first place where the professional and personal lives genuinely merged. The isolation, restriction of movement, and loneliness that I was incapable of handling in Darfur vanished here. Not being at the height of a disaster also slowed the pace of life. My research was fascinating and I enjoyed being part of a larger project and mission, especially when the study could contribute to something as significant as Taylor's indictment.

I loved my life so much in Sierra Leone that I invited Dad to come visit me. Before he arrived, I found the sole cardiologist in Sierra Leone, Dr. Kamara. He was an older man, his face flat and his skin dotted with deep pockmarks. He wore thick glasses that made it difficult to look him in the eyes because you never really knew where they were focused. I located his office in the largest hospital in Freetown and told him I would introduce him to my father, a cardiologist from the United States.

"Oh, this is excellent," he said. "Can he bring things over?"

"Sure," I said, expecting him to want drugs or

medicines he could not get here. But what Dr. Kamara wanted most were EKG papers. He shuffled me into the room where patients were examined and their heart rates monitored. I remembered my childhood visits with Dad at the hospital, where spools of skinny, shiny white paper printing heart rates would pile on the floor. Dad would rip them off, review them carefully, and hand me the long sheets. I spent hours drawing mountain landscapes with the zigzag heart readings. Dr. Kamara was using something that looked more like toilet paper to get the printouts. He pulled up one of the crumbling papers and looked at me. "I can't do much with these," he said.

Dad arrived with a large suitcase full of medicine and equipment but he wasn't able to get EKG papers that fit with Dr. Kamara's outdated machine. I could tell he was excited about his contribution. He reached into the bag, saying, "I brought as many antihypertensives as I could fit into this suitcase." But his spirits deflated when Dr. Kamara took us to the pharmacy where he handed over the supplies. "This will barely treat five people for a year," Dad said in dismay. He sighed. "These people need far more than just medications. They need access to basic health care. There aren't echocardiogram machines or other ways to even diagnose heart disease. There are no preventative measures."

Dr. Kamara shook his head. "I know."

Dr. Kamara boasted about the new ICU and made us put on clean gowns over our clothes and scrub our hands before entering. At first, Dad was impressed by these Western standards of sanitation. Yet once we were inside, he saw the mildew-lined curtains, the bugs swirling around the lightbulbs, the dust settled on the beds and floor.

We met another Sierra Leonean doctor at a more rural Catholic medical facility in Bo, about an hour outside Freetown. Dad had a chance to visit with the head physician there, a European-trained doctor. The hospital was cleaner and more modern and than the one in Freetown but beset by the same problems of access to modern treatments. The doctor who Dad visited with took him on a tour and was aware of the short-coming in treatment modalities in Sierra Leone. Here again Dad saw patients with advanced forms of neu-rologic and rhematologic diseases. There were stroke victims and those with arthritis. Physical therapy was not readily available. We met a young woman who had a treatable malignancy and yet was doomed to an early death because there were no chemotherapeutic agents available to her. I could see the sadness in Dad's eyes as we left. He gave the doctor his card and they spoke about contacting each other. As we left the hospital, a girl was carried in by her mother, who shouted some-thing to him in Krio. "This one," he said, sighing. "She just drank lighter fluid. You can see her lips puckering."

We thanked the doctor for his time and let him get back to his work.

FOR TWO OF THE DAYS Dad stayed with me my apart-ment didn't have water. Although this had become regular practice for me, for Dad it was new. He handled it jovially, putting a baseball hat over his dirty hair before we went to town. Dad may have been worried about his own safety and mine before he left, but any anxieties quickly disappeared. "The people here are so friendly!" he kept remarking, as we strolled through town, stopping to talk to the butchers and fish sellers. We bought some vegetables from women who liked Dad and his smiley nature so much that they padded our bag with extras. "That never happens to me!" I told him. He was flattered.

Dad had brought I ♥ NY shirts and gave them to some of my Sierra Leonean colleagues, who all showed up to work the next day wearing them. By the end of my father's visit, I could tell he felt at ease with my decision to work in Sierra Leone, and knew now that it wasn't the kind of place where you had to worry about making it out alive. It was the kind of place you could have a life, and I did.

What I hadn't yet realized, however, was that having a life wasn't the same as *making* one.

During the first few months I was in Sierra Leone, the Taylor case had been moving along at a slow crawl. The prosecution was trying to track down someone who could testify about the use of children as soldiers during the war. They needed two types of witnesses for each of Taylor's eleven crimes: one to verify that the crime took place, and the other to link Taylor to that particular crime. Finding the latter type was difficult, as many people were too intimidated to testify. Taylor had done a good job of maintaining plausible deniability. As he said in the courthouse that first day, he couldn't be held responsible for the atrocities that happened in another country.

Anna, a tall, lean, and hysterically funny British lawyer on Taylor's prosecution team, was exhausted. She often worked late into the night and could be found at the office most weekends. We were friends, and one evening she managed to get out and meet me and a few other expats for a drink at the local bar. The place was like any bar you'd find at home, with a pool table and foosball table, but it had only one kind of beer on tap and played the same gnawing soundtrack of Kylie Minogue and Shakira. The walls were painted with local proverbs: "Ehn pus no de, arata tak chaj" (When the cat isn't there, the rats take charge); "News no have fit but it de wak" (Rumors don't have feet, but they walk).

Anna mentioned that they were having trouble finding a witness who could speak to the number of children who participated in the conflict. They had children who could testify, just as they had other victims— amputees, rape victims, people who had watched their relatives be murdered—but they needed more evidence and research to establish that child abduction was a widespread, systematic activity.

We all knew that files at the Ministry of Social Welfare, Gender and Children's Affairs (known locally as
the Ministry of Social Welfare) recorded the histories
of children who were demobilized. These were the
forms that social workers filled out when a child entered an ICC. Social workers transcribed details about
the children's whereabouts, their activities during the
war, where they came from and how old they were
when they were captured. They needed someone to
weed through the thousands of files that sat in boxes in
the Ministry and find out what information was stored
in them. It seemed like a natural extension of my work,
and Anna wanted to hire me to get more data. Working
on the Taylor case and contributing to his conviction,
even in a marginal way, was about the most exciting
opportunity I could imagine. Anna said I might even
have to take the stand.

The defense was going to have questions, she said,
regarding the validity of these forms. Most of the children didn't have birth certificates, and many of them
lied to enter the program. It was my job to find as much
information as possible to verify that the abduction of
children during this conflict was a widespread occur-
rence, and that these kids were legitimate.

"Oh, and Jess," Anna said, after describing what
my job would be, "what's Article 14 of the Convention
on the Rights of the Child?"

"I don't know!" I said, laughing. I thought she was
kidding.

Anna was serious. "What's Article 15?"

I didn't know that, either.

"You're supposed to be an expert. The defense is already going to be suspicious because you're so young. Memorize the CRC."

Having seen the Special Court in action and be-friended a number of the lawyers who worked there, I knew the brutal tactics they used on witnesses who took the stand. I once saw a retired man outside the court-room after a particularly vicious cross-examination, during which the lawyers attacked his career, personal life, and expertise. He paced outside the courtroom, patting his forehead with a handkerchief and devour-ing cigarette after cigarette. I was scared.

SO I RETURNED TO THE field, revisiting the children and social workers I had just met, this time with more questions. The communities knew me and welcomed me with gifts—one time it was live chickens, handed to me by their feet, bound together with string. Another community offered me a cow's head. It came in a card-board box stuffed with old newspaper, like a delicate Christmas ornament. The head smelled like sardines, and the box was soggy at the bottom. But the com-munity was excited by their offering, so I smiled and accepted the package.

"My children like the brains the best," my driver told me on our way back to town.

"It's yours," I said, passing him the box. "I hope they'll enjoy this one's brains."

Besides collecting assorted animal parts, I still had to find a way to prove that the ages recorded on the forms were legitimate. The forms showed that more than two thousand of the children had been fifteen or under at the time they were abducted. But without birth certificates or any sort of written record of their ages, how could we be sure? Any ambiguities in our report would permit the prosecution to assert that the people whose stories were recorded in the files were, in fact, adults at the time of recruitment.

I interviewed social workers who had received children and asked the same questions that I anticipated being posed by the defense. In Kailahun, a district in the East, I sat down with Fatima, a social worker who now dealt with child protection issues—cases of abuse or neglect, labor violations, the trafficking of children as domestic workers—for the local Ministry of Social Welfare. We met at her office, which was a small room with some papers scattered on a large desk. No computer, no electricity. It was no wonder that so little got done in these places, which lacked even the most basic resources. Fatima barely had enough credit on her phone to schedule our appointment.

The efforts Sierra Leoneans made in the face of these obstacles and the victories they managed to achieve impressed me time and again. I sat down in the plastic chair across from her and we began to talk. A solid, motherly woman with a stern voice, Fatima had been in charge of the reunification process after the war for this province and she explained the system to me: "When a child entered an ICC, he received services depending on his age. We didn't know how long this child would be with us and we needed to provide age-appropriate activities, maybe schooling. Usually he didn't know how old he was. We asked them to try to remember what grade he was in when he was abducted. What major milestones of the country he could remember. Like who was the paramount chief at the time you were born? How old were you when this city council building was built? We asked whether he had younger siblings and how many. Did he care for these siblings before they were abducted?"

They took note of physical signs as well. "We looked at their teeth," Fatima said. "Did they have molars? Did they have their front teeth in?" She pointed to her incisors and grinned widely, so I could see her back teeth. "You listen to their voice. You can tell if they've been through puberty yet. For boys we measured the size of their calves, looked to see if they had an Adam's apple or underarm hair. For girls we looked if they had breasts." It may not have been the most scientific approach, but it was the best they could do, and it sounded pretty reasonable. "You can tell a ripe corn by its looks," she said. The mean age of the twenty-three hundred children entered on the Ministry forms—each one filled out by someone like Fatima, who'd carefully estimated the child's age as nearly as possible—was still only eleven years old. Eleven was four years away from fifteen, the court's designated cutoff age. So even if the approximations were off by a year or two in either direction, it wouldn't make a difference. These were children.

The defense was also likely to question the validity of the children's stories. When these centers opened, suddenly demobilized children were everywhere. "If I see my friend demobilized and getting access to education, I will want to come and lie and say I was demobilized, too. Some were opportunists—those who wanted something to put in their stomachs," Brima, a neatly put together male social worker who worked in the northern town of Kono, told me. The ICCs didn't have a lot of resources. They couldn't afford to accept children who weren't eligible. "So," Brima continued, "all you have to do is ask a lot of questions. He will get confused. The story won't add up."

The social workers who questioned these children survived the conflict themselves. "I know exactly when that town was attacked, because it was my village! Now this boy comes and tells me it was last year? No, no. He was not a soldier," Brima recalled. "He may have gotten some information from a friend, but if you go a little further and ask what kind of conflict took place, he won't know," Brima went on, leaning his head back as he recounted the stories. "Also, if they say they used an AK-47, then they were given training. So we'd ask— how do you use it? Can you draw one for me? What is a magazine? How many cartridges will go in a package? If a child has fired a gun for three years, he will have a mark on his finger." He pointed to his index finger. "If he has been using a big gun, he will have a mark on his shoulder." He patted his right shoulder.

"Or you ask who was his commander? Was he tall? Short? What was his complexion like? Ah, my dear, you say you worked with Foday Sankoh (the Sierra Leonean warlord), you don't, in fact, know Foday Sankoh—you can't discuss him with me. You are lying," Brima said, chuckling.

After about forty interviews across the country and peeling through more than two thousand sticky, mildewed forms sitting in the Ministry of Social Welfare, I compiled a report detailing my findings. After some scrutiny from the Special Prosecutor—queries about my methodology, the people with whom I met, the way I found them, and the questions I asked—they accepted my report as evidence into the trial. But I never did have to take the stand.

While I was doing my interviews, I had asked a few children what they thought of the Special Court, if the ones living far from Freetown even knew of it. One boy, not even thirteen at the time I met him, put it best: "For some of us, our lives were miserable, they trained us to come up in a bad way. By trying them, it shows people that if you do bad, there will be consequences."

In 2012, when the trial finally came to a close, Charles Taylor was convicted on all eleven counts of aiding and abetting the atrocities of the war and received a sentence of fifty years in prison.

❖

When Claudetta and I weren't traveling in the field, we spent days in the office eating lunch, talking over family photos, telling each other stories about our lives. Our birthdays were one day apart, and in August she invited me to her house to celebrate with her family.

Claudetta would ask me what creams would make her skin white and if she could use my shampoo so that her hair would be smooth like mine. She knew America from movies and the Internet and wanted to come work with me there. Even though Claudetta longed for the things I had in my life, I realized that I was the envious one.

One night after work, I accompanied Claudetta to the market. A woman hissed when she saw her, and Claudetta stopped to chat. The woman was her cousin. "Mit mi padi Jessica,"—Meet my friend Jessica—she said, introducing me.

I shook the woman's hand.

"Yu de enjoi yu ste?" she asked, wanting to know if I was enjoying my stay.

"Yehs, a lehk Salone tumohs," I replied in my broken Krio, telling her I liked Sierra Leone so much.

Claudetta said good-bye to her cousin and the two of us continued on our way. As we walked, Claudetta turned to me and told me her cousin's story. Her husband had left her and was now coming back, begging for forgiveness. "Yu no go meso snek te I dai," Claudetta said.

The phrase was a popular Krio expression: *"You can't measure a snake until its dead."* Or, as someone in the United States might put it, "You don't know what you've got 'til it's gone." It's true everywhere in the world: we realize people's worth only after we've lost them.

As we moved through the market, Claudetta spotted a young girl carrying her backpack home from school. She shouted her name. The girl turned around, raced toward Claudetta, and gave her a big hug. They talked and Claudetta reached into her purse and handed her a few bills. The girl was ecstatic. "OK, sista," Claudetta said. "Tehl a du to Musa for mi."— tell Musa I say hi.

"Yes, ma," the girl agreed, and I watched as she skipped away.

Claudetta told me the girl was her niece, who was having some trouble in school. Some nights, Claudetta helped her with her homework.

After Claudetta and I parted that evening, I realized that I wanted what she had—a community, a sense of belonging, and the closeness of loved ones. Dad's visit was great, and I had made friends, but my life here was all just temporary. I wasn't going to stay forever. One night over drinks I asked my Swedish friend Carmen where she planned to go next. She worked for the United Nations Development Programme (UNDP) and had been in Freetown since I arrived over a year ago. Her contract would be up in a few months and she was looking for jobs.

"I don't know. Depends . . ."

"On what?"

"Well, where I get a contract, of course."

"Where are you looking?"

"The Middle East would be cool. Where do you think the most men would be?"

"Right now? Probably Lebanon." Tensions between Israel and Lebanon were flaring. Aid workers were sure to be flocking there in droves.

Susan, another friend who worked on human rights, had just been offered a job in Juba, the capital of South Sudan. "The woman who interviewed me said that I'd even get my own container to live in," she said, laughing. "As if that's supposed to be a draw! My friends at home are buying houses and on their second babies. I'm supposed to get all excited about a prefab box to live in for a year?"

Finding long-term companionship in this field seemed like a fluke. Some people's relationships did last overseas, but they were the lucky few, able to continue this life, fulfilled both personally and professionally. Couples living apart trying to have babies ended up planning their R&Rs around ovulation cycles. If they were stationed together, reproducing in a bunker in Iraq, a compound in Sri Lanka, or a tent in Myanmar wasn't easy. Some made it work, and those who did called their offspring "tsunami babies," "cyclone babies," even "conflict babies." Some people tried to hold onto long-distance relationships, but most couldn't maintain the passion over crap phone connections and unreliable wireless signals. As we worked hard to re-build other people's lives, our own were falling apart.

"George is going to Iran," my friend Muriel told me one night over dinner. She was a French nutritionist working in a clinic downtown. She and her boyfriend had been dating for two years, since they met in Malawi.

"He didn't even consult me! He just told me one morning over Skype. What am I supposed to do with that? I don't want to go to Iran."

"Then don't."

"And then what? This is over? He got an amazing job there, so it's hard to blame him for wanting to go. But we were supposed to make these decisions together now. I want to talk to him, but, tell me, what are the rules for communicating when one person is in post-conflict West Africa and the other is in a failed state on the verge of a revolution?" I didn't know what to tell her. The problem was that there were no rules—or if there were, nobody knew them.

Everything felt fleeting—jobs, friends, romances, apartments, countries, even our sanity. Our belong-ings were strewn all over the world, packed away in the basements of our childhood homes or storage facilities on distant continents. ("I have my winter clothes at my friend's place in Amsterdam, most of my books are still with my ex-girlfriend in Nairobi, and my ski jacket, hat, and mittens are in Geneva," Scott once explained to me. We were standing in his bedroom, which was empty save for some shirts and slacks and two pairs of shoes. "That's really about all I own.") Building momentum in a romance that was going to be cut short anyway just meant asking for heartache; investing in material things just meant paying more for overweight baggage.

Sam had been shipped back to Afghanistan, and Facebook continued to blast photos of weddings I had missed at home. Every week it seemed, babies were born, engagements announced, new apartments moved into with new partners. Seeing all these happy couples with their kids and houses made me wonder why I didn't simplify my life. Sure, I had accumulated more stamps in my passport and made friends from places I didn't even know existed a few years before. But the catalogue of countries I had been were memories that I shared with people scattered across the globe. The work I found so rewarding threatened to destroy everything else meaningful in my life. I loved a job that made loving anything else seemingly impossible.

Years later, I saw a Facebook posting that perfectly captured why I decided to go home—and how hard it was to make that decision. A friend from grad school who shared my nomadic existence posted pictures from his recent trip to India. Someone he knew, probably from childhood, wrote on his wall: "*You've been across the Sahara, to Petra, to the Taj Mahal, and most of Europe. You've crossed off 75 percent of MY wish list. What exactly does YOUR wish list look like?*"

My friend replied: "*Having a lovely wife and a gaggle of children like yours . . . and being able to build a 12-square-meter back patio on which to sip cold beers and grill lamb chops. Grass is always greener, my friend.*"

Saving Lives One Keystroke
at a Time

"Jessica. How are you? It's been ages." It was James, an old acquaintance from college, calling. I hadn't spoken to him in years. Since we graduated, James had made a career financing and developing five-star restaurants around the world. He had done quite well. "I heard that you've been living in Africa, and I want to do something in Africa. You can help me!"

As soon as I'd returned to New York in 2008, I immediately applied for headquarter positions. It would provide the stability I craved while allowing me to remain engaged with the field. I now had the sunny apartment in Brooklyn that I could only have imagined a few years before, and I was happy to shove my suitcases under my bed and put my passport in a drawer. I missed the thrill and unpredictability of my life abroad, but there was a new excitement to coming back. Instead of having just a place to stay—a guesthouse, a shipping container—I had a place where I might stay indefinitely.

I'd also worked abroad long enough that I'd accrued some authority, at least to people at home. When there was an emergency, friends asked me where to donate; if someone wanted to volunteer overseas, she came to me for advice.

"Where in Africa?" I asked James.

"I don't know. I just want to do something in Africa."

"Why don't you find an organization that works there and donate to it?"

"No, no. I want to do it. I want to go there with some friends and do something."

"Are you going to live there?"

"No, just go for like a week and give things out. We're basing it on the one-for-one concept. Eat at our restaurant and you buy a pair of glasses for someone who needs them or something like that. We'd then go and distribute the glasses to people who can't see."

Since I'd been home, I'd noticed aid was getting a lot of attention, far more than when I had first set about applying for jobs so long ago. This newfound aware-ness was both due to and sensationally embodied by the celebrities who now attached themselves to various aid projects. Angelina Jolie was an ambassador for the refugee cause. George Clooney had a hand in the Sudan peace accords. Bono was now treated as a legitimate expert on development and even wrote the foreword to renowned economist Jeffrey Sachs's book *The End of Poverty*. UN agencies boasted celebrity spokespeople who raised the profile of the organizations: UNICEF

had David Beckham and Jessica Lange; UNDP en-
listed Antonio Banderas; the World Food Programme
drew Christina Aguilera, Drew Barrymore, and Penel-
ope Cruz. A young, single male friend of mine working in the outreach section of an ambassador-less UN
agency was trying to recruit one. "You think we can
get Megan Fox? What about Rihanna?" he asked with
a hopeful grin. In Hollywood, being linked to a charity
was as important as having a good agent. And it had
a ripple effect, providing aid work with a sheen of sex
appeal and giving the impression that anyone with a
heart and some money could do it.

"Why don't you come over to my apartment and
I'll explain it to you," James offered. He wasn't a bad
person; he wanted to help, but just didn't know how.
So I went.

The elevator opened directly onto his five-bedroom
Upper East Side apartment. The three bathrooms were
big enough to be confused with day spas. The cost of
the artwork that hung on the enormous walls alone
would have been enough to feed a rural community in
Africa for a decade.

James passed me a sheet of ideas that he had been
working on: giving away glasses and solar-powered
stoves, building houses for Africans, sending orphans
to school. "Simple recipes, simple solutions," was one
of the taglines.

"What are the good ideas here?" he asked.

"I don't know. Africa's a really big place. The needs
are different everywhere."

"Well, let's pick an idea and figure out where they need it."

I didn't know what to say. James had the classic misconception of aid, that it was just charity. People had good intentions, but they assumed that Africans were so pathetically poor that they would want anything we threw at them; that we could predict what they needed from afar. James was tacking on a solution before even knowing what the problem was.

I UNDERSTOOD WHERE HE WAS coming from, though: the West's idea of Africa has been shaped by years of misleading generalizations and sentimental imagery. All people can picture are those Sally Struthers infomercials, in which Africa is always portrayed as a lack: a place where people are defined by what they don't have, a hole that needs to be filled. And by us—by our lifestyle, education, and values. What these infomercials never showed was what they did have: community, tradition, resilience, and pride.

"Well, just giving people things isn't going to really solve their problems. You'll want to work with an agency that's already there and knows the issues and the best way to approach it," I said. "Or you should start very small. Go to a community, do some research to find out what would really make a difference in people's lives. I bet you they will say jobs, or health care, or even sanitation. It's not sexy, but before you go distributing these things, find out if people actually want them, or need them."

He took a sip of his tea. This isn't what he wanted to hear. But I continued.

"And the sending-the-orphans-to-school idea will surely tug at heartstrings for the people who eat at your restaurant. But orphanages are the worst place for children! A lot of times children in orphanages aren't even orphans—their parents send them there because in an orphanage, at least, they know that their child might receive three meals a day, some kind of schooling, and maybe even a bed. So the day after your orphanage is set up the number of 'orphans' will increase tenfold. Work with families in the communities to raise their quality of life so that they can care for their children and pay for them to go to school."

He looked at me like I was a heartless bureaucrat, wondering why I couldn't just be *nice* to orphans? I think he wanted me to tell him how amazing I thought his ideas were. But all I could think was, *Don't use some African family as an advertisement for your fancy restaurants.*

"Well, isn't it better than doing nothing?" he asked instead.

I didn't know how to explain what had taken me years to learn. Similar to the boxes of DVDs and stuffed animals and platform sandals that arrived after the tsunami, his plan could end up doing more harm than good. Powdered milk, for example, was often

310   JESSICA ALEXANDER

sent to help mothers nurse their babies after a disaster, when it was feared that the traumatization would result in an inability to lactate. But mothers mixed the powder with water, water that was contaminated, water that could end up killing the babies. Even liquid formula could be harmful: nutrition experts advocated for breast-feeding in almost all circumstances and rarely gave formula to nursing mothers because when that supply ran out, the mothers—who were no longer producing milk—would feed children rice or other foods that the infants couldn't digest. Also, cans of liquid formula need to be kept cool, which can be impossible or at least prohibitively expensive in places that are baking deserts, where there isn't much in the way of refrigeration.

Aid procedures weren't developed out of a lack of compassion; in fact, they specifically took into account how easily compassion could lead us and people like James astray. Aid workers aren't just a bunch of people doing the first nice thing that came into their heads. Sympathy was a shortsighted emotion: it told you to make the pain stop *now*, and so you went with the quick fixes. Because you wanted your pain to stop, too: you didn't want to be someone who stood by, seemingly idle, while human beings suffered.

But aid workers couldn't afford to be impulsive. People affected by crisis deserved more than just our working on a whim. They deserved the respect that went with providing services based on best practice and thought-out plans. To outsiders like James who wanted a quick win, we may have appeared callous, but over the years aid organizations had learned the value of foresight and patience, after seeing so many ostensibly well-intentioned initiatives create perverse incentives. The outcomes in those cases could be truly appalling: I'd heard of an agency working in the Central African Republic that inadvertently increased the HIV rate when they provided microcredit loans to HIV-positive mothers. Suddenly women who had previously tested negative for HIV were getting rescreened, and the results were coming back positive. The man who worked on the program was convinced that these women had contracted the disease deliberately, in order to be eligible for the loans. These were knotty issues, and to address them one needed to possess a high tolerance for nuance and ambiguity. In this case, I didn't think James had it.

"LOOK, IF YOU WANT TO do this yourself, it will take a significant investment. Why don't you help small businesses that already exist grow their own retail operations, help them reach international clients, help them market their own products? Handing stuff out just competes with local vendors and undermines small businesses. A lot of times the cost of shipping this stuff over, paying for clearing customs, and trucking the goods to communities costs more than if you bought things in the local marketplace. Plus that way you put money into the economy."

"That's really complicated, though."

That was exactly the point. Helping people required pinpointing what needed to change, and actually changing it, and both often raised difficult logistical, ethical, and economic issues. James's handout mission wasn't going to address these issues and could very possibly interfere with the work of people who were. He may have had a catchy tagline for his project, but aid is more complicated than that. It takes time and it takes an investment. You couldn't just come up with a good title—you had to actually write the book. Sitting at his granite kitchen counter, I could tell he wasn't getting it.

"If you want to do something," I said, "I really think you should find an organization that is good, is working there already, and donate to them. If you want me to help you find some, I can do that."

"Thanks. I'll let you know," he said, as he walked me to the elevator. I never heard from him again.

James's very human impulse—to help others in need—is centuries old. It became an actual industry in the mid-nineteenth century when a Genevan businessman witnessed the death and dying of forty thousand soldiers in the Battle of Solferino. He returned to Geneva and founded the International Committee for the Red Cross with the mission to provide relief to all those in need, regardless of which side they were on. But only in the last few decades has aid become an actual profession. The aftermath of the Rwandan genocide in 1994 is considered a watershed moment for the industry, where it was publicly called out for its chaotic, ad hoc, and poorly coordinated response to the massive refugee crisis that followed. The industry reacted to this extreme criticism by acknowledging its weaknesses and underwent significant reforms, including developing rules and regulations to govern themselves. By the late 1990s, wars were being covered by twenty-four-hour news cycles bringing the world horrific and real-time images of state failures and civil war, ethnic cleansing, and genocide. People were moved and through the early 2000s, the size of the humanitarian community increased significantly in terms of its budget, reach, and modes of providing assistance.

Today, the aid world is a highly professionalized industry consisting of large, networked International NGOs, UN agencies, local NGOs, think tanks, consortia, and academic institutions. There are at least eighty different global master's-level programs focusing on humanitarian and development studies, and hundreds of professional training programs. The aid community resented amateurs, "voluntourists" like James. But when they scorned people like James they were also reassuring themselves, justifying their place in the profession and that what they did *was* a profession. Whenever a dilettante screwed up or revealed his ignorance, it was once again confirmed that experience and master's degrees were the only ways to be legitimate. But as self-serving and smug as the critics could be, they were also usually right.

Yet it was easy to point at the flaws within the aid community; certainly I had made many mistakes, and I saw my colleagues and the institutions we worked for make them, too. No one had the perfect answer, the magic bullet. Doing good aid required a time commitment—not a week, not a month, but years. It meant focusing your efforts rather than trying to solve everything at once, and tackling what you could do well. It also meant fessing up to mistakes, learning from them, and sharing them with donors or the general public. Too often we hid behind shiny reports that glossed over the complexities of certain situations and the trouble we might have navigating them.

"No one wants to hear the truth about aid," a friend who had just come back from assessing an education program in Niger told me that winter. Over several cups of coffee in her Brooklyn apartment, she detailed the problems she'd encountered during the trip. "The donor government spent fifty million dollars of taxpayer money on this education program. You think they want to hear that it went badly?" she asked. Negative press and scathing headlines would follow if it turned out that money had been invested in projects that were poorly administered or proved otherwise ineffective. "The agency spent the money, so they want to be able to report that they spent it well. The office in the country that actually implemented the program, well, they don't want to look bad, either, so they will present it as going well, too." It was one big merry-go-round of denial.

Now that I worked in New York, I saw her point. At headquarters, we relied on reports from the field for much of our information. We trusted the agency staff out there to tell us how it was going, but they were incentivized to report success and cover up or excuse problems. Numbers could be massaged, made to suggest a positive outcome: X amount of money was spent on Y number of buckets, which were distributed, or Z number of teachers, who were trained, these reports would tell us, and everyone would be happy. But rarely did people follow up on the Ys and Zs. What if the buckets had holes in them? Or what if the teacher training program didn't make a difference in literacy rates of schoolchildren? In the private sector, a bad investment shows up in the numbers: if you lose money, you know, and somebody's held accountable. But in the aid world, it was hard to see, let alone measure, impact. Our time lines were often too abbreviated to be sure if an investment was bad or good. After the emergency stage came to an end, humanitarians passed the reins to development professionals like my friends in Sierra Leone who would be there longer.

"Who, at the end of the day, is really interested in whether the project went well or not?" my friend asked as she took another gulp of her coffee and looked up with raised eyebrows from her large mug.

"The people who we're there to help," I said.

"Yes. Of course, they are. But we don't really work

like that, do we? I mean, we work *for* them, but at the same time we don't. Organizations can fire people, and donors can stop giving, but what can the people we help do, if we mess up?"

It was true. Accountability to beneficiaries, to the people actually affected by disasters, didn't fit into the equation anywhere. As long as donors paid for services, they would have the final say about whether or not the program continued. Although humanitarian actors preached "community participation," and "ensuring affected voices are heard," at the end of the day it came down to pleasing donors who kept aid agencies in business. The people receiving the services almost never got a say in what was offered in their communities during an emergency response. "We come with hammers and so we look for nails," a colleague once admitted. "It doesn't matter if what we're seeing are screws, we're going to find those nails so we can get to work as we know how."

This isn't to say that there weren't very passionate or committed people on the ground. And it's also not to say that people were actively misusing funds, or spending them with deliberate carelessness or indifference. Although a strong movement to improve quality and accountability was growing and gaining traction within the humanitarian world, there was no getting around the fact that the system was set up so the end user wasn't in a position to select what he received or to evaluate its benefit.

From New York headquarters, it was even easier to lose sight of my connection to the field and affected populations. This was classic office grunt work—I sent e-mails, wrote reports, circulated memos, developed log frames. My job was to evaluate a new method for financing aid which supposedly delivered money to disasters faster. People at headquarters wanted to know whether the streamlined process was turning into speedier aid delivery at the field level. My job oversaw a painfully inefficient process, requiring input from at least two dozen people at different agencies scattered across the globe. The perpetual overreliance on consensus slowed proceedings down even more. "It's one big *kumbaya* session," my boss said, frustrated that before we could move on with anything we had to wait for feedback from Geneva, Rome, Nairobi. "This place needs a dictator to just lay down the law and make decisions." Meanwhile, we had to play the never-ending game of interagency politics, appeasing all vested parties in order for anything meaningful to occur.

My daily routine in New York—going into the office, contacting people, negotiating with them, waiting for people to sign off on a decision, then starting all over the next day—was admittedly far less exciting than the life I had lived abroad. But if you wanted some of the steady normalcy of home, working at an agency's domestic headquarters was an attractive option. What I didn't realize until I was working in New York is that the more senior you become in this profession, the less interaction you have with the parts of the job that keep people motivated: seeing human resilience in some of the toughest situations imaginable, knowing that children are back in school due in part to work you've done, giving people a place to sleep, even if temporarily. Several years later, I still remembered the expressions of people standing in line for food distributions in Darfur, the interactions that I had with children who had been assisted after the war in Sierra Leone, the names of asylum seekers in Rwanda. Even though it was flawed, the work there helped people at the times when they needed it most. Writing reports and drafting memos from headquarters, I had to remind myself of this every day.

AND IT TOOK TIME TO adjust to headquarters bureaucracy language, too. Words not recognized by a proper English dictionary were regularly passed off as actual vocabulary, adding to the already brimming bowl of bureaucratic alphabet soup. *Complementarity* of processes, *sectoral* coverage, *evaluability* of impact, *operationalization* of the concept—eventually enough of these invented phrases were dropped in documents or e-mails that people stopped wondering if they held actual meaning. "Modalities are in place" was the response you got almost every time you asked how a project was progressing. I never got a clear answer about what a modality actually was or how you would go about putting one in place. But eventually I was able to translate it from aid-speak to actual English myself: it was an admission that we'd put that one on the back burner, indefinitely.

These words not recognized by Microsoft spell-checker or any other dictionary, were used to compose what were basically nonsense sentences, which resulted in e-mails literally devoid of any actual meaning: "*The Inter Agency Real Time Evaluation Interest Group (IA-RTE IG) is meeting for a full-day workshop to agree on procedures and methodologies for IA-RTE (to be presented to the Inter Agency Steering Committee Working Group—IASC-WG), inter alia also a 'logic model' that could be used to assess effectiveness and results. Reading all the issues and options for discussion with the Consultative Group, I feel that there are clear linkages between the two 'Working Groups' and that we shall strive to maintain and strengthen the relationships so that each can benefit from the other's work.*" Years later, I still have absolutely no idea what that e-mail means.

Every agency had an Evaluation Office that analyzed the effectiveness of the agency's response to a particular disaster or crisis. But then someone else would be hired to evaluate the quality of the Evaluation Office's evaluations: these reviews were called "meta-evaluations." The reports issued by the meta-evaluators often recommended that they create a sub-committee to review the recommendations and create another report to summarize and report back on actions taken.

No one could make up their minds about what language we should use when referring to ourselves or the people for whom we were working. "Beneficiaries" was widely used until it was deemed disempowering and people started using "affected populations" instead. Some agencies called them "people of concern." Others used words like "clients," "aid customers," "aid recipients," or "program participants." The humanitarian community was referred to by some as "change agents." Others made this distinction: they were "rights holders" and we were "duty bearers."

Days were assigned causes: World Refugee Day, World Humanitarian Day, United Nations Day. Even this practice quickly came to seem like a parody of itself—it wasn't long before we started getting e-mail reminders about World Breastfeeding Week, Global Handwashing Day, World Toilet Day.

But a lot of the time only people who worked in the UN could understand the lingo. A typical sentence from a UN e-mail: "The initial phases of the CERF (Central Emergency Response Fund) evaluation will need to consider CHF (Common Humanitarian Fund) countries where there has been a CAP (Consolidated Appeal Process) or CHAP (Common Humanitarian Action Plan). The NURD (Northern Uganda Recovery and Development) donor group will be funding part of it but we'll have to rely on the ERFs (Emergency Relief Funds) and HRFs (Humanitarian Relief Funds) to finalize the rest." When I read a report that Violence Against Girls had been shortened to VAG it was undeniable: the absurdity of the bureaucratic speak had gotten completely out of hand.

Some aid workers made cracks about the impact we were having from so far away. Someone would get up at the end of lunch and declare, "Well, guess I'm going back to my desk to save some more lives now," and everyone would laugh. "Saving a life one keystroke at a time" became the running joke. We all missed life on the ground. Daily field engagement is critical to making the issues real and giving legitimacy to the work of the international agencies. But as time goes on, it's harder for aid workers rising through the ranks and wanting a life in the West to have regular access.

There was constant jockeying among HQ staff to be selected for short missions in the field. Meetings would get tense as soon as the announcement was made. "You just got back from Afghanistan—give someone else a turn!" someone would snap. "I haven't been to Asia in months," another person would say mournfully, while others rolled their eyes. All of us needed to go back and be reminded of what drew us to this career in the first place. Because it certainly wasn't what we were doing from New York.

That year for my job, I often traveled from New York to Geneva—the "Peace Capital" of the world and seat of the UN's humanitarian assistance and human rights operations, as well as host to a vast assortment of other international agencies. In graduate school I read somewhere that when you're in a place like Geneva, you can't imagine a place like Africa even existing. And when you're in a noisy hectic African capital, a place like Geneva cannot exist. The idea stuck with me, and when I landed in Geneva for the first time, it was clear. In Geneva, the air smells of croissants, chocolate, cappuccinos, and wealth. It's a place obsessed with time; clocks are everywhere, from the bus stops that tell you the minute the next bus will arrive, to the Rolex and Tissot stores on every corner. Litter doesn't exist in Geneva, and the city streets are scrubbed clean of life and character. Shops close exactly at 6 p.m. each night, except Thursdays, when they stay open until 8 p.m. The whole city shuts down on Sundays. A friend told me that she was given a list of rules when she moved into her apartment: vacuuming was not permitted, except on Saturdays, and flushing the toilet after 10 p.m. was absolutely forbidden.

Such a pristine city, so governed by rules and so admiring of orderliness: nowhere on earth was farther away from Africa, with all its haphazard chaos, its constant upsetting of even the best-laid plans. Yet life in Africa was affected by the decisions made and policies implemented at meetings in Geneva. The UN building was a palace, with long echoing hallways and offices adorned with Persian rugs. The walls were lined with maps and photos from Africa and Asia, but they may as well have been postcards from other planets: places so far away, and so hard to imagine. The manicured lawn outside the United Nations overlooked the still and silvery water of Lake Léman, and the white Alps glowed pink at sunset. Some days I'd come out of a meeting about aid distribution in African countries and seeing the lake and the mountains made me feel like I was living in a snow globe—a cold and perfect sphere, a world unto itself, apart even from our own.

A few months later, I got another chance to travel abroad when I was sent to Jerusalem for two weeks to plan the logistics of an upcoming evaluation. It wasn't until after I landed that I realized it was the ninth anniversary of Mom's death.

My mother died in Israel. She wasn't there for spiritual reasons, to be closer to God or to be in the Holy Land. When the cancer returned after the first bone marrow transplant, the doctors at home shrugged and shook their heads. They said we were out of options. But Dad, refusing to give up, found a doctor in Israel who offered to perform a kind of bone marrow transplant that was not yet approved in the United States.

I remembered a night nine years ago, when all five of us—Mom, Dad, my two younger brothers, and I—had cuddled next to each other in Mom and Dad's bed, talking about whether Mom should go. She was scared. We were all scared. She didn't want to live out what might be her last few months or weeks in a foreign place, far from friends and family. But as we lay there discussing the options—Mom and I under the covers, the boys sitting among overstuffed pillows—my younger brother, Ben, his head resting against my mother, got to the point. "If you stay here, there's nothing left to do, right? You'll die. So there's really not a choice, is there?"

"No, I guess there isn't," Mom said softly, staring blankly at the ceiling and mindlessly stroking Ben's hair.

A week later Dad left work and Ben transferred to an international high school in Jerusalem. When they moved, Dan and I stayed behind—he was in college and I had just graduated and started my new job. Mom refused to have us join them. "Look," she said, when I pleaded with her. "This is already disrupting Dad's and Ben's lives. You don't need to come. I don't want you quitting your job. It will make me sadder having you there than if I know that you're getting on with it in New York. What are you going to do there anyway? Sit by my bed and watch me? Stay. Live your life."

She spent that last week packing and tying up as many loose ends as she could—making last-minute phone calls, sending e-mails, showing me where she kept her jewelry, closing out professional obligations and appointments. She wrote a letter to each of us. There was so much to do. How do you prepare to leave your life, potentially forever?

The day of their flight came at last, and while Ben and my father were carrying all the suitcases down the stairs and packing them in the trunk of the car, my mother crouched to stroke our cat good-bye. Then she stood up and hugged me for a long time. I was crying. "Don't worry, honey. I'm coming back," she whispered in my ear as she turned to get into the car. The procedure and the recovery period were to take five months. Dan and I waved good-bye from the porch as Dad pulled out of the driveway. Through the window, I saw Mom turn around and look back at the house, taking it in for the last time.

We wrote e-mails regularly and spoke on the phone every day. At first, Mom was too weak to get out of bed, but eventually she was sturdy enough to do laps around the hospital wing. She made friends with all the nurses and they left little gifts for her in her room. One of them ran a 10K race in Jerusalem and gave her his medal. Dad bought colorful posters and hung them on her walls. After the pope visited Jerusalem, Dad bought a pope costume and wore it to the hospital one morning to surprise Mom. They kept each other's spirits up this way, watching Woody Allen movies and listening to Bob Dylan CDs, playing cards and Scrabble. After Mom died, I found a "100 Things to Live For" list that Dad told me they worked on together during one of the roughest stretches. "More time with Jon" (my dad) was Mom's first entry. "Jessica's wedding" was number two.

I flew over to see her twice. One night, I stayed in with Mom while Ben and Dad went out to dinner. We were lying in bed watching a movie when she turned to me and said, "There are just so many things I want to tell you. I have so much I need to say to you. To all of you." She was crying.

"Mom, it's OK. You'll have time to tell us everything."

"I don't know. I just don't know. My dad died when I was sixteen. And I don't remember him. Of course, I remember what he looked like, but the details, his personality, who he was . . . I can't remember. I can't remember my own father! You guys, my children, you aren't going to be able to remember me." She was sniffling into a tissue.

I guess I expected it to be like in a movie. Music would swell and I'd be able to say to my mother all the things I had been meaning to say for so long. Tell her that I loved her, tell her everything that I admired her for, thank her for my life. But it was nothing like that. I held her hand silently, unable to speak. The only thing swelling was the lump in my throat, which choked off anything profound I might have said. I gathered myself together and made a pitiful attempt at a response: "Of course we'll remember you. But we won't have to. You're coming home."

But that wasn't to be. A few weeks later, although

her cancer was officially in remission, the treatment had so debilitated her that a slight infection turned into full-blown pneumonia overnight. Her body was too weak to fight it. Five months after they arrived, Dad and Ben flew back, and my mom went home in a box.

Sometimes I still can't believe how much my mother has missed, how much she doesn't know. She wasn't here to see Ben get into college, to witness George Bush elected president (twice!). She wasn't alive for September 11. She didn't get to vote for Obama. Even trivial things could give me pause. I'd be watching *American Idol* and all of a sudden the thought would appear in my mind: *Mom never knew what reality TV was.*

And Mom never knew who I had become, either. When she died, I was still in New York, working at a marketing firm and leading focus groups about Sunny Delight. Mom didn't know that I went on to graduate school or worked in Africa and Asia. The last time I saw her was in Israel, four months before the Second Intifada. Still, she warned me, "Don't go into East Jerusalem." My parents were cautious and didn't want me going anywhere that posed even the slightest risk. I obeyed them and stuck to Ben Yehuda Street and the Jewish neighborhoods.

When I returned to Israel this time, a UN administrator had similar words of advice: "Don't leave East Jerusalem, the Palestinian section. Eating or staying at a hotel in West Jerusalem is supporting the Occupation and we can't do that." It seemed like a silly distinction, and I'd heard from other aid workers that one of the chief consequences of the rule was that housing prices in the West Bank and Gaza had gone up, since there was now a new pool of wealthy aid workers looking for places to live, and some former residents were getting edged out of the market. Still, the instructions seemed apt, somehow—a mirror image of the ones my parents had issued so long ago, the other end of the yardstick measuring just how far I'd come in the years since. And although I could still remember my mother, I knew now she had been right that night she cried to me at the hospital, admitting that she couldn't remember her father and worrying we would forget her. Nine years later, the details were lost. I couldn't recall her voice or the subtlety of her movements. I still had a shirt of hers that I never washed because it smelled like her. I would open my drawer every so often to get a whiff of her, but even that smell was fading into a musty memory. My brothers and I watched home videos and looked through photo albums, and those helped a bit, but they were from when we were children. Mom never knew me as an adult.

When Dad visited me in Sierra Leone, we took a boat ride down a river near the coast. "I wish Mom was here," I had said to him then, and he had tapped me gently on my shoulder.

"I picture her sitting right here everywhere you go."

I thought of that now, as I walked the streets of Jerusalem, wanting to tell her how much I had changed in the past nine years, and all about what I had chosen to do and why. It was her death, after all, that had set me on the path to this career. I wished I could talk to her about what the work had been like and who it had made me. What idealism still remained within me and what had been chipped away. I wanted to talk to her about everywhere I had been, so she could imagine me there—imagine me living a life she never would have envisioned for me when she was alive.

But maybe Dad was right. Maybe she already knew.

I'm Headed to Haiti,
Where Are *You* Going?

HAITI, 2010

Haiti is a mystery for most Americans, despite being scarcely seven hundred miles from US shores. The American population has been historically apathetic toward its French-speaking neighbor on Hispaniola. Haiti sits directly in the center of a collection of other places that, in contrast to Haiti, are very familiar to

Americans: the legendary Communist island of Cuba, the magical fountain of baseball talent from the Dominican Republic, favorite vacation spots such as Turks and Caicos, Jamaica and the Bahamas, the famous international financial haven in the Cayman Islands, and America's own commonwealth of Puerto Rico. Incredibly, precisely in the geographical center of this collection of well-functioning Caribbean paradises lies the nation of Haiti, a nation of ten million people that has been dysfunctional longer than any other country in the New World.

With its long history of bloodshed, disease, oppression, and the ongoing poverty and disenfranchisement of its masses, one might think that the people of Haiti had served their penance for whatever imagined cosmic crime they had committed. Haitians deserved to turn the next chapter of their history, hopefully a chapter of growth and prosperity. At a minimum one would think that things couldn't, or at least shouldn't, get any worse for the Haitian people and that gradual progress must be made. But while few thought Haiti could be worse, almost none thought that it could ever be as bad as it became in the early days of 2010.

Little did I know it either, but I was about to be thrust back into the turmoil of an international disaster response.

On January 11, 2010, my cell phone rang. *Unknown Number.* I was busy and not particularly interested in hearing the canned ramblings of what I thought would be a faceless telemarketer, so I decided to wait until later to listen to the message.

When I got home that evening, I listened to a familiar voice crackling through the phone, and I was thrilled to hear it.

It was Charles, calling from Port-au-Prince, where he had been working for the past two years. It had been seven years since we last saw each other in Rwanda and almost a year since we had spoken over the phone. I loved his sense of humor, and as I listened to the voicemail a second time, I laughed out loud as he joked about me being married with kids after only two months of e-mail silence between us. He finished the message casually. "Just wanted to say hello to my favorite *muzungu.* Bye-bye!"

I had met plenty of people at postings over the years and many of them were special to me, but after our jobs ended we always lost touch, save for regular Facebook updates. Gradually our lives moved on and those friendships dwindled. But that was not the case with Charles; Charles never faded.

I was busy, so I didn't call back right away, and I went to bed that night without returning his message. I had a boyfriend in New York, Jack, with whom I now spent my evenings. We had gone to college together and became reacquainted at our tenth reunion. Meeting Jack was one of the best things about having come home. Charles could wait.

By 6 p.m. the next day news of the earthquake began trickling onto television screens and websites across the country. The initial headlines were benign: *"Earthquake Reported in Haiti," "Port-au-Prince Damaged by Earthquake," "Injuries Reported in Haitian Earthquake."*

The existing telecommunication structure had been wiped out, so details were sparse. I was aware of the news media's habit of crying wolf in situations like these, so I assumed things were probably OK and that I would be able to talk to Charles as soon as a few broken utility poles were repaired. But the headlines became more foreboding. And then I saw one that gave me chills: *"Earthquake Destroys Haitian Capital."*

I was beginning to get scared.

BY THE NEXT MORNING, all of the major American media outlets had invaded the streets of Port-au-Prince with their armies of production infantrymen and their cavalry of mobile broadcast vehicles. Instead of firing bullets and shells, they fired volleys of verbal and visual speculation that landed in the living rooms of disaster-obsessed consumers across the United States. The favorite blood sport of the media—predicting the number of casualties caused by a disaster—had transitioned seamlessly into its Blitzkrieg phase. Ten thousand dead. A hundred thousand dead. Three hundred thousand dead. Half a million. One million.

In fact, it was much too early to predict anything, especially while the city was in chaos, individuals were impossible to account for, and there was no way to know at that point how many people were trapped beneath rubble, how many had already died, and how many would soon be dead because they were not found in time. Others would be rescued only to die while waiting outside the overcrowded hospitals.

But I didn't care about any of that or the thousands or millions just yet. At that moment there was only one person who I was thinking about, and my mind was filled with terror.

Fixed in front of the television, I watched replays of buildings collapsing in waves and people running down the streets screaming, their bodies and faces streaked with blood and ash and mud. Reporters said that the UN building had collapsed. I knew there would be many UN buildings in Haiti. Was this the one that Charles worked at? Why hadn't I called him back earlier? Had he sensed something and called me to say good-bye? No, that was obviously impossible. But was it really impossible? Did he feel something? My mind was obsessed with these questions, and my heart was full of sadness and fear. I dialed Charles's number, compulsively, over and over again. There were no answers, only the disgusting heartlessness of electronic beeps, followed by the ghastly coldness of mechanical clicks. I pictured his phone under a pile of rubble, smothered by the roof, the walls, the furniture, and the bodies—everything that had collapsed in those thirty seconds. No signal would reach it. My stomach was sour. It was the first time someone I cared about was at the scene of a disaster when it struck. I wrote e-mails and sent texts, hoping somehow something might make its way through. I couldn't believe Charles was dead.

Finally, on January 15, three long days after the earthquake, a call: "It's a huge mess. You can't imagine. I'm not even sure what is going on." Charles's voice sounded strong, but tired.

"What do you need?" I pleaded. "Where are you sleeping? Is it as bad as it sounds? What can I do? Are you leaving? Can you get to New York? Are you safe? Please stay safe. Are there aftershocks? Where are people living?"

"I can't talk long, my dear. I'm fine. You would have felt pretty guilty, huh, if something had happened and you didn't call me back!" He was able to muster a joke. Charles was really fine.

"I will be staying. I've lost so many friends. People from work keep coming in missing a kid, a spouse. It's horrible. Horrible. It's worse than what you are seeing on TV."

For once, the reporters may not have been exaggerating.

The job offer came a few weeks later. I was in the middle of my first year in a PhD program and planned to be done with long missions in the field, at least for the next few years. My life in New York was finally starting to feel real: I was happy to be back and excited about my relationship with Jack, who worked in finance. I enjoyed spending time with someone who wasn't tied up by the knot of professional and social concerns I had been tangled in for so long. For some time I had suspected the threads would never come loose, but now they were, and I found that not only was there a world beyond aid but that I liked inhabiting it. When the earthquake happened, though, I remembered something a mentor had told me long ago: aid work isn't just a profession, it is a lifestyle. You never clock out of the field, or not really.

I told Jack, "I got a job."

"Great. What are you doing?" he asked.

"I'll be doing monitoring."

"Monitoring what?"

"The response."

"What response?"

"The Haiti response."

"From here?"

"No."

"You're going to Haiti?" Jack had become used to my peripatetic ways. In the months we had been dating, I had been to Kenya, Uganda, and Jordan for various weeklong consulting projects, and I could tell he assumed this was simply another one of those short trips. "For how long?"

"I don't know, six months?" I knew this was going to come as a shock. I had applied for the post secretly, telling myself I just wanted to see if I'd get the job, never expecting it would come through so soon. But when it did, the same reflex kicked in. I felt a familiar tug in my stomach, and I realized how badly I wanted to go.

"Six months!?" He sighed. If we were going to stay together, these surprises were something he'd have to adjust to somehow, and I could tell he was trying. We hadn't been dating long enough for him to put his foot down and demand I stay. But the relationship was meaningful enough that one of us leaving for a foreign country wasn't something that we could take lightly, either. At least *I* didn't take it lightly.

But my resolve was clear. Watching the response unfold on television, I knew, after having seen the aftermath of similar situations, that whatever the final death toll was it was more than just a figure. It was people—people with families and friends, people who were loved. People like Charles, who could have been a number but wasn't. He was still Charles—and I was so grateful.

Part of me, though, didn't think that going off to Haiti was jeopardizing anything at all. In my mind, I could justify my decision easily. Haiti was close; I was only going for a few months; it was a good job; and Jack and I worked out a plan to see each other every three weeks. Unlike Darfur or Sierra Leone or anywhere in Asia, where the journey home was a grueling global marathon, the flight from Haiti to New York was an easy three hours or so. I could eat lunch in Port-au-Prince and dinner in SoHo, if I wanted. If this hadn't been possible, I wouldn't have gone. I thought I could have one foot in my professional life and one foot in my personal, and maintain good standing in both. And I promised myself that if things started to fall apart with Jack, I'd quit.

When I look back now, my actions do seem reckless. The thought that I could move fluidly between worlds was ridiculous. I had everything that I had imagined wanting from afar: a boyfriend, a sunny apartment, a life with some steady direction. Convincing myself that I could assuage the tug to follow another disaster while also maintaining a normal life at home was foolish. Sheer adrenaline was what was pulling me to Haiti— the addictive rush of being part of a major response. I loved that my career was intertwined with the most urgent events in the world. Sitting around in New York, I felt like a football player on the disabled list, watching the game unfold in front of me, but not being able to get off the bench. All my other jobs now felt like practice runs. In Haiti, I'd be in a position of seniority, with the chance to contribute more than I ever had before. So when I got the call, how could I refuse? This disaster was bigger than my nice life in New York; the allure was too powerful to ignore, and its force helped me rationalize my decision, as I persuaded myself I could have both the job and the relationship.

❖

When I arrived in Port-au-Prince that winter, I had never seen anything like it. Iron rods jutted out from slabs of concrete like broken bones—looking at them you'd think, *I was never supposed to see that*. Facades had been ripped off buildings, exposing the insides, and concrete walls were shot through with cracks. If a building was clearly beyond repair, it was demolished, and every day more of the town came down, as people slowly chipped away at the places they once called home.

And these chips added up. My first morning on the streets, I stared out the window of the van transporting me and the rest of the staff to our office. They had done this trip for a few weeks now and sat silently with their laptops open, somehow managing to type as we bumped along the rubble-filled streets. Meagan, the young red-haired British nutritionist who had been there since day two of the quake, looked up from her spreadsheet and saw the expression on my face. In the understated way that only a Brit can pull off, she nodded slowly and said, "Yeah, it's a bit shit, isn't it?"

I nodded back, unable to imagine a force powerful enough to cause all this damage. With just a thirty-second flick of its tail, *le grand serpent* (the great snake, as Haitians called it) brought down schools and homes, crushing classrooms and entire families. More than 220,000 people were killed and approximately 180,000 homes were wrecked, leaving 1.5 million Haitians homeless. Close to four thousand of the roughly five thousand schools affected by the earthquake were leveled completely. January 12, 2010 would be a turning point for the nation: now people referred to events in Haiti's history as having taken place "before"—or "after."

The damage caused by the earthquake, however, was not merely the consequence of its magnitude, which measured 7.0 on the Richter scale. The 8.8 magnitude earthquake that hit Chile in February 2010 was significantly less destructive, despite being *five hundred times stronger* than the Haitian quake. So why was the earthquake in Haiti so much more devastating?

One answer was that the fault line ran directly beneath Port-au-Prince, which was vastly overcrowded and teeming with poorly built structures. There was almost a complete absence of building codes and regulations. Construction companies forewent expensive materials such as rebar, the steel bars used to reinforce concrete. And the concrete itself was cheap, made from salinated sand in the hills. In order to get more for their money, builders also added too much water to the cement mixture, which meant it didn't actually bond.

After the quake, more than half a million of Port-au-Prince's two million residents skipped town to live with family members in rural areas. The rest pitched tent camps all over Port-au-Prince, until it seemed as if every stretch of open land—parks, parking lots, even the dividers down the main highway—were patched in plastic sheeting.

And when the rainy season started, there wasn't much more than a few flimsy plastic sheets, tattooed with humanitarian logos, already muddy and frayed, between people and the tropical storms. Gutters turned to whirlpools and roads became gray foaming rivers. Bodies stood stiff against walls, staring stoically outward at the road, trying to stay dry under over-hangs. When people had to duck out into a downpour, they wore shower caps or held plastic bags over their heads. People moved a tire, a piece of concrete rubble, a bundle of wood: anything sizable enough to obstruct or divert the water rushing down from the hills and keep it from getting under the tents was repurposed as a makeshift dam. But still the brackish water managed to seep into everything. The stench, like the rain, was relentless. Mothers told us that some nights they held their sleeping children in their arms to protect them from the inescapable wetness.

"I'd rather be dead than living like this in five years," a woman said to me one day, when I visited a camp. "When I am deeply thinking about life, I ask for death because I find there is no hope for my chil-dren," she added, brushing away tears as her young son peeked out from behind her legs. "Life does not have sense for me anymore." The earthquake had stripped her of everything she'd relied on. Her child's school collapsed. Her house crumbled. Her husband died. She used to sell sweets in a local market but the market had fallen apart and her supply dried up. "Neither in two nor in five years, I do not know where I will be; only God knows. I need a way to survive with my children so that they can be something in the future." Once again, just like Darfur or Aceh, Port-au-Prince was a giant puzzle to solve, the ultimate professional challenge. And the people were truly desperate for help.

❖

I was in charge of monitoring the agency's response in the seven sectors we covered: health, nutrition, water and sanitation, child protection, education, shelter, and food. While people at home were writing me e-mails that said "The work you do is incredible" or "You're an inspiration to us all," I was doing what people in offices everywhere did: I sat behind a desk and stared at a computer. My first weeks in Haiti were spent squinting at spreadsheets that listed the number of jerry cans distributed in Delmas 31 Camp and the number of tarpaulins handed out at Gaston Margon Camp. I questioned the contents of the hygiene kits we delivered. I sorted through requisition forms when the number of blankets didn't add up.

"Were these the hygiene kits with the toothbrushes donated by the Brits or the sanitary pads from the Danish?"

"Were these bales of blankets or individual blankets received? How many blankets are even in a bale?"

"Are these the drugs that came through Miami or Santo Domingo?"

"I don't know. I got here two weeks ago," was the usual response. Staff turnover in a place like Haiti was high.

I spent at least a few hours every day in a fugue of frustration. I didn't know what people saw when they imagined me at work, but surely they didn't picture a glorified bean counter, which is what I felt like most of the time. Regardless, being there and being able to respond and help organize this massive effort was worthwhile. I knew that the tents we distributed, the food that was handed out from our warehouses, and the water we trucked into camps were providing some relief to that woman I met in the camp and the over one million homeless people just like her. They may have been rudimentary, but the temporary schools we built helped keep children in school and may have attracted others who weren't in school before the earthquake. Our nutrition services gave support to lactating mothers and their newborns. People who had never seen a doctor before were now able to visit our clinics and receive treatment. It was basic, and it was messy, but it was *there*, and people were grateful.

Now in a position of relative seniority, I was able to guide strategic planning within our organization and meet with directors of other organizations to devise plans to improve the overall humanitarian response. Donations of millions of dollars came in every day, and part of my role was to help determine how that would be spent and make sure our programs were of high quality. It may have taken time, it may have required patience and perseverance, but I was part of a chain that made progress. Just knowing that was rewarding enough.

❖

Given that my curfew was 6:30 p.m. and his 7:00, and that both of our days were consumed by work, Charles and I still had not been able to arrange a time to see each other. We spoke on the phone regularly, but that we could be living in the same city after all these years and not see each other was unbelievable—and unacceptable. Finally, after three weeks of trying to make plans, I told him just to meet me by my compound after work one afternoon. The plan lacked a certain ceremony, but if I got to see Charles, that would be enough.

I waited for him outside the compound gates in an impatient sweat, checking my watch over and over again. Fifteen minutes after he was supposed to arrive, I called him. He didn't even say hello.

"I know, my dear. I know. I know. You're a very

busy *muzungu* lady now. I'm stuck in traffic five minutes away. These guys don't know how to drive."

I laughed. It was the same old Charles.

I'd only just pocketed my phone when a white Land Cruiser turned the corner and came racing toward me, its lights blinking and horn honking. Charles rolled down the window and waved.

"Look at my favorite *muzungu*!" he shouted out the window as the car sped past me toward the parking lot.

I ran over to his car and he opened the door. We embraced.

"Look at you!" he said, standing back, holding my shoulders. "You're a grown-up lady now!" When I met Charles in Rwanda, I was a twenty-five-year-old intern. Now I was thirty-two and a "Senior Specialist," at least according to my job title.

"You look exactly the same!" I said.

"Ha, my dear. You should see these gray hairs I have. Here, get in the car out of this heat." He guided me into the car and turned the air-conditioning up as high as it would go.

"So, how are you?"

"I'm good! I'm . . . My God, it's been so long!" There was just too much to say.

"It has."

"So, are you married by now?" he asked, pulling my left hand to see if I was wearing a ring.

"No, not married," I said. "But I do have a boyfriend in New York."

"That is very good, my dear." He was being genuine.

Charles was married now, with children back in Rwanda. For the past two years, he had been living and working in Haiti, where he was earning quite a bit of money. In Rwanda Charles had been a local employee, but here he was an expat, which meant a significantly higher salary in addition to the daily allowances for food and housing that agencies provided to foreign workers. So although Charles could now afford to send his children to the best schools, he couldn't see them more than a few times a year.

"Don't you miss them?" I asked.

"Yes, but this is life," he said, shrugging his shoulders. "And anyway, with that Skype business these days, I see them more than I would if I were at home. You know, at home they would be playing with their friends and have no time for Dad. Now we sit and chat for an hour every night."

"They must have freaked out when the earthquake happened."

"They thought I was dead. And I couldn't get through for so long." He looked down. Then back at me. "It was horrible. I was on the phone and it all started shaking. People were screaming. It was so hard to run, but everyone in my office got outside. There wasn't much damage to my building. I went home and found that the wall to my bedroom had caved in. No one slept that night. Or for nights after that. Everyone was too afraid to get under a roof. Even now I'm still afraid."

He continued, "But the next morning, that was the

worst. That was when we realized who hadn't made it. On the UN radios they kept calling out the names of people they found dead under the rubble. I heard colleagues crying with every name that was called. I knew a lot of them. I just sat there outside the office, listening. One woman I had gotten into an argument with the day before. She was walking into her office when the building collapsed on top of her."

His phone rang.

"Look, my dear, I have to go. I'm supposed to be off panicking somewhere about something." He turned to me. "How long are you here for?"

"I don't know. Six months?"

He laughed. "You think this shit will be picked up after a few months?" he said, motioning to the rubble all around us.

"No. But I can't really stay longer."

"Yeah, yeah, your boyfriend will be upset. I know." He slapped my thigh. "So, when can I see you again?" We made plans to meet for lunch that weekend.

❖

Charles was right. The rubble would not be cleared in six months. An estimated 19 million cubic meters of debris clogged Port-au-Prince—enough, some said, to fill a line of shipping containers stretching end to end from London to Beirut. To start the process and get cash in people's hands, many NGOs hired teams of day laborers, who were given rubber boots, shovels, wheelbarrows, and hard hats, and assigned areas to clear. They dumped the rubble into the backs of massive pickup trucks that the government was in charge of taking away. Often the trucks never showed up, so they left the rubble in enormous piles on the sides of roads. Eventually, we had to change our route to the office because when it rained there was risk of a landslide.

Since getting big machines such as jackhammers and Caterpillar loaders up many of the narrow streets was nearly impossible, the day laborers dug the city out by hand, tossing one brick at a time down the steep hills. In a handful of areas where the ground was more level, the big trucks could pass, but when one agency brought in heavy machinery, some day laborers protested. In a city with widespread unemployment and underemployment, rubble clearing guaranteed people an income for months, maybe years. To stretch the work out as long as they could, some laborers craftily cleared rubble from one area and slowly dumped it in another, where a different agency would then hire them to move it out of that neighborhood—and so on, and so on. It was an *ouroboros* of rubble, a whirlpool of trash spiraling around us—but nobody even noticed. Yet the image of all that rubble, moving endlessly around the city, struck me as a bad omen. The universe couldn't have made itself clearer if it tried: we thought we were making progress in Haiti, but really we were just going in circles.

"HAITI WAS AN EMERGENCY BEFORE the emergency," my Haitian colleague told me one afternoon over lunch at our office. We were sitting at his desk, looking at a report citing Haitian human development indicators. In every major category—education, health, and living standards—Haiti ranked the worst of any country in the Western Hemisphere. In short, 80 percent of the population lived below the poverty threshold and only 50 percent of children were enrolled in school. Almost half the population had no access to basic health care or potable water. The country had been plagued by political instability and associated violence and civil unrest for so long that the UN peacekeeping force had been stationed there since 1993, and in 2012 the worldwide corruption perceptions index placed Haiti as the 165th most corrupt country out of 176. Corruption was so endemic in Haiti that they used New York lotto numbers because if the Haitian government ran the lotto, no one would believe that it wasn't rigged. Given these preexisting conditions, we had to ask ourselves: What, exactly, did "building back better" look like? If we helped increase school attendance by 10 percent, was that success? How much did we expect from ourselves here, and were those expectations reasonable or insane?

In crisis situations, the immediate response was emergency relief, which eventually gave way to long-term development planning. The boundary between emergency aid and development aid was always a little fuzzy. But two goals we all worked toward were strengthening the ability of people to meet their own needs, and helping them develop the capacity to withstand future shocks on their own. In Haiti, however, many of us wondered: How long could an emergency response last before it became routine? When did living in the aftermath of a disaster turn into simply living? Agencies provided free water to people living in the camps, but it didn't come cheap to us; the water had to be trucked in, since it wasn't feasible to start drilling boreholes throughout the middle of a crowded city. Just getting rid of human feces was also a huge cost to agencies. Much of the excreta was disposed via emergency latrines and had to be desludged daily. This was by no means a sustainable solution, but in the short term we had no other option. We wanted to divert our support to relocation sites, but since they were still undetermined, these expensive but necessary interventions had to continue. But many people openly went to the bathroom all over Port-au-Prince—we used to make bets on the way to work about how many people we'd see peeing on the side of the road. The "flying toilet"—shitting in a plastic bag and throwing it anywhere, in a ditch, in the air, on the side of the street, a method commonly used in Africa—was widespread.

Some of the ongoing crises were predictable, but no one was attacking the root causes. The hurricane season, for example, came every year and always caused mass destruction and flooding. Port-au-Prince had canals that were supposed to evacuate the excess water.

But because there wasn't a regular garbage disposal system, people threw their trash in the canals, creating enormous mounds where you'd see fat pigs literally rolling in piles of shit. Every year agencies cleared out the canals in anticipation of the heavy rains. But what Haiti really needed was a sustainable trash collection system, so that these Band-Aid solutions wouldn't have to be repeated year in and year out. But rebuilding water, septic, and garbage collection systems in a capital city that had been functioning poorly even before the earthquake wasn't going to happen overnight. Meaningful change—rebuilding the house from the ground up—took much more time. And it took cooperation and leadership from the government, the same government that had been ill-equipped to deal with the country's struggles even before disaster hit.

"The UN should just run this country," my boss declared. "This is ridiculous." An older Danish man in charge of the emergency programming, he was furious after coming out of another fruitless meeting. Thousands of people were living in makeshift tents, and the government was supposed to find somewhere for them to resettle. But no site had been selected, and nobody knew how long it would be until one was. At times we questioned whether the government was working with us or exploiting us. Our agency had new cars, for instance, which arrived safely in the port but, for reasons that remained less than clear, could not be properly registered and, therefore, had to be impounded. In the meantime, we spent more than $100,000 a month to rent vehicles. People speculated that the government was taking kickbacks from the car rental companies. As long as our vehicles were stuck in the ports, everyone profited off our inconvenience. "Giving the government money," my boss said, sighing, "is like putting Dracula in charge of a blood bank."

❖

There were moments in Haiti, moments of hard work and dedication that I will never forget: a colleague coming out of a coordination meeting collapsing onto a plastic chair, lighting a cigarette as if in a trance, and slowly smoking it while debris—dust and tattered plastic bags—blew behind him; a health worker putting her hands on her hips and pausing to catch her breath before returning to the line of patients that snaked outside the clinic gates; the face of a seething logistics manager who arrived at a locked warehouse to find that the contingency stock of nutritional supplies had been stolen; the head-in-hands frustration of an education officer who learned that five of her tented temporary schools had collapsed overnight in a rainstorm. Some of us worked fourteen, sixteen, eighteen hours a day, seven days a week, and although it could be hard to see, the work was making a difference. In some places, a child who had been getting zero meals a day now received two. Pregnant women could get stronger and healthier. A girl who was once a *restavek*—a form of domestic child labor in Haiti, which some UN officials have deemed "a modern form of slavery"—enrolled in a school we rebuilt and had now risen to the top of her class. Simply knowing how to read could save a child's life the next time there was a disaster, and our education programs did just that. "It's massively frustrating," Margaret, a Canadian woman my age in charge of programs for children, stated one night after returning from a visit to a completed child-friendly space that she had worked months to set up. "But then you go meet those kids, and you're like—that's amazing. And it makes it all worthwhile."

I think we all came to Haiti thinking there would be more moments of gratification like that, that there would be clearer connections between our efforts and improvements. But a lot of times we took one step forward and then—*bam*!—the unexpected would happen and we'd take a leap back.

Take the schools we rebuilt. Tom, our cheerful British construction manager, worked tirelessly for months to rebuild a school in Port-au-Prince. Tom was careful to design the one-story school to code, with reinforced wood paneling and a solid foundation made of high-quality concrete. He never thought that as soon as he handed over the keys—the day after a big ceremony where the children sang and the senior staff gathered to take pictures—that the headmaster would strip the roof and begin constructing a second floor. It was a private school—80–90 percent of schools in Haiti are—

and the more children who enroll, the more money the headmaster makes. A second story would double the number of students and, therefore, the headmaster's income. But if there were another earthquake, the foundation wouldn't support the additional height and the school would collapse. Tom removed the agency plaque from the school wall.

Wellness staff tried to help us manage stress by giving us cards listing the signs of burnout. Excessive drinking? Check. Exhaustion? Check. Short temper? Check. The burnout we were experiencing certainly wasn't going to be identified on laminated wallet-sized checklists or be treated by lavender oil and antitrauma body spray, which they also generously doled out. Signs placed around the office ordered us to "Take care of YOU!" Although we may not have been taking care of ourselves, Haitians were taking care of themselves, visibly and busily getting back to the business of daily life. They called their country *"Ayiti Cherie"*—My Dear Haiti—and as one of our young colleagues told me: "We know that the world thinks our country is a mess. But we still have pride." And they flaunted this pride: colorful art markets returned to the streets, where painters strung their art along the sides of roads, and loud Haitian kompa music wafted from bars and clubs. The vibrant Creole scene was alive and couldn't be buried under all that concrete and pain. While we the expats were busy stressing, smoking, and swearing, our local colleagues ate their lunch on benches with friends. They took time to tell a joke, laugh. It wasn't because they weren't working just as hard as we were, but because they chose to celebrate being alive. "By the grace of God, we survived," one said.

Moments like these left me humbled. A friend of mine once went to a shelter distribution where his driver recognized one of the beneficiaries standing in line, a tall, slender man with a carefully groomed beard. The driver stopped the car in the middle of the road, got out, and ran over to hug him. The bearded man turned around and, realizing who had greeted him so enthusiastically, bent over with laughter. They embraced for a while. Our driver later informed us that Groomed Beard was an old school friend. Each thought the other had died.

Every day I drove past a pancaked five-story building, next to which a woman had built a small shack made of a piece of tarpaulin draped over corrugated metal. The shack leaned to the side, and its open front could barely protect the occupants from even a light rain, but it provided the illusion of shelter, which was enough to comfort many Haitians at that time. Inside, the plump woman had placed two folding chairs, one of which she sat in and the other of which was always empty. Beside the chairs were small cardboard boxes, which she used as tables, on which she placed an array of colorful hair combs. Above the open door she had placed a hand-painted sign that said BEAUTY PARLOR.

Other people were busy clearing the rubble near

their homes. They didn't have much to work with, but they were resolved to get the job done with whatever instruments they could find—sometimes removing rubble using rubble itself. I saw one man using a ripped piece of corrugated metal to push large chunks of gravel away from his home like a snow shovel, while another man used pieces of shattered wood to pry up slabs of concrete just enough to get his hands under. I even saw one man digging out his home with a large soupspoon that he had found in the heap. They had a look of determination, all of them, and instead of being bitter, they had compassion for others in similar situations. When the Pakistan floods ripped through the spine of that country later that summer, I passed walls of graffiti written by Haitians: "Pakistan needs help."

BUT HAITI STILL NEEDED HELP, too. We learned that cholera was stirring in the central plateau just 100 kilometers from Port-au-Prince. It was a vicious disease whose victims died from dehydration, caused by severe and unrelenting diarrhea and vomiting. Health practitioners started preparing rehydration salts, telling communities how to prevent and detect the disease, and making beds with strategically located holes, under which they'd put buckets to collect the mess. Nurses drew lines across the buckets which measured the amount of liquid waste so that they knew how much the person lost and how much they had to replenish him with.

Back at our residence, a few colleagues sat on the stoop under the hazy moonlight, the buzz of the generator gently lulling in the background, fearing the what-ifs. Would cholera make its way to the capital? Could Port-au-Prince handle a disaster on top of the disaster? Marie, our resident house doctor, remembered her work in Goma, Democratic Republic of the Congo (then Zaire) in the mid-1990s when cholera stole the lives of tens of thousands of people in what seemed like an instant. "It's the easiest thing to cure—if you get there in time," she said. With cholera, prevention is everything, and the tragedy was just how simple it would have been to prevent. "Soap and clean water. That's it. None of this wipe-your-hands stuff (she was referring to hand sanitizer) or Dettol. No, no, no." We sat quietly as cigarette smoke drifted above our wineglasses, and the cat chased a cockroach. "If you get to them in time, it's just about rehydrating. An IV in this arm and an IV in that one," she said, hitting the inside of her arm at the elbow like a junkie. "And if it's really bad, then you stick them behind the knees, too," she added. In the end, cholera did arrive in Port-au-Prince, and by May of 2013 over 650,000 cases and 8,000 deaths had been reported. (The cholera strain was found to have been introduced to Haiti by UN Nepalese soldiers who arrived to assist the earthquake recovery efforts. The UN has come under considerable criticism for denying compensation for cholera victims.) But the work that Marie and other health workers like her did to educate children about washing and to teach mothers about clean water helped prevent what could have been a crisis of even vaster—and graver—proportions.

❖

But not everyone was committed to doing the heavy lifting required to make a substantive difference in people's lives. "Look at those people," a colleague said to me one day when we were out in Port-au-Prince, pointing to a group of Americans wearing matching blue shirts and crisp khaki pants, cameras hanging from their necks and inexperience dripping from their sweaty faces. "If we want to get it right, we need to stop encouraging every volunteer out there who can pick up a shovel and throw some rocks on the back of a truck to come down here. If it were you and your family, would you want amateurs coming and just using their whims to determine how to respond? I mean, it's like giving people shotguns and sending them to Afghanistan to fight the war."

In other emergencies, various travel constraints—visa restrictions, the cost of the plane ticket, the length of the flight, the fact said flight would end with them landing in the middle of a war zone—combined to dissuade most would-be humanitarians from just dropping in. Haiti, however, was only a one-hour flight from Miami and did not require an entrance visa, which made it an ideal destination for people who wanted to come "help out" for a week. We'd see flocks of Americans sporting shirts commemorating the trip they were currently on. The Haitians knew the groups were there to help clean up, and presumably the groups themselves knew why they were there, so the brightly colored billboard T-shirts were only there to remind the weekend warrior do-gooders and their friends what great people they were.

Their chests would proclaim: *"Haiti Relief 2010: June 16–22"* or *"Haiti Project Spring Break 2010."* Most were worn by missionary groups: *"Forward Edge International: Ordinary People, Extraordinary Purpose," "World Hope International: Making Disciples of All Nations," "Southwest Haiti Christian Mission: Rescue, Restore, Redeem," "Angel Missions: Relief, Recovery, Rebirth," "Love Haiti Missions: Keeping Hope Alive," "Southern Baptist Mission: Raising Children from Poverty with Compassion in Jesus' Name."* And last but not least: *"Church of the Brethren: I'm Headed to Haiti, Where Are You Going?"*

Meanwhile, the Vegan Food Relief Team had matching baseball caps, while the Scientologists favored identical orange ponchos. No matter what their members wore, every group's agenda was always the same: they cleared some rubble, said a few prayers (except for the vegans), took a lot of pictures, and left.

If their shirts weren't brazen enough, their conversations were. On one of my flights back from New York, I was joined by a bunch of firefighters. After the

baggage carousel in the Port-au-Prince airport stalled
for a third time, some of the firemen started to get rest-
less. The group leader admonished them: "I told you
guys, it's like a fourth-world country down here! You
gotta just be patient!" Standing directly to his left were
several Haitians, who understood him perfectly well.

A few weeks later I was on a field mission in Jac-
mel, a lazy seaside town about three hours from Port-
au-Prince. Two vacationing American teenagers who
were staying at my hotel struck up conversation with
me. The best part of their trip, they agreed, had been
the orphanage and playing with some of the children.
The orphanage was a tourist stop for these boys, who
now sat on hammocks by the beach drinking Prestige,
the local beer. For them, going and giving out candy to
kids hadn't just felt normal—like handing out pellets
to goats when you're at a petting zoo—it felt *noble*.
But while these boys may have thought they were doing
good, putting smiles on the faces of children, and creating "lasting bonds," I imagined the kids they had left
behind, who had to interact with and potentially form
attachments to the stampedes of foreigners that rolled
through the orphanages every day.

"Real" aid workers hated these folks. We called their
trips "hug vacations." "They're on spring break! This
trip is for them, not for Haitians! Let's be clear, they're
the beneficiaries of this whole thing. They're here to
have a story when they go home, to feel good about
themselves," complained one aid worker. "Seriously,"
bemoaned another, "all you need is a good heart and a

Bible and you can get away with anything these days."
Another friend told us about a group she knew of in
Cambodia. "There are tour operators who you can pay
to go on a tour and hand out food to 'poor people.'"
We all turned to look at her. "No," she protested, see-
ing our incredulous expressions. "I'm *serious!*"

One afternoon I arrived at a camp clinic to check on
our infant feeding program and saw a bunch of these
tourists wandering around, shaking their heads in dis-
belief. They photographed everything, especially children; whenever some kids were spotted, the whole set
would take turns posing with them. They looked like
a tour group at the Grand Canyon—or Disneyland.
I was surprised there wasn't a coach bus waiting for
them outside the camp.

"Hey, Claude." I turned to my driver. "Can we actually go back?"

Claude looked at me, confused.

"You forgot something?"

"No, I just can't be here with this going on," I said,
pointing to a group of white women holding babies and
taking photos of themselves with them.

Claude smiled. I wondered what he thought of this
spectacle. Of all of these people—myself included—
stomping through his country, there to "make a difference." To Claude and to the rest of the Haitians, I was
probably just another white face among the thousands
of do-gooders, no different from any of the other disaster tourists. Revulsion clenched my stomach whenever
I thought of the people I saw at the camp, and yet still I

knew I recognized myself in them. Perhaps my motives
for coming here weren't so different from theirs. These
church groups wanted to *see* Haiti, wanted to touch
it—wanted, in other words, to be part of an extraordinary experience. But so did a lot of the people I worked
with, who updated their Facebook statuses every two
minutes in order to keep everyone they had ever met
apprised of their latest activities in Haiti. Why should
Claude have been able to distinguish me from them, or
from anyone else working there?

❖

As they did in every emergency, organizations in Haiti
competed with each other for funding from big gov-
ernmental donors. Agencies—mine included—needed
these multimillion-dollar grants in order to carry out
their projects. But watching these contests play out in
real time was like moving from the nosebleed seats to
the orchestra: for the first time, I could see what this ma-
neuvering actually entailed, and it struck me as crude
and shameless. As field workers scrambled to hand
out tents and provide water and rebuild schools, staff
from headquarters in the United States and the United
Kingdom flew in to take pictures and cherry-pick details for the profiles they would write about the people
we helped, which would be featured in press releases
and websites. Once, someone from the PR/Marketing

team asked a program officer if he could put Christmas lights on the tents in a camp where he was shooting a promotional video. "We know it's not Christmastime now, but the video will be airing at Christmas, and we think it would have a better impact," the producer said.

"First of all, there's no electricity in the camps," the program officer told him. "And anyway, you can't string lights up on people's tents and take their photos like they're props."

That much was obvious, but the argument went that if the video tugged at heartstrings at Christmastime, more people would donate money, and that money could then be directed back to those people living in the camps. Celebrities were also part of the equation, as a single photograph in *People* could boost donations significantly. But celebrity visits took work, since whole teams had to rearrange their schedules to be available to fulfill requests from the visiting luminary on a moment's notice: What is the make and model of the helicopter we'll be using? Can you accommodate vegetarians? Do the vehicle and hotel have air-conditioning? Can someone who speaks English drive with us to the Dominican Republic and explain the sights?

"Demi Moore makes a statement about vulnerable children in Haiti and I have to spend half my day responding to her in the press?" fumed one of my colleagues, who had been conscripted to manage the fallout from a *New York Times* article that criticized our organization for not doing enough to support vulnerable children. He was furious. "What the fuck do you know about vulnerable children, Demi Moore? Go back to Hollywood!" Some journalists were no better. One photographer asked a bunch of children to sit in a partially collapsed school so he could take pictures whose message would be impossible to mistake: look how eager Haitian children were to return to their educations! When the child protection team heard about this, they forbade the photographers from working with their programs again.

The fundraising worked exactly like a business except in one critical way. Because Haitians weren't paying for what they received, their requests and opinions were rarely taken into account. Although Haitians were the "consumers" of the aid industry's "product," agencies didn't rely on them for their own institutional survival. Only the donors could put an aid organization out of business by refusing to fund it. In a typical free market relationship, consumers have a choice of goods. If you don't like Crest, you'll choose Colgate. If enough people choose Colgate, Crest will either go out of business or adapt to the demands of the marketplace. But in the world of aid, the "customers" don't choose what kind of soap they receive or the quality of the tarpaulins that are distributed. And they don't decide when these things arrive—or if they arrive at all. In almost any other circumstance, businesses couldn't survive if their end users repeatedly criticized their products. No company that wants to stay in business would conceive of not asking its customers how they were experiencing their product.

But in aid, that's exactly what we did. "It's basically a take-it-or-leave-it relationship," an older female colleague once told me. "There's no situation where the power between two groups is more lopsided. Except," she added carefully, "maybe prison."

Later, on another mission, I would meet a woman who told me how she handled the imbalance. As an individual, she felt powerless to change the backward dynamics that made the overwhelming pressure to answer to donors and the media more acute than ensuring quality services to the people who needed them. When the bureaucracy felt more pressing than the work, when reporting to headquarters was prioritized over going to the field, when she was scolded for not cc'ing people in the right order on e-mails—those were the times, she said, that she looked at a photograph she kept on her desk of a child she had met on a field mission. "I look at that picture," she told me, "and I think: *This is my boss.*"

❖

Seeing Charles in Haiti was like opening a time capsule that I had buried years ago in Rwanda. He reminded me of the person I had been in those days: idealistic and energetic, intent on making things better and undaunted by the work that would require. It was exactly that enthusiasm—and that patience—that had made me good at my job. I had been in Haiti a few months when Jenna, a young blonde woman, was hired to work on PR. A bubbly Canadian, she had only just completed graduate school, and this was her first field mission: Haiti was where she'd cut her teeth. I introduced myself and asked how long she would be in Haiti. She smiled and said, "One year."

A year was a long time, longer than Jenna probably realized. I had been that naive once, too—we all had—and now I was treating her as I felt I'd been treated in Rwanda, when I sat alone in my room wishing somebody would be my friend, or at least talk to me. I should have been kind and welcoming to Jenna, but I wasn't. I was tired and worn out, and I couldn't muster the energy to show her the ropes. She would figure the job out for herself, just as we all had.

Still, I was glad that Jenna was there—people on their first field postings brought a certain kind of urgency to the work. The shock of what Jenna was seeing allowed her to challenge people who had already seen it all and had become complacent and burned out. New people, even if they were young, provided a foil to our cynicism.

Meanwhile, after six months away, my phone conversations with Jack were starting to grow tense. The

longer I was in Haiti, the harder it was for us to communicate with each other, and the clearer it became
that the situation was unsustainable. Before I left, I
had promised Jack—and myself—that I could success-
fully inhabit two worlds at once, living a life in Haiti
while maintaining the one I'd left behind in New York.
But that had been wishful thinking. Not only was three
weeks a long time to go without seeing each other, but
our everyday realities couldn't have been more different. I'd often text him from a chaotic food distribution
where people were on the verge of rioting, pushing
each other up against barbed-wire fences, while others
were collapsing in the sweltering Caribbean heat. Picking their way through this chaos would be uniformed
MINUSTAH soldiers, assigned to patrol the crowds.
I tried to picture Jack receiving these texts: he would
be at a board meeting, wearing a tailored suit and sitting around a polished table with a bunch of other
white men in equally nice suits. I imagined platefuls
of bagels and pastries, trays stacked high with fresh
fruit, thick carpeting, and unobstructed views of the
Hudson River. New York was only a three-hour flight
from Haiti, which sounded close enough, on paper. In
reality, leaving one city and arriving in the other felt
like traveling to another planet—and Jack and I were
worlds apart.

After six months in Haiti, I realized our one-year
anniversary was approaching, so I came home to spend
a weekend with Jack. We drove up to Lenox, Massa-
chusetts, near Tanglewood, to spend the night.

"It's been a year, I can't believe it!" I said, toasting him.

"Well, it hasn't really been a year."

"What do you mean?" I had been of the opinion that I had a boyfriend who I had been with for a year.

"Jess, you've been away for six months of it. The relationship's stalled. We're not where a couple who has been dating for a year would be."

I had taken time for granted: a year was a year, I told myself, the same no matter how you spent it. The months I was in Haiti I was also in a serious relationship—or so I had been able to delude myself. I knew I didn't want to end up as one of the Sheilas of the aid world, so I had convinced myself I could have both a career abroad and a stable relationship at home. But that equation became harder to understand. And now it was clear: one of the two had to give.

❖

Charles met me at the airport and before I got on the plane we hugged for a long time. Charles would stay in Haiti as long as he could—he knew that the benefits he reaped as an international aid worker were worth holding on to. I thought that in another time, another life, things maybe could have worked out differently for us.

"Bye," I said softly, as we pulled away from each other.

"Good-bye, my dear," he said.

"Do you remember promising you would see me again when you left me at the airport in Kigali?"

"I do."

"Can you make that promise again? Please?" I didn't want to let go of Charles again. I wanted him in my life.

He laughed. "I will see you again. Of course, I will."

Epilogue
2013

It's now been three years since I left Haiti and I'm living in New York. When I got back, I picked up my PhD right where I had left it. I also began teaching courses on humanitarianism at three New York City universities and consulting for various humanitarian organizations. Aid is still my profession, but my role is different. For now, having a home base feels satisfying. It's not the same thing as living in the field, but it allows me to contribute on my terms.

And I still travel. I led program evaluations in Pakistan after the floods of 2010, and in Ethiopia and Kenya after the severe drought in 2012. These trips, even though they only lasted a few weeks, allowed me to touch the field and stay connected to new trends in humanitarianism. But now, instead of unpacking my bags and digging in for months at a time I can return home and wake up in my own apartment and get coffee in a city I know. It's a compromise I can live with. Friendships aren't interrupted every few months, romances don't die over Skype, and family problems can be squabbled about over turkey and stuffing rather than summarized over a hopeless phone connection. These things matter more to me now.

Yet, I didn't say good-bye to Haiti for good. I go back every year around the anniversary of the earthquake, and spend a week helping write the annual report for the office in Port-au-Prince. When I returned in early 2013, much of the agency's emergency programming was coming to an end, and our field offices were shutting down. Most of the 1.5 million people who had flocked to tent camps in and around the city had been relocated to more permanent housing.

But in Haiti, where for years the government was characterized by corruption and general inefficiency, circumstances tend to be difficult, and difficult circumstances bred difficult choices. Take the cholera treatment center the agency built in Port-au-Prince. Two years after cholera hit the capital, donor governments discontinued funding to the clinic. Their attention had moved on to the more recent events in Syria and Yemen. The Haitian Ministry of Health had neither the resources nor the capacity to pay clinicians, maintain the building, procure the necessary supplies, and keep the place running properly. Without outside funding, the doors of the clinic would be secured shut with a padlock.

Health care, like education, is a social service that is the responsibility of the government or the Haitian people themselves. In the long term, we can't take these over and create a parallel system entirely dependent on the international community's support. Otherwise, there's very little incentive or demand for the ministries to provide these things themselves. You sometimes wonder by doing this whether you are just allowing political leaders to avoid dealing with problems that are theirs to solve. But when there is no stable government, or when the one in charge doesn't have the resources or capacity to run these most basic services, and without them people will die, what choice are we left with?

Although our agency didn't plan well for this abrupt ending, the circumstances reinforced what I had begun to feel toward the end of my time in Haiti. Even though my role was more senior, I was only a cog in a large wheel whose spokes were twisted and interconnected—a tangle of aid agencies and governments sometimes working together, sometimes at cross-purposes. In the immediate term, emergency aid funded by foreigners could help save lives, but agencies took on tasks that in the long run would be the responsibility of the local government. Our work in Haiti, like aid work in any failed state, is just a Band-Aid stuck on larger political problems, ills that can't be fixed with food rations and jerry cans, and that don't heal quickly. The needs are urgent and pressing, but they are also recurring and seemingly endless. Even the most thorough emergency response wasn't going to cure Haiti of the years of neglect and international indifference it had endured until the earthquake. There are critics who suggest that our presence just prolongs the government from having to rebuild the country and repair its decrepit infrastructure. Some even say that it's better to let the disaster and recovery run its course without us. I'm not one of them yet, but I do believe that saving lives today without critically thinking about saving lives in the future can just perpetuate a dysfunctional situation.

But over the years I learned to be realistic in my expectations of what aid could achieve. Whatever the context we're working in, it's never simple. Things take time, it's messy, there are always mitigating factors and extenuating circumstances. But to focus on just the negative aspects of international aid work—of which there are many—and conclude that aid is a failure is not the solution. Our work in humanitarian settings matters, and to wait for broader social, political, and economic reforms to address the needs of the most vulnerable is not an option. Systemic change is only possible through an amalgamation of short-term/long-term, micro/macro, national/subnational, policy/project investments. We will never be able to prove a counterfactual argument—What would people's lives be like without aid? Would they be better, or worse off?—so in some ways it is a profession based more on belief than empirical evidence. And I stay with it because I believe in the purpose of aid: to alleviate suffering of people when they need help most.

As I tell my students, we need to remind ourselves that aid is still a nascent profession although its roots are centuries old. The industry is now bigger than ever with $17.9 billion spent to respond to humanitarian crises in 2012. That may sound like a large number, but when you compare it to other figures—the $114 billion the US government has provided to Katrina relief, the $50 billion pledged to Sandy relief, and the $13.7 billion spent on the 2012 London Olympics—and when you consider that the $17.9 billion is a figure of *all* donations combined—from government donors ($12.9 billion) and private donors ($5.0 billion)—used to respond to all global humanitarian crises, it no longer seems all that impressive.

Prior to the 1990s, few humanitarian organizations measured the effect of their actions, assuming that the mere fact of having provided assistance was itself evidence of positive outcomes. Today, the industry is teeming with standards and certifying bodies to make agencies more accountable to affected populations and ensure minimum standards of aid delivery. We are also becoming more transparent about the money we spend, more honest with donors about our failures, and openly reflecting on our work and the impact it is making. Aid may be an unregulated industry, but it's also highly self-reflective and self-critical. And there are a lot of smart people committed to improving the way we deliver aid to make it more effective and relevant.

THE LATEST OF THESE EFFORTS is cash transfers. The use of cash in emergencies is one of the clearest examples of empowering beneficiaries and allowing *them* to decide for themselves what they need most. A lot of times, the food, shelters, kitchen sets, and soap we ship from our warehouses somewhere halfway around the world are resold so people can get what they want: cash in hand. Agencies provide people with either vouchers or incremental cash transfers (sometimes with conditions attached). Cash might not make for a nice press-release photo, but it can simplify the logistics of distribution and eliminate many of an agency's expenses. People spend at their own discretion, buying locally, thus ensuring that local suppliers aren't cut out of the market. Advocates of cash transfers call it the future of aid. And for those who worry about where the money will be spent, the aid community has come up with a semiofficial rule, which some in the industry refer to as one of the Ten Commandments of cash transfers: Give the money to women. Women will spend it on the family. Men might be more likely to spend it on alcohol and prostitutes.

Another change in the industry has come with the advent of mobile technology, which is pervasive in the developing world. People may not have eaten for a day, but you can bet they have a cell phone. Twitter and texting enables affected people to have a greater say over the services they receive and communicate with the world about the aid response. Agencies are only one YouTube video away from being called out for bad practices, and aid recipients are becoming savvier about using these vehicles to demand what they need.

But people don't *want* to need help. The aid community is investing in making people and communities more resilient and better able to manage and recover from disasters themselves. When we go in, we need to work with development actors to strengthen national capacities so that humanitarian aid can phase out. We still need a system that underwrites a humanitarian intervention when national governments are overwhelmed. But aid should leave people and their governments in a position to better cope next time disaster strikes.

It is exciting to be part of these developments, even from afar. Of course, I'll always feel the pull to go and respond. Being in the field means living in an intense, driven environment, surrounded by all kinds of ambitious people, with moments of extreme connection and accomplishment. That life is hard to beat. But if I wanted a stable life, I had to actively choose one, because the path of least resistance would have been to continue working abroad. When I returned from Haiti, though, I was tired. Not tired in the way I had been when I came home from Darfur. Tired of running around and putting what *felt* like real life on hold. I no longer *needed* to be part of the latest breaking emergency, and not only that, I didn't want to. But I did want to remain involved in the profession I loved, and I found ways to do so here. It's been a spectacular and surreal journey, and some days I find the destination—my life as a humanitarian aid worker—nearly as astonishing, particularly when held against the distant backdrop of the life I might have had.

When the conflict in Syria began earlier this year, so did the Facebook updates—"Headed to Amman tonight," "On my way to Lebanese border—tens of thousands of refugees there already," "Packing bags for Southern Turkey"—I couldn't help but feel tempted. Syria and the neighboring countries to which Syrians were fleeing were about to have a do-gooder invasion on their hands. But I'd read this storybook before. I knew what it would mean for me, for my life if, once again, I dropped everything to join my friends and former colleagues.

Then one afternoon, a Skype message popped up on my screen from a former boss—"I'm putting a team together for Syria, you in?" My hands were perched over the keyboard, ready to start firing back questions—When? Where? For how long? But I stopped myself, chuckling at the same old predictable reflexes. I sat back, sighed, and knew what I would tell him.

Author's Note

The stories in this book are written from my memory. It is a true account based on my best recollections of the events and my experiences. In a few instances, I rearranged and/or compressed events and time periods in service of the narrative. I have changed the names and identifying features of all of the characters in this book and in some instances I created composite characters based on real people I met. Dialogue matches the exchanges to the best of my memory. Finally, for many of the statistics and figures cited, it is difficult to find precise numbers. For the most part, I have used UN sources.

Acknowledgments

This book was written over several stages of my life, in multiple countries, passing through the hands of many friends, loves, and family members. So many people have helped shape these stories and the book could not have materialized without them.

First, I'm grateful for the people and families from the places I have worked who took in an often clueless young American, and who were so open, generous, and eager to help, and asked for nothing in return. I remember the faces of your children, the rooms of your homes where we sat to eat or drink tea, and the stories you told about your lives. I recall, above all, the bravery and humor you showed despite having to endure some of the most horrific circumstances imaginable. The time I spent with you made it feel like what we were doing, despite the frustration and the constant obstacles, was worthwhile.

Katie Dunn, Seth Searls, Ben Tishler, Christian Lewis, Ed Sien, Keith Gessen, Trish Rapaport, and

Jesse Samberg read early, messy drafts which I'm now embarrassed I let ever leave my computer. Your enthusiasm gave me the confidence to continue.

Kasia Laskowski and Laura Risimini, thoroughly fact checked the manuscript. You were both so positive and smiley even on those long days when I wasn't nearly as perky.

Charles Salzberg believed in this book from day one of writing class and helped me first imagine this could actually happen. He and fellow students who provided affirming feedback—especially Julia Scully, Corey Maloney, Diana Ventura, Dean Gordon, Whitney Dangerfield—made the writing process so much more fun. Vivian Conan read the entire manuscript with a careful eye and offered smart edits. Laurence Klaven also provided wine and constructive feedback.

Jane Dystel had confidence in this project even when I didn't and helped me navigate the publishing world as an enthusiastic and determined advocate.

She connected me with my editor and friend Meagan Stacey, who regularly took frantic calls with the calming words, "I'm sensing anxiety, what's going on?" She patiently reassured me through every worry, coached me through every question, and continually pushed me to make the book better.

The gifted editor Elizabeth Gumport took a red pen, a smart eye, and some serious elbow grease to the manuscript and cleaned it with care, good judgment, and talented writing.

I'm grateful to have been mentored by the best: Les

Roberts, Dirk Salomons, and Neil Boothby. You taught me to keep questioning, and fostered my passion for this work. Neil especially, you have been instrumental in shaping my career and I'm grateful to you for taking me under your wing. I'll never forget the wisdom and compassion you showed me through a rough period after Darfur.

Zbysek and Barbara Szulc, so much gratitude to you both for the many times you helped me pack, unpack, picked me up at an airport, dropped me off at another, always with energetic hugs and smiles over these years.

Colleagues, and friends from overseas, it is extraordinary that our paths crossed in some of the most unlikely of places, but I'm so happy that they did. You have influenced the way I think about the world, this line of work, and the stories I have to tell. I'm especially grateful to have met and lived with such special people in the Millicom house and the Bungalows. Cynthia Koons, Paule Neale, Charlotte Balfour-Poole, Kristy Baughman gave useful comments on Haiti and Amy Brathwaite let me borrow some of her beautiful language and images to make that chapter much more rich. I'm grateful to have had my dear friend Anne Althaus with me in Sierra Leone and even more grateful for your continued friendship and generosity as you welcomed me time and again to Geneva.

The entire SIPA crew with whom I graduated: you are the most adventurous, spirited, engaging people I know. If it weren't for your friendship over the years—couches to crash on overseas, late-night Skype sessions from around the globe, reunions in some of the most extraordinary settings for weddings or work, New Year's celebrations, or R&Rs—these experiences might not have been possible and they certainly would not have been so much fun. I'm lucky that our lives intersected so permanently that fall of 2002.

Lesley Bourns accompanied me during my early days abroad and was the silliest of travel partners and tent sharers. You somehow managed to keep cool and support me even when I ruined our vacation in Zanzibar during a thorny time. Natasha Kindergan kept a spare bed, a hot shower, and a cool glass of boxed pinot grigio waiting for me in Khartoum whenever I came back tired and dusty from Darfur. I was lucky to have such a close friend just a helicopter ride away during the lonely stretches. I'm grateful to you both for reading multiple drafts at home and helping me accurately recall our times overseas.

Luke Garman, you selflessly worked with me to rewrite my initial pitch over and over until it was perfect. Your help shaping up the Haiti chapter is evident on those pages. I'm so thankful to have had your steady support when I nervously threw myself out there with this book.

My grandmothers were the most comforting women I have known. Nana Hannah—who gave me my earliest writing lessons and my first books—the playful imagery you conjure in your poetry inspires me today. Nana Elsie—who supported my graduate school education—you taught me to have courage and be kind even in the face of tragedy. I only wish that you both were able to read this book.

Sophie and Nathan Mittleman, I know many a family dinner was consumed with "Jess's book" talk. Thank you for tolerating it graciously, offering advice, and not rolling your eyes.

My brother, Ben, you instructed me to "Stay here this year!" a mantra you left on voice messages, in texts, as subject lines of e-mails. Although I didn't heed your request, I appreciated you caring and you kept me laughing with your e-mails while I was away.

The book was conceived one breezy night in Istanbul where I told you, Suzy Hansen, that I thought I could turn it around in six months. You nodded and said, "Let's see how it goes." And for five years now, you have patiently tolerated hours of Skype-whining (about book- and non-book-related crises) and had the patience and stomach to slog through some of my worst writing and provide intelligent feedback. This book could not have been written without your brilliant editing and clever ideas. You have truly been the best of friends and I'm blessed to have you in my life.

Andy Wyllie, thank you for being so consistently patient, thoughtful, and wonderful during these final, nail-biting months.

Julie, our bike rides, power walks by the water, yoga classes and chat-sessions were the best therapy for writer's block. Your comfort cooking and upbeat attitude (I can still recall the enthusiasm in your voice when I called to tell you I got a book deal), kept me afloat these years.

Dan, your wit and humor are sprinkled throughout these pages. As a brother and friend, whenever I've been in a tight spot you've reassured me with the words from our favorite childhood movie: "Don't worry, Pooh Bear, we're gonna get you outta this hole." And you have, every time.

Mom, before being admitted to the hospital for your first bone marrow transplant you wrote a letter to me and the boys in which you doled out "some words that I want to tell you because I may not think of telling you again." In that letter, you told us, among many other pieces of wisdom, to "Keep safe but don't always play it safe. Take good, worthwhile risks in your lives . . . Be tolerant of others in the world . . . Don't ever, ever compromise your values . . . Remember that time is a most precious commodity and use it wisely." These are words that have guided me since. Oh, how I wish you knew me now.

Dad, the night before I left for Rwanda, you toasted me and my upcoming trip with a quote from William Shedd: "A ship in a harbor is safe, but that is not what ships are built for." I know it wasn't easy for you to watch me leave the harbor again and again, going off to such distant and scary places. You have stood by me through every trip, every return home, taking calls in the middle of the night from around the world layovers, with your signature calm, patience, and optimism. If I didn't have such a solid home to return to, I may not have had the courage to go so far. I love you.

About the Author

Over the past twelve years, Jessica Alexander has worked for the United Nations and various NGOs. She has responded to crises in Rwanda, Darfur, Sri Lanka, Indonesia, Myanmar, South Sudan, Pakistan, Haiti, and the Horn of Africa. Alexander is a Fulbright Scholar who received the award to research child soldiers in Sierra Leone in 2006. Her research there was used as expert evidence in the case against Charles Taylor, former president of Liberia.

Alexander is an adjunct professor at Columbia's Mailman School of Public Health, the Institute of International Humanitarian Affairs at Fordham University, and the Wagner School of Public Service at New York University. She received a master's of public health and a master's of international affairs from Columbia University in 2005. She is currently pursuing her PhD at the London School of Hygiene and Tropical Medicine, focusing her research on accountability to affected populations in humanitarian action.

She currently lives in Brooklyn, New York, and works for the United Nations.